THE FIGHTING JEW

HUMPHRIES & MENDOZA.

In their third public contest for Superiority, on Sept. 29: 1790.

Publish'd Sep. 16: 1813, by G. Smeeton, 139, St Martins Lane.

THE FIGHTING JEW

THE LIFE AND TIMES OF DANIEL MENDOZA

WYNN WHELDON

AMBERLEY

To my own Mendoza

Page 1: Humphries and Mendoza at Doncaster, from *Boxiana*.
Page 3: Daniel Mendoza, from *Boxiana*.

First published 2019

Amberley Publishing
The Hill, Stroud
Gloucestershire, GL5 4EP

www.amberley-books.com

Copyright © Wynn Wheldon, 2019

The right of Wynn Wheldon to be identified as the Author of this work has been asserted in accordance with the Copyrights, Designs and Patents Act 1988.

ISBN 978 1 4456 8573 1 (hardback)
ISBN 978 1 4456 8574 8 (ebook)

British Library Cataloguing in Publication Data.
A catalogue record for this book is available from the British Library.

Typesetting by Aura Technology and Software Services, India. Printed in the UK.

CONTENTS

ACKNOWLEDGEMENTS

Thanks are due to the following, for all manner of help, advice and actual work:

Melanie Arnold, Martin Austwick, Elbow Room, Michael Herbert, DNM, Dr Alex Moghissi, Giles and Emma O'Bryen, Tom Overton, Stephen Paul, Kathrin Pieren (Jewish Museum), Kate Summerscale, David Snowdon, Connor Stait, Caleb Wheldon, Jacob Wheldon (Flux), Brian Whipp, staff at the British Library, London Metropolitan Archives, and National Archives.

All errors and infelicities are my own.

AUTHOR'S NOTE

Where I thought old styles of spelling, and typography (chiefly CAPITALS and *italics*) distracting, I have modernised (usually dispensed with) both. I have also tried to render spellings of names consistent throughout, even when using quotations in which these are at variance. 'Humphreys' therefore becomes 'Humphries' throughout, 'Crib' becomes 'Cribb' (the spellings favoured by the Oxford Dictionary of National Biography).

When available, I have used the copy of the 1816 'New Edition' of the *Memoirs of the Life of Daniel Mendoza*, kept by the British Library. Otherwise I have scribbled all over my own copy of the 2011 edition prepared by Alex Joanides, an altogether more accurate version of Mendoza's own than is Paul Magriel's popular edition of 1951.

INTRODUCTION

The great object of life is sensation – to feel that we exist, even though in pain. It is this 'craving void' which drives us to gaming – to battle – to travel – to intemperate but keenly felt pursuits of every description, whose principal attraction is the agitation inseparable from their accomplishment.

– Letter from Lord Byron to Annabella Milbanke,
6 September, 1813

I first came upon Mendoza in a pub in Wardour Street in London's Soho. Nearby used to be the Jolly Brewers, run or owned by Jem Belcher, champion bare-knuckle pugilist of England from 1800 to 1805. Belcher died, an alcoholic, around the corner from Wardour Street at another pub, the Coach and Horses in Frith Street. If you walk south back down Wardour Street you come to Leicester Square, on the other side of which is St Martin's Street, where a pub called the Horse and Dolphin used to be, more or less on the site of the National Gallery extension (Prince Charles's 'carbuncle'). The proprietor for a while was Bill Richmond, the great black bare-knuckle boxer who in 1805 very nearly beat the reigning champion Tom Cribb. Cribb's pub, The Union, was a one-minute-walk away from Richmond's in Panton Street (the pub now bears Cribb's name). The two boxers became great friends; it was at the Union that Richmond quaffed his last drink, in Cribb's company, before dying an hour or so later at his home in Wardour Street. The Fives Court, too, was in St Martin's Street. This was boxing's chief testing ground, where sparring sessions and 'benefits' for boxers were held from the earliest years of the nineteenth century. A rival establishment was the Royal Tennis Court in Windmill Street, back over on the other side of Leicester Square. Around the corner, in the Haymarket, Jack Broughton, whose 'seven rules' provided the ground rules for the sport for almost a century, had given private sparring lessons decades before. Further west, at Number 13 Bond Street, 'Gentleman' John Jackson, so-called 'Commander-in-Chief' of British boxing in the first quarter of the century, had a room where, with precious little knowledge of the art, he taught grandees – including Lord Byron – how to box. So, when I first met Mendoza I was in the heart of the world of prize fighting. And I must say, I took to Mendoza – generous, with a brilliant and ready smile and a fine figure – so much so, indeed, that, reader, I married her. My wife is the first cause of my interest in Daniel Mendoza. Daniel's grandfather, Aaron, was her five times great-grandfather. She is descended from Daniel's Uncle Moses. Her uncle Victor boxed in his youth. My son has done some sparring. There's a boxing gene at work.

The great American novelist, Joyce Carol Oates, doesn't think of boxing as a sport. She has described it as 'the only human activity in which rage can be transposed without equivocation into art.'[1] I daresay Daniel Mendoza, author of *The Art of Boxing*, would have agreed with that. It is an activity that either fascinates or repels. It can also, uniquely, do both at the same time.

My first reliable memory of 'the sweet science' (the phrase coined by Pierce Egan, the father of sports journalism, from whom we shall hear frequently in the pages to come) was that great trilogy of fights between Mohammed Ali and Smokin' Joe Frazier. It punctuated the first years of the 1970s, and what I recall watching on the television is the sweat gleaming and spraying, the darkness around the lit ring, the intensity and the drama, and the huge contrast between the two men. Of the brutal third fight, the decider, the 'Thrilla in Manila', which Ali described as 'the closest thing to dying that I know of', *Sports Illustrated's* Mark Kram wrote: '…once more had Frazier taken the child of the gods to hell and back'.[2] David Halberstam wrote that Ali and Frazier were 'men who, like it or not, have become prisoners of each other and those three nights'.[3] The same might be said of Daniel Mendoza and Richard Humphries, who fought a similarly epic trilogy of fights, a landmark in the history of the sport, referred to decades later and not infrequently, as the *ne plus ultra* of pugilistic art and science. Of course, Mendoza and Humphries fought in daylight, in the depths of the pacific English countryside – nevertheless the intensity of the occasions must have been the same, the fans as fervent, the attendant grandees, if anything, even grander.

Dan Mendoza was a secular Jew. His first contest for money was fought on the Sabbath. His piety was nugatory, but in his writing his ethnic pride is palpable; how could it not be, he was so much the hero of his 'tribe', and constantly reminded, certainly before he became a national celebrity, that he was a 'little black bruiser', or 'the fighting Jew'. Joyce Carol Oates again:

> If boxers as a class are angry one would have to be wilfully naïve not to know why. For the most part they constitute the disenfranchised ... they are the sons of impoverished ghetto neighbourhoods in which anger, if not fury, is appropriate ... boxing ... is a way of transcending one's fate.

We shall see that Daniel Mendoza was infuriated, enraged, by the insults he and those he cared for suffered because they were Jews. The fate that Daniel Mendoza sought to transcend was not poverty but contempt. He certainly shared this ambition with others, but why is he in particular worthy of a full biography, this commoner who had the gall to write his own?

Daniel Mendoza is important for three reasons. He modernised bare-knuckle boxing; he wrote the first proper autobiography by a sportsman; and he raised the social status of poorer Jews.

His lifespan coincides almost exactly with that of George, Prince of Wales, later George IV, and substantially with the history of what was called the prize ring (its 'golden age' is generally regarded as having run from about 1787 to 1824). In that period boxing changed from an excuse for gambling organised by the aristocracy to a sport largely operated by its practitioners themselves, in league with powerful and sympathetic journalists. It was an age and a sport given dramatic colour by an astonishing cast of rakes, ruffians, rogues, aristocrats, swells, showmen, millers, hammerers and professors. In short, what became known as 'the Fancy'.

It was an age too when wealthy Jews came to the centre of British political life, in the form of men such as Nathan Rothschild and Abraham Goldsmid, and when poorer Jews found protectors from the contempt and violence of the street in the form of Mendoza, Dutch Sam, Aby Belasco, men it was unwise to argue with or offend.

'Mendoza' was a well-known name for a long time. Throughout the nineteenth century it was used as a synonym for the violent resolution to an argument. The phrase '*a la* Mendoza' lasted long after Daniel threw his last 'facer'. As late as 1934, in Leslie Howard's movie *The Scarlet Pimpernel,* Mendoza gets a name check. He even gets a mention in a list that includes fellow acculturated Jews Mendelssohn and Spinoza, in James Joyce's masterpiece, *Ulysses* – Mendoza was popular in Dublin. It is not impossible that Joyce had access to the *Memoirs.* However, with the advent of photography, film and television, new boxing celebrities arrived, and the star of the east was dimmed.

In recent years Mendoza has exerted a new fascination as academic fashion has turned towards matters of identity, considering the roles of nationalism, ethnicity, religion and gender in forming it. Daniel Mendoza has been held up as an agent of Jewish integration into mainstream English culture, as a Jew who to some small degree emancipated his community from physically expressed anti-Semitism, but who also represented the particularly 'British' virtues of manliness and patriotism.

What follows does not pretend to understand Daniel Mendoza as an individual. He is too alien a figure for that. Though much written about as a fighter, there is little that tells us of him as a person. He was full of apparent contradictions. His *Memoirs,* jaunty and indiscriminating as they may be, give us only a vague sense of the man who wrote them. He was proud, querulous, honest, and, one feels (but no more than feels) good company. He very obviously enjoyed attention. Above all he was a 'natural genius' with his fists. Almost every commentator attests to his supremacy as a theorist, as, indeed, he saw himself. He liked to put the initials 'PP' after his name, in mocking (but perhaps not that mocking) imitation of less robust fields of learning. PP: Professor of Pugilism.

A resurgent nationalism, seemingly throughout the world, the reappearance of anti-Semitism and, in the West certainly, what has been termed 'a crisis of masculinity', elements of our contemporary scene, were no less talking points at the end of the eighteenth and beginning of the nineteenth centuries. Daniel Mendoza's life is full of sharp reminders of our current concerns. Having said that, fighting and anti-Semitism are of course as old and seemingly as permanent as jawbones or monotheism. It is worth adding that boxing too, in the United Kingdom at any rate, with the rise of Anthony Joshua and Tyson Fury to the heights of the game, is enjoying something of a revival.

This is neither a work of popular psychology nor of academic inquiry. There is no 'Life' of Daniel Mendoza in existence, other than his own (possibly ghost-written) words. A very good educational comic book entitled, infuriatingly, 'Mendoza the Jew' (my own preferred choice of title) really covers only the great trilogy of fights with 'Gentleman' Richard Humphries, at the beginning of Mendoza's career, the bouts that made him famous. But Daniel Mendoza was to live through both the glory days and the decline of prize fighting. His story is worth telling in full, both for itself and because such a record ought to be readily available. Full of faults – impetuous, proud, quick to anger – he was also heroic, in Britain and Ireland perhaps the most famous Jew of his day, a name mentioned in America and France, a boxer who began his career as 'a little black bruiser' and ended it as 'the Nestor of the Ring', but also in pathos and despair. His is a story of public, historic triumph and personal misfortune. Perhaps our fates can never quite be transcended.

Prologue

MURDER IN CHELSEA

Late on the evening of 11 June 1771, Mrs Elizabeth Hutchins, widow, was sitting in the parlour of her farmhouse in Chelsea on the outskirts of London, thinking about retiring to bed. Her two manservants had just done so, when her dog started to bark alarmingly. She called two maidservants to see what the commotion was. Hearing subsequent screams from them she ran to investigate. She was suffering what is nowadays called a home invasion. Her maids had been set upon and tied up by three or four men dressed in greatcoats 'so long they reached down to their heels'.[1] Mrs Hutchins herself was forced to sit, her petticoats pulled over her head. The men went exploring. A scuffling from upstairs was followed by a shout for mercy. Two pistol shots rang out, at which point Mrs Hutchins decided to make a run for it. Opening her back door she found the way barred by several other men waiting outside. She was returned to her chair, struck across the face with a pistol and had her shoe buckles removed. She was then led around the house, a pistol at her head, and forced to hand over 64 guineas in coin. With that and all the plate silver they could find, the gang made off.

One of the pistol shots from upstairs had hit one of her manservants in the back. Joseph Slew crawled downstairs, more or less naked, bleeding profusely. Mrs Hutchins remembered that 'his shirt was on fire close to the wound, and I put it out. The blood ran down his legs.'[2] Slew died the following day.

The invaders were identified as Dr Levi Weil, a surgeon and apothecary who had trained at the University of Leiden, his brother Asher, Hyam Lazarus, and Solomon Porter. They had been aided and abetted by Marcus Hartogh, Abraham Lineval, Lazarus Harry, and Daniel Isaacs. This last, seeking the handsome reward offered by the government (an unusual practice, suggesting the gravity of the crime) turned the gang in. All were Dutch, though Dr Weil was well established in London and spoke fluent English. And all, it will be guessed from the names, were Jewish.

Levi and Asher Weil, Hyam Lazarus, and Solomon Porter were convicted on a Friday, and on the following day, 7 December, 1771, they were anathematised (formally cursed) in the Synagogue. They were hanged on the Monday 'attended to the place of execution by immense crowds of people'.[3] The appointed Rabbi declined to accompany them. The four men reportedly 'sang an hymn in the Hebrewe language' before being 'launched into eternity'.[4]

Referring to leaders of the Jewish community who had played a part in identifying the culprits and in persuading witnesses to speak up, the judge had prefaced the sentence with a 'judicious and just compliment to the principal Jews, for their very laudable conduct in the course of this prosecution'. He 'hoped no person would stigmatise a whole nation for the villainies of a few'.[5] His hope was in vain. The *Newgate Calendar* reported that this crime 'long roused the public indignation against the whole Jewish people'. According to William Jackson, a barrister, 'a Jew could scarcely pass the streets, but he was upbraided with the words 'Hutchins' or 'Chelsea', and many of them were pulled by the beards, while those who ought to have taken the insulters into custody stood calmly by and triumphed in the insult'.[6] Jew baiting became a sport.

As the Industrial Revolution had sucked the population into the cities, so crime had increased, Jewish criminality too, chiefly at that petty level that encourages contempt and casual violent attack. The Chelsea murder amplified the perception of Jews as essentially disruptive, alien, beastly. To put it romantically, they were in need of a hero, and on 17 April 1787, in the unlikely setting of Barnet Racecourse they found one in the form of a 5 foot 7 inch twenty-one-year-old by the name of Daniel Mendoza.

I

TYNE

According to his *Memoirs*, Daniel Mendoza was born in Aldgate, then the easternmost area of the City of London, on 5 July 1764. The *Memoirs* are probably wrong. The De Paiba Register at Bevis Mark Synagogue gives the date of his circumcision as 12 July 1765.[1] The ceremony, called a *bris*, is performed by a *mohel* on the eighth day of a Jewish boy's life. Dan's birthday was probably 5 July 1765. Various other sources – the distantly related George Rufus Isaac's biography of his own father, and a Masonic record that gives Daniel's age as twenty-two at the end of 1787 – support the later date. And frankly, throughout the *Memoirs*, Daniel's grasp of dates is flimsy at best. His godparents were Jacob Del Mar and Deborah da Costa,[2] which is to say that Jacob Del Mar held the new-born Daniel on his lap while the *mohel* went about his business.

The year 1765 was a big one for the forces of mutability. It was when James Watt worked out how to make the steam engine efficient, thereby more or less kick-starting the Industrial Revolution; it was the year in which the British Government imposed the Stamp Act on the American colonists, thereby inflicting taxation without representation, amplifying American revolutionary fervour. Daniel Mendoza's more modest but no less revolutionary credentials include first Jewish boxing champion of England, and first sporting autobiographer. He was to kick over a few traces himself.

Where did he come from? Daniel himself was a fourth-generation Londoner, and a proud Englishman, but his seventeenth-century roots were in the Iberian Peninsula.

Jews had begun gradually to return to England during the Protectorate of Oliver Cromwell. While Oxford and Cambridge had had Regius Professors of Hebrew since 1540 (with the new Reformation emphasis on the Old Testament), it was not until 1655 that the readmission of the Jews to England was formally recognised. Almost all the Jews in England for the next few decades were Sephardi, originating from Spain or Morocco, though generally by way of Amsterdam.

One such newcomer was Daniel's great-great-grandfather, David, born in Seville in 1655. He married Abigail Penhra Castro in Amsterdam in 1684, and died in London in 1722. David would have found in London a boom town, where the constraints of an organised Jewish community were very much less in evidence than elsewhere.[3] Unlike on the Continent, where traditions were long established, the relatively recent resettlement of Jews in England meant that there was no formally (or legally) recognised organisation to which all Jews were required to belong.[4] This was to make acculturation more pronounced in England than on the Continent. David and Abigail's son Daniel, probably born in London, was the father of the boxer's grandfather Aaron (born 1709), who was probably the Aaron Mendoza who became *shochet* (ritual slaughterer) to the Sephardi community in the city. Aaron wrote a book on the subject, illustrated by his own hand. There may have been, then, literary expertise in the boxer's genes, later to manifest itself in the *Memoirs*. It's a 'maybe'.

Aaron married an Italian Jew, Benvenida Tobi, in 1730, and their son Abraham married Esther Lopez in May 1752. Daniel Mendoza was their seventh child. Three of his siblings had died before he was born. In 1765 those living were sister Benvenida, who was thirteen, brother Isaac who was seven, and sister Sarah, five.

Mendoza is an extremely common Spanish name. It derives from a village in the province of Álava in the Basque country and means 'cold mountain' from the Basque 'mend(i)' (mountain) plus 'oza' (cold). There was a powerful aristocratic Catholic Mendoza family much involved in the upper reaches of Castilian politics from the fourteenth to the later seventeenth centuries. The family, and the name, spread throughout Castilian Spain. The Jews expelled from

Spain in 1492 under the Alhambra decree moved, some to the eastern Mediterranean, Salonica in particular; others went to the Netherlands where the mercantile culture and its concomitant tolerance proved conducive to their success. But many chose to remain, pretended to convert and to live nominally as Christians. They were known as Marranos (meaning 'swine' or 'pigs'), and were assigned names by the *Santo Officio* of the Spanish Catholic Church or by noble patrons or masters. This is very likely how the Jewish Mendozas got their name.

Dan describes his parents as 'of the middling class of society'. Most of the Sephardi Jews who had entered England in the century or since Cromwell rescinded Edward I's expulsion decree of 1290 were relatively well off, so perhaps there is a hint of the genteel about 'middling', as though the family had once been better off. Dan's father was possibly a craftsman or small shopkeeper, or may have had stalls in one or two markets. One of Daniel's brothers was a shoemaker, so too was one of his sons. Daniel himself wrote that he wanted to be a biscuit maker – perhaps his fighting nom de guerre would have been 'the Confectioner'. The family was certainly not rich enough to allow the children to be educated into their teens; even the education they did get was a mark of relative affluence, for most Jews – generally the newer influxes of Ashkenazi from Eastern Europe – were poor. But a good education, then as now, was understood to have an importance for the children's 'future welfare in life'. Daniel was educated at 'a Jew's school', possibly 'The Gates of Hope', a school for London's Sephardi congregation. Here he was taught 'English grammar, writing, arithmetic [and]…also instructed in the Hebrew language, in which, before I quitted school, I made considerable progress'. He was evidently proud of his Hebrew.

If his ancestor David had come to England from Spain, it is probable that he would have been living as a Marrano, and would already have cast off the 'look' of a Jew long before arriving in England. The Mendoza males were likely clean shaven, and the women would have dispensed with *sheitels* (wigs). Dan himself had a distinctly Spanish look, dark and gimlet-eyed. A 'little black bruiser', one newspaper, the *Public Advertiser*, called him.

Before he was thirteen years old Dan, English-speaking with some fluency in Hebrew, was apprenticed to a glass cutter. Or at least that was the plan. He lived with the 'honest good-natured man' and his wife and son (almost certainly Jewish) but found the son to be 'of a very haughty disposition'. Daniel Mendoza was to spend his entire life taking against haughty dispositions. It is one of the several attractive elements of his personality. He had a certain peacockishness himself, but this was closer to pride than haughtiness. No one pushed Daniel Mendoza about, by word or by force, without having made a mistake:

> Having one day taken the liberty of remonstrating with him on the subject, hoping thereby to induce him to amend his conduct, I found that, so far from such being the effect, he became highly exasperated at my *presumption*, as he was pleased to term it, and made use of such insolent threats, that I determined no longer to submit and therefore gave him a severe thrashing (though in his father's house) and having done so, thought it prudent to imitate the manners of the great – I resigned my situation, to avoid being turned out.[5]

It is impossible not to hear, in Mendoza's italicisation of 'presumption', his extreme indignation. Where the teenager had learned what 'the manners of the great' were is unknown, though an earlier passage suggests that 'the great' may have included his father, of whom he writes that 'he would often declare, how gratified he felt in seeing resolution and fortitude displayed upon proper occasions; though at the same time no one could hold the character of a bravado or quarrelsome man, in greater abhorrence.' Whether Daniel was a disappointment to his father is not known, but reading the *Memoirs* it is occasionally quite difficult to think of Daniel Mendoza as entirely an unquarrelsome man.

No longer cut out for glass, Dan then went into service with a local Jewish fruiterer and greengrocer, from whose family he received 'very kind and liberal treatment'. Many Jews made a living selling citrus fruit on the streets of London, though they were regularly abused while doing so. Mendoza doesn't make clear whether his mistress sold from a shop or peripatetically, but he does report frequent anti-Semitic insults, which of course required him to enter into 'contests' with butchers and others whom he felt had gone beyond the pale. Quite when or why he left the greengrocer is not recorded, but one imagines the reason was a contest too many.

His next 'situation in life', around 1780, was with a tea dealer. Tea was the cause of much vexation to drinkers, dealers and government alike. Contrary to what one might expect, the tea that was so popular came not from India or Ceylon, but from Japan or China (the English introduced tea to India in order to challenge the Chinese monopoly). By 1801 the British were importing £28 million's worth a year. Its popularity, driven, it is said, largely by women, had an effect on the consumption of spirits and the government found itself losing revenue from taxes and duties on alcohol.[6] As tea's popularity grew, so a tax on it as a 'luxury' grew. By 1750 it had increased to a preposterous 117 per cent. An obvious consequence was a healthy trade in the smuggled item. Not until 1784 was the tax cut to 12.5 per cent.

Needless to say, it was only a matter of time before Daniel, sufficiently incensed by insults aimed at his master, fought again. A porter had brought a chest to the dealer's premises. Daniel had offered him 'the price of a pint of porter' as a tip, which the porter had rejected 'in a contemptuous manner'. This was only going to end badly. The dealer entered the shop, the porter challenged him to a fight, young Mendoza stepped in, the pair stepped out, a ring was formed by the gathering public, and a fight ensued. The porter 'most probably flattered himself with the hopes of gaining an easy victory over a youth (being himself a stout athletic man in the prime of life)'. The 'severe contest' lasted about 45 minutes before the stout athletic man in the prime of life gave in. A man named Richard Humphries, five years older than Daniel, therefore still quite young himself, had acted as Dan's 'second'. Whether Humphries had simply been passing or whether the two knew each other already is unknown. It is possible that Humphries had already made a name for himself either as a boxer, or as a boxing teacher, or both. Certainly, he was to have noted victories over a man named Bentley in October 1784, over a Dick Smith the following year, and, most famously, Sam Martin in 1786.[7] His name was to become inexorably linked to Daniel Mendoza's.

Soon afterwards, Dan fought his first professional bout, arranged by a friend without his knowledge. It was to take place on a Saturday, the Jewish Sabbath, at Mile End, a little east of Aldgate in the East End of London.

In 1820 Mendoza made a list of the men he had fought during his career. The first on the list is one Thomas Wilson. Whether Wilson is the man he fought 'with some reluctance' that Saturday on the Mile End Road, we do not know. Legend has it – *Pugilistica,* Henry Downs Miles's history of British boxing, published in 1866, appears to have the earliest mention – that Mendoza's first battle was with 'Harry the Coalheaver'. It took the young Dan an hour to win. Again, Humphries acted as his second. Years later, Mendoza remembered, obviously with some pride, a reply Humphries gave to a spectator who suggested he tell Mendoza where to aim his punches: 'There is no need of it, the lad knows more than us all.'

The downside of this particular triumph was that Dan was sacked the following morning, whether for his impiety or his pugnacious inclinations is not known. Mendoza's decision to fight on the Sabbath was not entirely scandalous. English Jews, especially the Sephardi, were generally fairly lax in the observance of *Halakha*, the set of Jewish rules that was supposed to govern their behaviour. As Todd Edelman writes in *The Jews of Georgian England*, 'English Jews tended not to throw religion overboard altogether but to practise it in a haphazard and non-rigorous manner.'[8] Rabbi Hart Lyon, imported from Holland on the death of the Rabbi of the Great Synagogue in 1756, was outraged. He warned his congregation

> … against the small sins you have fallen victims to. The shaving of the beard, a non-Jewish custom, strictly and repeatedly forbidden in our Torah … but you regard them as minor matters, not realising that they are pillars on which Judaism stands. You direct a non-Jewish servant to light the fire, to make fresh tea or coffee on Sabbath. Do not forget the punishment for this sin is that fire breaks out in your houses …[9]

He despaired at the fact that 'Christmas pudding … is more favoured than the Mazzoth.'

The festival of *Purim*, celebrated in March, commemorates the saving from extermination of the Jews of ancient Persia. It is celebrated with a kind of mandatory raucousness that commences with dressing up. Daniel, soon after losing his latest job, decided that for the festival he and his pals would dress as sailors. Not a clever idea in the age of the press gang. Contrary to the public image suggesting kidnap and arbitrary shanghai-ing of ne'er-do-wells, press gangs were strictly limited to conscripting among 'eligible men of seafaring habits'. Dan and his friends looked just the thing. Not for the last time, Daniel found himself in a jail. In due course extricated, the gang made it back to Aldgate in order to be present at a theatrical event based on the biblical story of Esther (she having been responsible for persuading her husband the king to spare the Jews). Invited to perform in an interlude, they agreed. Unfortunately, Daniel, a natural performer, opened with a song he could not sing for hoarseness, having spent the previous night convincing his captors they had taken a desperately unseaworthy gang, and to let him and his pals go free.

> I was scarcely audible when I came on the stage, and this circumstance, together with the awkward and embarrassed behaviour of my companions at the time, so excited the disgust of the audience, that they would not suffer us to proceed, and we were finally hissed and hooted off the stage.[10]

Worse still, the gang didn't get paid. Dan himself refused to return a 'valuable epaulette' he'd been given by the company manager, presumably part of a costume, until properly remunerated. Money was important to Mendoza, and was the cause of several of his fights, but he would prove himself quite incredibly bad at looking after it.

He now took a job as a travelling tobacco salesman, coming from and going to a base in Whitechapel, the area contiguous with Aldgate, though beyond the City. Tobacco was at that period smoked in pipes (cigarettes were introduced to British soldiers in Spain during the Napoleonic wars), so Daniel would have been carrying not only tobacco but also all the paraphernalia that attends the business of pipe smoking: pouches, flints, tampers, reamers, picks, pokers, seals and 'smoker's companions', a contraption that combined many of these tools. Dan would have been fairly laden down as he walked into Chatham in Kent, a town with military connections, and a Navy dockyard, and therefore likely to be a fruitful market. However, before he could begin selling or taking orders, he was accosted by a man leading a body of soldiers, and told to 'get out of the way' in 'a peremptory tone', and, having remonstrated, was struck with a halberd, a kind of pike no longer used in war but denoting its carrier as a sergeant. Rudeness was as bad as haughtiness in the Mendoza list of reasons to thrash. The two men fought for an hour, Mendoza prevailing.

An officer who witnessed the fight presented the young man with 5 guineas, and 'exerted his influence, with effect, in procuring orders for my employer'. A group of sailors who had also been impressed 'carried me with them in triumph to Gravesend', thence to London, where the tobacconist heard the story with pleasure, and sent Dan straight back to fulfil the order. Despite his success, Dan found that he did not earn enough 'to procure [the] many little enjoyments I wished for'. It is a curious remark, suggesting that he was used to such enjoyments – it suggests leisure. It is irritating not to know what those little enjoyments might have been.

Daniel's inability to hold down a job was very far from unusual. The fortunes of almost all trades fluctuated with the seasons; war and winter didn't help. Earnings in London were 'often high, but nearly always uncertain'.[11] Given his almost constant lack of funds, despite earning well from fighting, it is hard not to believe that Mendoza was a gambler. 'Temptations to drink and gamble were interwoven with the fabric of society to an astonishing extent,' wrote M. Dorothy George. She quotes the social reformer Francis Place's *Autobiography*, in which he is describing Bell Yard, Temple Bar:

> It was inhabited by many men whose businesses were such as would have enabled them to bring up their families respectably and to put them out in the world with fair chances of success, yet scarce anyone did half as much as he might have done, and nearly all did the contrary.[12]

It is possible the young man frequented brothels of which there were many (Jews were much favoured by prostitutes, as they were considered both more considerate and more generous), religious tolerance having released both Christians and Jews from certain moral constraints. Somehow I think this unlikely. There is something a little too proud in Daniel Mendoza for that kind of lowering. So gambling seems more likely. Horse racing had become immensely popular, and there were numerous card clubs that met in inns and taverns.

He may also have enjoyed seeing shows. Theatres were attended by all classes except the very poorest. We've already seen

Mendoza at one; he liked to perform, and later in his career he was frequently in and out of theatres for one reason or another. A little after this period, the Royalty Theatre in Wellclose Square, not far from where Mendoza lived (probably White Street, off Houndsditch, at this time), opened in 1787. 'Theatre' included everything from rope dancing to ballet, from magic to horsemanship, often all on the same evening. And while the age of David Garrick, who had dominated Shakespearean acting and the London stage, was passing, new stars were arriving on the scene, such as Edmund Kean, Charles Macklin (one the great Shylocks) and John Kemble, Mrs Siddons, Mrs Jordan and Mrs Wells. There were Assembly Rooms and Pleasure Gardens, like Ranelagh and Vauxhall, and even art exhibitions to spend time in. Bull-baiting and cockfighting were popular, the latter especially in Scotland (a country that appears to have produced no first-class prize fighters in the period). They were banned in 1835, when Parliament passed the Cruelty to Animals Act.

Dan Mendoza, though the victor now in several public fights, was still, in essence, an apprentice and 'London apprentice boys seem to have had no legitimate outlet for amusement and exercise'.[13] One popular escape was to hire, buy or steal a 'cutter', or small boat that could be sailed or rowed up to Kew and Richmond, on the Thames to the south-west of London. It was an expensive recreation, and had somehow to be paid for. Criminality was never far away.

There is no suggestion in the *Memoirs* that Daniel went cutting up river, but he did find himself briefly involved in crime. Promised a situation that paid a guinea a week, with board and a horse, he accepted with alacrity, only to find that he was being hired to escort smuggled property. I'm not sure if it was the illegality or the threat to his life that put him off. Certainly he 'remained therein only four or five days'.

Shortly after this (at least according to the often wonky chronology of the *Memoirs*) Mendoza was walking with a friend in Kentish Town. The friend was insulted, and I think by now we know what the consequence was. The familiar words loop round again: 'we accordingly set-to, when after a contest of about half an hour, he was forced to give in.'

There is another possible reason why Mendoza's chronology around this period of his mid- to late teens is so unreliable:

he was in Africa. A longish report in the *London Chronicle* of 17–19 September 1782 describes the trial of a Daniel Mendoza, who on the evening of 7 September had attempted to remove a pair of shoes from the pocket of a man called William Forest who was walking in Aldgate Street. Mendoza had been caught and marched to a local shoemaker's where there was a light, and where Forest intended to get help to hold his captive. However, grabbing hold of a door frame, the latter drew a 'long knife' – reckoned at 18 inches by Forest – and stabbed his captor two or three times in the hand, chopping off one of his fingers. He escaped but was caught the following day. The jury at the trial found Mendoza guilty. The Recorder, James Adair, sentenced Mendoza to be transported to the west coast of Africa, reprimanding Forest for not asking for the death penalty.

The newspaper gives the name 'Mendoza', but the trial records give 'Mondoca', which is closer than it looks, when the 'c' is pronounced softly.[14] The defence was that at the time of the offence the accused was in the company of butcheress Sarah Martin, in Petticoat Lane, helping her chop meat for the forthcoming Jewish New Year meal. Daniel would have been seventeen or eighteen years old. His brother was a shoemaker. Making this link does not get us very far. There is the knife. Possibly a butcher's knife? Sarah Martin's husband was a confectioner. We know that Mendoza was drawn to that line of work. Was Daniel Mondoca Dan Mendoza? He probably was. Our Daniel Mendoza had a cousin called Sarah Martin (her mother was Hagar Mendoza). In 1791 she married Joseph Belasco. Their firstborn was Abraham, whom we shall meet later. The only other candidate was Daniel's uncle (and father-in-law to be), also called Daniel Mendoza, in his forties at the time.

Following defeat in America, where convicts had previously been transported, the coast of West Africa became the new host land. That honour fell to Australia in 1788. 'Mondoca' would have travelled on the second vessel to sail for Africa for the purpose, the *Den Keyser*, a slave ship. The convicts travelled 'with the woollen and cotton cloth, ironmongery, muskets and alcohol' that were swapped for the captives of victorious African tribes. The convicts travelled as the slaves later would: they were 'ironed' and put into the hold. The *Den Keyser* set sail on 6 November 1782.[15]

The attempt to use West Africa as a solution to the overcrowding in English prisons was a failure, for reasons we cannot address here. The last convicts were sent out in 1785. Many found ways to return to England, some went to the West Indies, others to Australia. We simply do not know what became of 'Mondoca'.

Although the evidence suggests that Dan and 'Mondoca' were one and the same, it is odd that this particular slice of his history was never mentioned in subsequent newspaper reports of his fights, or by enemies such as Richard Humphries, who knew him at this period. The episode remains open to speculation.

If it was the fighter, perhaps he learned a lesson and took to boxing as an antidote to knifing; and perhaps the African jaunt explains the recurring periods of malarial-like sickness that the boxer suffered throughout his life. The story also makes him a good deal rougher around the edges than the orthodox portrait presents.

If this was our man, he was back in England by the end of 1785 because at the beginning of 1786, not yet twenty-one, he set off for Barnet, about 10 miles north of Aldgate and a favourite 'milling' location, to watch the champion Tom Johnson fight a butcher named Bill Love. Dan cadged a lift from an old man in a cart going to the same place. Tom Johnson (real name Jacklin) had been fighting for three years and had won every contest he entered. He was not an elegant fighter – 'his appearance indicated, when stripped, more of strength than beauty of form' (Egan) – but he was successful enough to be regarded as the reigning champion of England.[16] To Daniel's disappointment Johnson finished Love off 'in a few minutes', and he and the old man started out back to the city. En route they encountered a young man driving another cart, who challenged them to a race. The challenge was accepted, and the old man won. The young man, put out, abused the older 'in very gross and infamous language'. Well: 'We stripped and set-to in an adjoining field, and having fought for an hour, the battle ended in my favour.' A passing gentleman paid Dan a guinea 'and raised a subscription for me among the spectators of between five and six pounds'. On they travelled. In Finchley the old man (who was this chap?) was recognised by a party of butchers, who began insulting him; was he Jewish? As a consequence another £6 or £7 joined the funds. The day's fighting ended in London when Daniel, now on a horse and fairly obviously and self-admittedly 'no very capital horseman', ran into a gang leader intent on frightening the beast. 'I was so much incensed at his endeavours to divert himself and his companions at my expense, that I insisted on his fighting me on the spot … we immediately set-to.' Though having 'set-to' three times during the day, Daniel Mendoza claimed that he had come through without a scratch 'or even any blow of material consequence'.

Despite his considerable earnings for the day, Mendoza was still in need of a job. So, as you do, armed with 'some slight knowledge of the confectionary business, being used to make Passover cakes and things of that sort', he set out with a friend to walk the 60-odd miles to Northampton. Apparently 'there was a likelihood of [his] obtaining a situation' there. The Jewish population of Northampton at this time has been estimated as non-existent. So why Northampton? As it happens, Northampton had indeed had a flourishing Jewish population, one of the country's leading Jewish communities, in the twelfth century. Flourishing Jewish populations usually result in acts of outrageous anti-Semitism, however, and even before the expulsion of the Jews from England, Northampton's Jews had suffered a number of attacks. Nevertheless, some remnant of the Jewish presence must have persuaded Dan to investigate the possibilities. If nothing else, his determination suggests the degree to which Jews were integrating, though on arrival Dan and his companion almost immediately ran into 'the bully of the place',

> … who observing two Jew lads, strangers to him, walking about and conversing together on different matters, thought proper to show a little consequence on the occasion; and therefore accosted us, observing that he supposed 'we were after no good', that he 'hated to see such fellows strolling about the place', that it was 'a pity we were not sent to Jerusalem' and using many other expressions equally absurd and insolent.[17]

His companion tried to dissuade him, so too the landlord of their lodgings, but Dan had determined to teach the bully a lesson, and so, 'accordingly', a ring was formed in the street and the two men set-to. The bully afterwards was confined to his bed for three weeks. The people of Northampton were surprised but 'gratified'. This included the bully's father, who himself had received 'very unbecoming and insolent replies' from his son when he had remonstrated about his violent conduct. In fact, so delighted was the father that he took in his son's opponent (there is no word about the companion). Dan didn't find his 'situation', but stayed with the man (and his son) for a month, before returning to London.

During Daniel Mendoza's life the vast majority of the Jews of Britain lived in the capital. Readmitted during the Protectorate after centuries of banishment, the first Jews to live openly were wealthy Sephardi merchants, but they were few, probably no more than 100 or so families at the beginning of the eighteenth century – perhaps 700 people in all.[18] By 1800 that figure had risen to 15,000, and the ratio of Ashkenazi (Jews from Germany and Eastern Europe) to Sephardi (Jews from the Iberian Peninsula and North Africa) had changed drastically.

The first purpose-built synagogue in London was the Ashkenazi Grand Synagogue in Duke's Place, Aldgate. Its erection in 1722 provided a kind of beacon to the distressed Jews of the Continent, of whom there were many. A resurgence of the Inquisition brought a new wave of Sephardi Jews from Spain in the 1730s, but there were persecutions in Bohemia and Poland, too, and even without such extremities, 'the conditions of Jewish life in eighteenth century Britain was more tolerable than elsewhere in Europe at this time.'[19] Still, in the 1780s there were no Jews in Northampton (with the exception perhaps of a peddler named Bernard Levy) because there were few Jews anywhere.

Anti-Jewish feeling as expressed in the outburst of the bully of Northampton had two upsurges during the eighteenth century. The first was that which greeted the Jewish Naturalisation Act of 1753. The second was the result of the murder in Chelsea in 1771.

The Jewish Naturalisation Bill, or 'Jew Bill', as it was familiarly known, had as its object 'the many persons of considerable substance professing the Jewish religion' who might usefully be naturalised.[20] They had to be rich because the process was deliberately expensive. And anyway, according to Horace Walpole, the Bill was 'purely for increasing wealth and commerce in the nation'.[21] It wouldn't make foreign-born Jews any more 'citizens' than native-born Jews, Catholics or Dissenters, none of whom, because they could not take the necessary Oath of Abjuration or pass the Sacramental Test, were allowed to vote, take a degree, or be called to the bar.

Passing without any great difficulty through Commons and Lords, the Bill became an Act in May, at which point a 'clamour

... was industriously propagated against it'.[22] Pamphlets and newspapers raised preposterous objections. It was suggested, for example, that one consequence would be the institution of mandatory circumcision. Genesis 34:15–16 was cited:

> If ye will be as we be, that every male of you be circumcised;

> Then will we give our daughters unto you, and we will take your daughters to us, and we will dwell with you, and we will become one people.

The grounds for objection were both religious and political. With an election due the following year the Tory opposition gladly jumped on the bandwagon, finding in it a stick with which to beat the Whig government. Jews were portrayed as 'professed enemies of Christianity', who prayed for its 'total extirpation'.[23] These were more or less medieval views, dragged up for political purposes, written by those who wished to stir the mob, which was always ready, as mobs so often are, to raise the flag of malice. It was especially easy to do so in light of the fact that only eight years previously Bonnie Prince Charlie had conquered England as far south as Derby. Fears of 'foreign invasion' were easily rekindled. The public reaction, out of all proportion to the provisions of the Act, included the threat of physical violence as well as name calling. The public furore was so great that the government, looking to the general election, repealed the Act in November. This didn't help Sir William Calvert, MP for the City of London, who lost his seat for having supported the Bill. A caricature had had him being circumcised on the steps of St Paul's.

Notably absent from any anti-Jewish sentiments was the accusation of criminality, which would surely have been the case had it been a talking point. However, by the 1760s the subject had become of concern to both Jewish elders and the authorities. A crackdown in 1766 did little to staunch the work of Jewish fences, receivers of stolen goods, who were becoming among the most active in London; with their contacts in Germany and Holland, loot could be swiftly removed from the capital. Otherwise, Jewish criminality was low grade, consisting of pickpocketing, passing bad coin, minor fraud, swindling and mock auctions. Most criminals were poor Ashkenazi, who made otherwise paltry livings by selling on the streets. Violent crime was not part of the picture.

Which is perhaps why the Chelsea murder caused such a stir in a city – Defoe's 'great and monstrous Thing'[24] – through which it was not particularly clever to walk home at night. Think certain parts of New York in the mid-1970s.

* * *

Tom 'the Tailor' Tyne, from Borough, 'was a pugilist of considerable activity and science, and, it is said, was equally as expert in using his fist in the ring as he was in throwing about the steel bar upon the shop-board; and in himself a contradiction to the old sentiment, that *nine tailors make a man.*' I believe the steel bar was a measuring instrument – a ruler; the shop-board was the table on which a tailor sat. Quite when Daniel Mendoza fought him, is unclear. The *Memoirs* states that it was 'the year 1783', when he had 'just attained the age of nineteen'. He places this some time after he had seen Johnson beat Love, a fight that certainly took place in January 1786. Mendoza's vagueness adds credibility to the Africa narrative. John Bee, in *Fancy-Ana,* his book on the history of pugilism, gives the year as 1787 – but it was certainly not after April, when Mendoza fought Martin, the Bath Butcher, in a much celebrated contest. The most likely date is 7 November 1785. The *Public Advertiser* of a few days later carried this brief report:

> Monday a pitched battle was fought near Wanstead, between Mendoza, the noted fighting Jew, and a tailor, of the Borough, which, after a severe contest of 40 minutes (during which time much real drubbing was given on both sides) was decided in favour of the tailor, to the no small disappointment and regret of the knowing ones.

It was Mendoza's first defeat. In his *Memoirs* he blames his friends for having pitted him against an older man, while at the same time declaring that he was at the time 'by no means convinced that Tyne would be able to maintain the superiority over me which he had on this occasion acquired'. Tyne may also have been the first left-handed boxer Mendoza had come across.

Shortly afterwards Mendoza beat John Matthews in a fight at Kilburn Wells, attended by the Prince of Wales; another fight was a result of a 'very gross insult from a man of the name of Richard

Dennis'. It was fought in Lock's Fields in Walworth, in south-east London. Dan didn't make a lot of money from the occasion, but then 'I fought not for the sake of money, but to punish Dennis for his insolence.'

Although unbeaten in these two fights, Mendoza did sprain an ankle quite severely in the latter, so much so that he was 'confined at home ... between three and four months', which suggests badly torn ligaments, perhaps even a fracture, but Mendoza interestingly remarks that 'one good ... resulted from my confinement':

> I lived now more temperately and regularly than I had been accustomed to do for some time before, and on my recovery from the lameness I felt both my strength and health materially improved and invigorated.[25]

Mendoza's recognition of his own immoderate way of life, his inability to hold down a job or let an insult pass without a set-to, suggests a movement into adulthood. Although prepared to 'practise the manly art' and make money doing so, Daniel Mendoza 'felt a repugnance' at making pugilism his profession. He fancied having a proper job, and the one he thought he would excel at, despite the disappointment of Northampton, was biscuit maker. He reckoned that 'a little time would suffice to perfect [him]' as such.

Before he could devote himself to biscuit making full time, however, he sought a rematch with Tyne. His first fight after his recovery was with a 'watch spring maker of the name of William Bryan' and was fought in Islington 'at a place then called the Hollow', by which we must imagine Highbury Corner, where the Holloway Road starts (or ends), near enough to town to attract 'a vast concourse of people, and almost every sporting character'. Mendoza 'gained an easy victory' but was accused of foul blows and the contest was declared a draw. The accusations were probably themselves false, and motivated by financial greed rather than any idea of fair play.

He was then challenged by William Nelson – 'an uncommonly large and powerful man'. It is important to remember that Daniel Mendoza, although strong, was not a big man. At a height of 5 foot 7 inches, and weighing a little over 10 stone (146 lbs or 66 kg, going up to 160 lbs in his heyday), almost everyone he fought in his career was heavier and taller than he was. Nelson, moreover, was 'in the prime of life', a state Mendoza did not reckon himself yet to be in (he was still only twenty years old). Mendoza accepted the challenge but had to raise 20 guineas for his stake. An advance was at first forthcoming from a Mr Elwood, a chief patron of Richard Humphries. Elwood invited Dan to train at a house in Epping Forest, owned by a friend of Humphries. Not, at this time (it was to change), being one for too much training, relying on his youth and 'the excellence of [his] constitution', he declined the invitation, having also discovered that the house was 'let out to women of a certain disposition, and that continual scenes of riot and dissipation prevailed there'. Not a place for the newly temperate Dan Mendoza. His refusal to go was 'much to the displeasure of Humphries, who afterwards caused his patron to forfeit the deposit'. This seems to have been the generative incident of a mutual antagonism that was to produce the most celebrated series of fights of the eighteenth century, rendering both men immortal in the annals of boxing. Mendoza borrowed the deposit money from a friend, at the rate of ½ a guinea a week, should he lose. Nelson's second was Tom Johnson, whom Mendoza heard say that Nelson wouldn't require one against 'such a youth'. Dan won after an hour and a quarter. He was now ready for Tyne II.

This was very different from the first fight. It was held in Croydon, to the south of London, in July 1786. A little older, a little stronger, the winner of several recent fights, Mendoza dominated from the start. Indeed, so little hurt was he that he decided to show off by afterwards running races against horses, in the rain.

As for Tyne, on 6 August 1788 he entered a ring put up on Brighton racecourse, to take on a fighter named Earl. 'Never were more fashionables assembled at a boxing match,' wrote Piece Egan. Most fashionable of all was the Prince of Wales. The fight commenced. Earl had the better of it until Tyne landed a blow on his temple. Earl was killed instantly.

It turned out that Earl had been 'in one continued state of inebriety' during an election campaign in Covent Garden, and had really been in no fit state to fight. Tyne went on, in March 1790, to defeat the very likely Mendoza-trained Jewish boxer Elisha Crabbe. The Prince of Wales never attended another fight. He characteristically arranged for a settlement to be made on Earl's immediate family.

It was now that a second incident occurred to ramp up the tension between Mendoza and Humphries. Mendoza's story sees him entering the Roebuck pub in Duke Street, Aldgate, to find Richard Humphries carousing with some friends. Humphries turned his gentlemanly eye on the ungrateful Jew. Mendoza remembers:

> He seemed very desirous of provoking me to strike him; for after using very scurrilous and abusive language, he seized me furiously by the collar, and tore my shirt with great violence.[26]

Temperate Dan suppressed his indignation, but made it clear that he would not forget the insult. Indeed it seems that Humphries was really the only person Mendoza would have considered fighting had his stab at full-time biscuit making not been forestalled by the arrival at wherever he was learning that peaceable trade of a man clad 'in the rich paraphernalia of royalty'. His name was Tom Tring and he had been sent by the Prince of Wales.

2

MARTIN

Tom Tring worked for the Prince of Wales, among other offices as a sedan chair carrier. At 6 foot 1 and 15 stone, he was apparently 'the finest made man in the kingdom', and being so was a favoured model of several painters, including Joshua Reynolds. He was also an occasional boxer, which made him the obvious choice of emissary when the Prince wished to bring fighters together, though 'as a boxer he possessed little science but excellent bottom'.[1] I suspect Tring's visit to Mendoza was at the beginning of 1787. Tring had fought and narrowly lost to Big Ben Brain, later Champion of England, the previous October. A newspaper report suggested that 'since the time of the Great Duke of Cumberland, there [had] not been a battle so severely contested, or so well fought.'[2]

The 'Great Duke of Cumberland' was 'Butcher' Cumberland, the victor of Culloden, the battle that in April 1746 had ended Bonnie Prince Charlie's Jacobite revolt. The Butcher was also a noted sponsor of bare-knuckle fighting, and the chief patron of a former Thames waterman, Jack Broughton, the man often regarded as the father of the sport. Broughton earned this epithet both by his predominance in the ring and by introducing a set of rules for the sport, which were to be largely adhered to for the next several decades. The sport itself began to flourish a little earlier than Broughton, its first great figure being James Figg, who in 1719 opened a school in Oxford Street where, among other martial arts, he taught boxing.

On 1 January, 1743 Broughton published his *Proposals for erecting an amphitheatre for the manly exercise of boxing* (the name consciously evoked classical Rome). The following August he announced his 'seven rules', pinning them up in the amphitheatre now opened in Marylebone Fields (the Angel in the Fields pub in Thayer Street is the remnant of the area):

That a square of a yard be chalked in the middle of the stage; and every fresh set-to after a fall, or being parted from the rails, each second is to bring his man to the square and place him opposite to the other; and till they are fairly set-to at the lines, it shall not be lawful for one to strike the other.

That in order to prevent any disputes as to the time a man lies after a fall, if the second does not bring his man to the side of the square within the space of half a minute he shall be deemed a beaten man.

That, in every main battle, no person whatever shall be upon the stage, except the principals and their seconds; the same rule to be observed in the bye-battles, except that in the latter Mr Broughton is allowed to be upon the stage to keep decorum, and to assist gentlemen in getting to their places; provided always he does not interfere in the battle; and whoever presumes to infringe these rules to be turned immediately out of the house. Everybody is to quit the stage as soon as the champions are stripped, before they set-to.

That no champion be deemed beaten, unless he falls coming up to the line in the limited time; or that his own second declares him beaten. No second is to be allowed to ask his man's adversary any questions or advise him to give out.

That in the bye-battles, the winning man to have two-thirds of the money given, which shall be publicly divided upon the stage, notwithstanding any private agreement to the contrary.

That to prevent disputes, in every main battle, the principals shall, on the coming on the stage, choose from among the gentlemen present two umpires, who shall absolutely decide all disputes that may arise about the battle; and if the two umpires cannot agree, the said umpires to choose a third, who is to determine it.

That no person is to hit his adversary when he is down, or seize him by the ham, the breeches, or any part below the waist; a man on his knees to be reckoned down.

These rules were more or less to govern the sport for the next 100 years. The English were busy formalising other sports too, notably horseracing and cricket; the Enlightenment reached deep into social forms.

Broughton's last fight, on 10 April 1750, was against a Norfolk butcher called Jack Slack. Having been unbeaten for the entire sixteen years of his career, Broughton had been the favourite. A lucky punch between the eyes levelled him. Cumberland is said to have lost £10,000. He apparently accused Broughton of throwing the fight and took steps to have the amphitheatre closed down and boxing outlawed. As Karia Boddy observed, 'a more striking demonstration of the dependence of the sport on aristocratic patronage can hardly be imagined.'[3] Within three years the amphitheatre had indeed closed, and boxing as a fashionable sport died with it. Broughton himself lived just long enough to see its revival and the early development of 'scientific' boxing. He died in 1789 and was buried in Westminster Abbey.

A primary, perhaps the chief, cause of boxing's resurgence was the interest of George, Prince of Wales. Born in 1762, his lifespan ran almost concurrently with Daniel Mendoza's, Daniel being three years younger. It may be that George was taught to box by his celebrated fencing master Domenico Angelo; more likely, Angelo's son, Henry, who inherited his father's fencing academy, introduced the young man to the fight game. Angelo was later to share premises at 13 Bond Street with John Jackson, another so-called 'gentleman' pugilist who would end Mendoza's career as champion boxer.

The young George was handsome, clever, and idle or, in the later words of the Duke of Wellington 'the most extraordinary compound of talent, wit, buffoonery, obstinacy and good feeling'. He gathered around him a coterie of like-minded aristocratic swells of often outrageous nerve, eccentricity and occasional malice, men like George Hanger, Banastre Tarleton, and Lord Barrymore; together they went to the races, and gambled. The English obsession with contest – 'Anything that looks like fighting, is delicious to an Englishman,' wrote a French visitor – fed the addiction to betting.[4] Dennis Brailsford maintains that pugilism 'would have been unthinkable without gambling'.[5]

Boxing didn't disappear completely in the dark post-Broughton years, and by the early 1780s it was again a common enough sight on London streets. An English correspondent writing from Rome complained that 'one sees every day the lower class of people stabbing one another in the street ... this happens as often as boxing matches do in London.'[6] From Norwich a correspondent remarked that 'scarce four-and-twenty hours pass without some dire mischance from these evils. – Duels, caning, boxing, and such like sports.' The same newspaper, however, carried a notice in its classifieds:

> A gentleman wishing to know the Art of Boxing and Defence, any person sufficiently master of that art, is desired to leave his address at the Somerset Coffeehouse, Strand.[7]

In June 1785 a proposed match in Hyde Park drew what one newspaper reckoned was 30,000 people. In fact so great was the throng that the bout could not go ahead. A man died falling from a tree. Later in the year the *Whitehall Evening Post* noted that boxing seemed to be reviving 'into as much notice as it attracted when Broughton kept the boxing academy at Hockley-in-the-Hole'.[8]

Hockley-in-the-Hole, now Ray Street in Farringdon, was 'the resort of thieves, highwaymen, and bullbaiters'.[9] On the site of what is now The Coach gastropub – 'a warm and welcoming place to eat, drink and unwind' – was the Bear Garden, where the noble art of self-defence was demonstrated. This was principally sword fighting. Mondays and Thursdays featured bear- or bull-baiting. The basic protocols of fighting with weapons were carried into bare-knuckle fighting: there was a stage, and only the fighters and their seconds were allowed on it. Broughton's amphitheatre was actually off Oxford Street, in the West End. 'Hockley-in-the-Hole' was shorthand for any place known for 'barbarous practices'. A modern analogy would be using 'Fleet Street' to signify the press.

Of course barbarism could as well be practised by the State, in the form of public hangings at Tyburn, where Marble Arch now stands, at the north-east corner of Hyde Park. These hangings ceased in 1783. They had been preceded by processions from Newgate Prison in the city of London, to which huge crowds flocked. The fight in Hyde Park may have promised some of the gruesomeness the crowds had been missing.

Into this renewed interest in boxing stepped Daniel Mendoza, a man for his time. One of the first newspaper mentions of Mendoza came on 10 November 1785, in the report of a fight with Tom Tyne mentioned in the preceding chapter. He is described as 'the noted fighting Jew', so clearly he was already on the radar, both as a boxer and as a Jew. By March 1787 he was 'the famous Jew-Broughton'. Mendoza's moment was not far off, but the fight that sparked the sport into fashion occurred a year before, and featured his mentor, Richard Humphries.

Boxing began to flourish again with the surge in popularity of horseracing, the sport of kings and, it would seem, princes. Newmarket's 1786 Spring meeting was forecast to be 'the greatest for many years'. There would be more horses and so more racing, hence more gambling. What was more, a fight was being arranged between Sam Martin, the Bath Butcher, and Tom Johnson, reckoned to be the current champion. Other reports named Martin's adversary as 'Norris the gardener of Suffolk'. 'Norris' was probably Richard Humphries, the man who had 'discovered' Daniel Mendoza. Humphries was a Suffolk man, very likely from Ipswich. It was reported that bets were already being placed as early as 23 March. Certainly Martin was to be one of the fighters. In the middle of April Colonel George Hanger informed the Jockey Club of the proposed fight, adding that it met with the approval of the Prince of Wales. It was accordingly added to the list of other matches on the racing calendar.

On the westernmost edge of Suffolk, a county in East Anglia, there is an odd pimple of territory sticking into Cambridgeshire. Here is Newmarket. It is as though some East Anglian lord in ancient times knew there would be a good reason for holding onto the place. It is, after all, where modern horse racing started.[10] It remains one of the principal centres in the world for equine health and training. A little to the town's north, about 3 miles, is the village of Exning. In April 1786 it was here that boxing gained a new lease of life in a match between the aforementioned combatants, 'Gentleman' Richard Humphries, champion of Suffolk, and Sam Martin, 'the Bath Butcher'.

Both fighters were known already, but this bout – or 'mill', to use the word of the day – was the first to draw serious crowds and, more to the point, serious money. Originally intended for the racecourse, Captain George Hanger, later Lord Coleraine, having arranged the matter with the Jockey Club, the plan was objected to by the Duke of Grafton, a former Prime Minister and prominent Unitarian, hence the move up the road to Exning. Such contests were, if not illegal, then thought likely by the authorities to encourage illegality.

The Newmarket race meetings in April and May of that year, 1786, were unusually well attended. There was a good number of French nobles in the crowds, perhaps aware of what was going to rumble into revolution in their homeland within a few years. There was even foreign royalty in the form of the anglophile Duc d'Orleans (who, despite his sympathy for the Jacobin cause, was to die in Robespierre's revolutionary 'Terror' of 1793–1794). He was an intimate of the Prince of Wales, who was also at the races. Both intended to attend the boxing. However, on the Monday before the fight, planned for the Wednesday, the Prince had a severe nosebleed. A local surgeon, Mr Sandiver, 'opened a vein', and suggested rest. But there would be no keeping George away. Steven Marcus imagines the prince 'sat wrapped in furs in his open carriage in the rain, corpulent, grumpy, suffering from a chronic nosebleed, engrossed by the bloody spectacle'.[11]

In Exning, inside a walled garden, a stage was erected about 5 feet from the ground, with viewing platforms at either side for the VIPs and umpires (three – one from each side and a neutral chosen by them). Price for admittance would be 1½ guineas, well over the average weekly wage of the period. This was of course chicken feed to the Whig grandees who surrounded the Prince of Wales.

The fight was fixed for 11.30am, and Humphries turned up at 11.15. By 11.45 Martin had still not shown, and messengers were sent to chivvy him on. In due course he arrived, and took to the stage. The *Ipswich Journal* reported that 'the two combatants walked backwards and forwards several times, looking at each other, and word being given to begin, they immediately stripped. A total silence then ensued,' and the fight began. They fought 'in buff and had on white silk breeches and stockings', crouched rather than erect. The term 'in buff' meant naked to the waist. They were not big men, though obviously they must have been strong.

Martin had begun as favourite, at odds of 6–4, but Humphries had been second to an opponent of Martin's in a previous contest (Martin had won two fights in the capital, having made his name in the West Country), and had learned how the Somerset man fought. And Humphries was intelligent. He put his mind and the experience to good use. It was a long fight, over an hour-and-a-half, but Humphries' victory was eventually emphatic. He had opened wounds above Martin's eyes, and across the bridge of his opponent's nose, and landed hefty shots to the loins.

The box office takings, after expenses, amounted to around £325 and mostly went to the victor – Martin took the £25. Reports vary wildly as to how much was won and lost in bets, anything between £4,000 and £30,000. The pickpockets had a field day: 'the French Ambassador lost an elegant gold watch,' reported the *Norfolk Chronicle*.

After the fight Humphries returned to the racecourse and spent the afternoon in a one-horse chaise, the kind of transport Jane Austen's Tom Bertram, in *Mansfield Park*, who liked the Newmarket races, might have been seen in. I daresay Humphries, like Bertram, did 'a good deal of drinking'. Humphries, for many years the champion Tom Johnson's second, was now a star of the first rank. His good manners earned him the soubriquet, 'Gentleman'. Boxing was suddenly fashionable.

A fortnight or so after the fight Sam Martin let it be known in an advertisement placed in a newspaper that he was ready for another challenge: 'Particulars may be known by calling on, or addressing a line to, Samuel Martin, Peter Street, Soho; who weighs 9 stone 9 lbs and measures 5 feet 3 inches.'[12] It may of course be that he was seeking a man smaller than himself, and therefore exaggerating his diminutiveness. The *Ipswich Journal* reckoned him at 5 foot 5 inches. Humphries was not much taller (and Mendoza perhaps somewhere in between). Perhaps think Tom Cruise versus Robert Downey Jnr (whose bare-knuckle bout as Sherlock Holmes in the film of the same name, given poetic licence for exaggeration and concertina of time, is perhaps not an entirely unrealistic reproduction of what such a fight may have been like, certainly in terms of brutality).

It was no surprise then for Dan to find that Tring's message was that now he, Mendoza, the fighting Jew, had been matched against Sam Martin, the Bath Butcher, and that the match had been 'arranged' (i.e. commanded to occur) by 'an illustrious personage' (i.e. the Prince of Wales). No surprise perhaps, but nonetheless Dan made sure during an 'interview' with the Prince that followed some days later. Obviously, he could not say no.

The first attempt to stage the fight was at Shepherd's Bush, at the end of March 1787. An 'immense concourse of people' met to witness the contest, but it was dispersed by a party of light horse, members of the 10th Prince of Wales' Own Regiment of light dragoons. Perhaps, theoretically, the Prince might have ordered them to desist. George was quixotic but not stupid. The fighters and the concourse decamped to Lisson Green, further in towards London, but were again stymied. Gravesend was mentioned, but that too came to nothing. Eventually the Bath Butcher and the Fighting Jew were to meet on 16 April at Finchley or Barnet, 'persons interested in the event thereof being averse to mentioning the spot, lest the sport of the day should be interrupted by the interference of the Magistracy'.[13] As it happened that didn't happen either, but the following day it did, at Barnet.

'It is astonishing,' reported the *Morning Chronicle*, 'how numerous the crowds of people of all ranks and descriptions were to be seen yesterday upon the North Road on their way to Barnet, to be spectators of the bruising match between Mendoza and Martin. Many a poor working man's family went without dinner in consequence.'[14] The *Public Advertiser* reckoned on the presence of 'the whole tribe of Levi' adding to that old familiar hyperbole, the 'innumerable concourse of spectators', which had 'assembled many hours before the combatants'.[15] Impossible to say quite when the Prince of Wales arrived, with attendant gadabouts, such as MPs Wilson Braddyll, Percy Wyndham (neither of whom ever made a speech in the House of Commons), and William Gage (who did make two speeches, one of which was in defence of his brother), as well as various other 'young men of distinction'.

It is worth making plain here what prize fighting involved, and I follow Lewis Edwards in quoting Bohun Lynch: 'The men fought to a finish; that is, until one or other of them failed to come up to the scratch, chalked in the mid-ring, or until the seconds or backers gave in for them, which last does not appear to have happened very often. A round ended with a knock down or fall from wrestling, and half a minute only was allowed for rest and recovery.'[16] It is obviously that word 'wrestling' which gives pause. It did not mean wrestling on the ground, but referred rather to making the opponent fall, one way or another. This was obviously another way of injuring or exhausting one's antagonist. It would also signal the end of a round. Often boxers went down of their own accord in order to gain themselves half-a-minute's respite. This was called 'shifting' and was considered rather low. Rival pugilists loved to accuse one another of it, and restriction against the practice were often written into contracts drawn up prior to contests.

The fight between Martin the Bath Butcher and Mendoza the Jew begins around 3 p.m., on a stage built 6 feet from the ground. Martin enters the ring with his second, Big Ben Brain, a coal porter at the Adelphi wharf, a coming boxer 'mild and sociable in his demeanour'.[17] Mendoza's second is none other than reigning champion, Yorkshireman Tom Johnson. (Several years later Brain is to defeat Tom Johnson, to become champion, though his early death was put down to the injuries inflicted by Johnson during that fight.)

Martin is the favourite with 'the black-legged gentry'.[18] He is known to hit hard and not to give up easily. He is nuggetty, rolling, Frazier-like. However, one of the conditions of the bout is that there is to be no falling without a knock down, no 'dropping' or 'shifting'. This is a 'play' at which Martin is regarded as being 'dextrous'. (The modern equivalent would be closing or grappling with your opponent, in order to stymie his momentum or to gain breathing time for yourself.) It is also remarked, which is evidence that the sport is in a new infancy, that the fight is 'to be quite genteel, as there was no quarrel'.[19] It is, in short, a professional boxing bout. A crowd estimated at 5,000 has come to watch.

Mendoza, though already with a reputation as 'the fighting Jew' is regarded as being deficient in strength. However, he is also neat and quick and as the fight progresses it becomes clear that Dan's greater reach and nimbler feet are beginning to prevail. Not everything goes his way. Tom Tring, his own bottle holder, twice supports Martin 'who would otherwise have fallen to the ground'. Mendoza has to push his own man – substantially larger than himself – out of the ring.[20]

The fight lasts about half-an-hour before Martin gives the battle to Mendoza. The Bath Butcher is unable to leave the ring without help. Dan is so little hurt that he leaps up onto 'a railing of the scaffold', acknowledging his adoring fans – the whole tribe of Levi. Hebrew and Yiddish yells and songs of triumph must have floated out across the English countryside. For this was a great day for Duke's Place, for Dan's community, for the Jews (what one newspaper described as 'his sable-visaged brethren'), and surely one of the greatest days in Jewish British history up to that date. The aristocrats' favourite had been beaten, a Jew had prevailed in front of the Prince of Wales. This had been Mendoza's first fight on a stage erected for the purpose. He was twenty-one years old.

He returned to town in glory. We have seen, in the televised celebrations that attend it, how important to communities victory in sport can be, whether it be World Cup or local triumph. We must imagine something of that fervour, if not that scale (there were barely 10,000 Jews in London). He arrived back in Leadenhall

Street in the heart of the city of London, address of the East India Company, around 9 p.m., his way lighted 'with torches and martial music'. 'See the Conquering Hero Comes' was sung over and over again. News of the Jewish victory over the Christian had travelled quickly. 'All his tribe went forth to meet him.'

> ... his mistress came out likewise to see the man who had beaten others, surrender to her black eye – more fatal than any that Martin could have bestowed.
>
> The arrival of the Messiah could not have diffused more joy among the tribe of Judah, than the victory that circumcision obtained over uncircumcision on Tuesday. The old-cloathesmen themselves kept holiday, and left their coats to hang upon their pegs – while they repaired to Houndsditch, to celebrate the triumph over the diminutive Philistine![21]

To celebrate his victory, Mendoza led '200 Levites' from the Three Nuns in Whitechapel (later notorious for its place in the Jack the Ripper narrative), to the Theatre Royal, Covent Garden. They went there to hear fellow Jews, Michael Leoni and John Braham, sing at the former's benefit, Linley and Sheridan's tremendously popular opera *The Duenna*, regarded by Byron as 'the best opera ever written', which featured a Jewish merchant by the name of Isaac Mendoza.

Daniel Mendoza found himself, at least for the moment, rich. He wrote that he 'suddenly came into the possession of wealth far beyond what I ever expected to be master of, having received altogether considerably more than a thousand pounds'.[22] Half of this had come from the Prince of Wales himself. However, the idea of Dan being 'master of' any money at all is risible. 'Apprehensive lest the bank should fail', he exchanged £10 bank notes for 9 guineas in coins each.

'Amongst the amateurs, the Jew was held to have fought as well as any of the gymnastic professors have thereto done, Humphries excepted,' opined one report. The *Memoirs* contain this:

> On our way to town we happened to meet Mr Humphries when Colonel Glover (who had been present at the battle) asked his opinion of me, and upon his replying that he thought nothing of me, the colonel observed to him, 'Take care Humphries, depend on it, one day or another he will beat you.'[23]

3

HUMPHRIES I

Atop a chalky hill in the county of Hampshire in the south of England, a little east of Basingstoke, sits the small town of Odiham. Midway on the royal route between Winchester and Windsor, it boasts a castle built by King John in the early thirteenth century. He stayed there prior to signing Magna Carta at Runnymede the next day. During the following century it hosted, for a decade and more, King David II of Scotland, against his will. Perhaps the Prince of Wales played some part in the town's selection as the place where Richard Humphries and Daniel Mendoza would settle their differences – the place where they would decide, with bare knuckles, who was 'the better man'.[1]

Despite its royal connections, Odiham was by 1788 an obscure place. It was to become, for a time at least, rather well known. One of the reasons this little town was chosen, and agreed upon by the two fighters, was that it was 'at the distance of at least 40 miles from London'. The idea was to prevent 'an excessive confluence of rabble'.[2] It didn't – Odiham's population was perhaps a little over 2,000 (bigger than Stockbridge or Whitchurch in the same county); an estimated 1,000 people came from London to watch the fight.

There was known animosity between Humphries and Mendoza, or 'jealousies' as *The World and Fashionable Advertiser* put it; a 'rooted antipathy' was the phrase of the *London Chronicle*.[3] Humphries had, in a sense, discovered Mendoza, and had possibly trained him, but the two had fallen out. It added piquancy to what was considered an inevitable showdown. Both men had beaten Sam Martin, the Bath Butcher, in fights that had reignited interest in the sport, and it was the view among many that Humphries and Mendoza were the most 'scientific' of the 'bruisers' who had recently come to public attention.[4]

Daniel Mendoza's victory over Sam Martin in April 1787 had made him famous, even rich – at least for a while. He was in demand as a teacher and 'invited to spar with several amateurs, and gentlemen much celebrated for their attachment to the pugilistic art'.[5] One such was Colonel Hanger, who arranged for Mendoza to fight his black servant, a man apparently 'who had acquired great repute for his skill in pugilism'. It has been reckoned that there were as many ex-slaves in London as there were Jews. Several black men became celebrated boxers, most notably the great Bill Richmond, and his protégé, Tom Molineaux. Boxing was a sport for the disenfranchised, whether Irish Catholic, Jewish or black. According to Dan, the fight lasted 20 minutes before his opponent 'declined the contest'.[6]

Mendoza cashed in on his fame by opening a school where he would teach the art of self-defence. This was in Bartholomew Lane, Capel Court, behind the Royal Exchange. Soon after the opening 'a circumstance occurred, which though trivial, tended greatly to widen the breach then existing, between Humphries and me'.[7] According to Mendoza a 'Mr R', a friend and patron of Humphries, had won 20 guineas on the Martin fight, and happily presented Dan with all his winnings. One day, at the Capel Court school Mendoza was arrested at the request of the same 'Mr R', 'who now pretended he had *lent* me the money'. Mendoza regarded this as a machination on the part of Humphries. Nevertheless, he did not fight the claim and paid up.

While known to 'gentlemen', Daniel was known to the less-than-gentle too, such as soldiers. In his *Memoirs* he reports commencing a set-to with a soldier in Richmond, near the Talbot Inn (there is still a Talbot Inn in the Richmond of North Yorkshire, though there is no suggestion that Mendoza was on one of his tours, so the Richmond in question was likely that of Surrey). It took the soldier a little while to recognise his adversary, but when he did he 'suddenly exclaimed that he knew me, and would therefore fight no longer'.[8] The soldier, it turned out, had been taught to box by one of Mendoza's pupils (though it does well to remember that Dan was then still only twenty-two years old and a battle-bruised fifty-something when he wrote his book).

On 22 May 1787 (the same day as the formation of The Society for the Abolition of the Slave Trade), Mendoza married his cousin Esther, daughter of another Daniel Mendoza, his uncle. They shared grandparents Aaron and Benvenida. Esther gets very little mention in the *Memoirs*, though her husband does say that 'the years of experience in which we have had to encounter, as well the deceitful smiles of prosperity as the terrific frowns of adversity, have never given me reason to repent my choice.'[9] Which I suppose he did not have to. He did promise her 'to seek no further contests, and even to decline all challenges for the future that might be offered, except from Mr Humphries'.[10] It wasn't a promise that Daniel Mendoza was constitutionally designed to keep, which perhaps suggests either a lack of self-knowledge or a deceitfulness he probably would not have acknowledged in himself. Self-deception is the most likely reading. Again, he was still a young man. He did, however, turn down a challenge from John Doyle, a fighter who had won a 'terrible conflict' with a boxer called Chitty the previous December.[11]

According to the *Memoirs* Humphries and Mendoza during that year had met 'frequently … at public places' and 'had spoken [their] minds to each other pretty freely'. They met, for example, at a cricket match between the White Conduit Club (later the Marylebone Cricket Club, perhaps better known as the MCC) and All England, attended by thousands, played at Lord's Old Ground, in Dorset Square, Marylebone, to which the club had moved that year. (All England won by 239 runs.)

Mendoza places the following incident much later in the year, and holds Humphries responsible. It actually occurred three or four days after the cricket match, about a month after his wedding. Perhaps Esther's condition explains Daniel's shifting of the date.

One evening being at Vauxhall gardens with my wife, my brother-in-law, and another friend, on our preparing to return, we were suddenly surrounded by a party of about twenty men, among whom I recognised my old antagonist Tyne; they immediately began to insult us, pushing against us in a rude and violent manner, and as their ill behaviour was particularly directed against my wife, who was at that time in a state of pregnancy, I became greatly alarmed on her account, and entreated them to suffer me to conduct her to some place of safety; assuring them, at the same time, that if any of them felt the least cause of complaint against me, I was ready and willing to answer it in any manner they pleased. All I could say, however, had no avail with them, and I was actually compelled to fight my way through them, which having effected with the assistance of my two friends, my brother-in-law conveyed my wife away from this scene of riot, and returned as soon as he had placed her in safety, to my assistance. I now singled out one who seemed the stoutest man of the party, and having told him he should give me satisfaction for the conduct of himself and his companions, we set to and fought for about ten minutes when he had evidently the worst of the contest. I was now assailed by sticks in all directions, but my friends and myself made such a desperate resistance, that we were on the point of gaining the victory, notwithstanding the superiority of numbers opposed to us, when I was, all of a sudden, seized forcibly by the arm, surrounded by several men, carried away from my friends to the servants hall and locked up in a room over there. From hence however I contrived to escape by dropping from a window, and with no small surprise, beheld my wife, at a short distance, sitting very disconsolate on a bench, from whom I learnt that my two friends were in custody on the charge of our antagonists, who accused us of being the aggressors. Highly indignant at this false and infamous accusation, but at the same time, being aware that my attempting to interfere would serve no purpose, we walked to the waterside, and took a boat with the intention of returning home, and on our way, happened to meet our adversaries upon the water who it appeared had been to take some refreshment, and were on their return, for the purpose of making good the charge against my friends. Having accosted them, considerable altercation ensued between us, and on their evincing a disposition to insult me further, I felt so much irritated, that seizing a staff which lay in the boat I aimed a blow at them with such force, that had I not fortunately missed my aim by striking too high, the consequence would probably have been fatal to some of them. I believe they now regretted they had molested me, for some of them had suffered severely in the course of the conflict in the gardens, and conscious of having acted very wrong, proposed to settle the affair amicably, and professed great regret for what had happened, and their willingness to compensate myself and my friends, in consequence of which I consented to let the matter drop. I was dreadfully cut in the head in the course of the affray, the ill effects of which remained for a long time after.[12]

Newspapers reported the incident somewhat differently. 'On Saturday evening Mendoza, the fighting Jew ... having a quarrel at the garden-gate at Vauxhall, with Warr the famous bruiser, the latter agreed to fight the former, when the Jew received a most complete drubbing, and was obliged to be taken home in a coach.'[13] So reported the *Morning Chronicle*. *The World and Fashionable Advertiser* was closer to Mendoza's own memory:

A violent affray happened at Vauxhall on Saturday night, between a knot of Gentlemen and some Jews, headed by Mendoza. After a contest that lasted near an hour, the Israelites, with their champion, were defeated, and Mendoza conducted to the round-house, in the custody of the constables who attended.

In the course of the affray, Mendoza stripped, and challenged any two in all the gardens – but his late success at Barnet has given so much terror to his name, that none were bold enough to accept the challenge.

Several gentlemen were violently bruised – and the Jew himself received more dry blows than he even got from the Bath Butcher.[14]

Many years later a third account appeared, although so different is it that it probably describes another occasion. In May 1811 a sometime flunky of the Prince of Wales, Captain Felix McCarthy, died, and a long anecdote appeared in the newspapers concerning a fight he had had with Mendoza. The *Chester Chronicle*, for example, published this account:

Many extraordinary feats are told ... of the punishment ... which he inflicted on the petulance of those who were so silly ... as to fasten quarrels upon him ... the most celebrated of these affairs was a rencontre with the celebrated Mendoza, at Vauxhall, during the period when that celebrated hero of the fists held the proud station of what is called 'The Champion of England'. Mendoza was taken to Vauxhall for a freak by a party of amateurs, who selected Mr McCarthy, from his size and apparent strength, as the object upon whom Mendoza might most conspicuously display his science, to the surprise and amazement of the surrounding assemblage. A row was accordingly kicked up, and a set-to took place between Mendoza and Mr McCarthy, in which Dan had the advantage, but without making any material impression on his robust and hardy opponent. But the gentlemen who ran from all parts of the gardens on hearing of the affray, recognizing Mendoza, and thinking it unfair to suffer anyone, of whatsoever apparent strength, unless a professed pugilist, to be involved in a contest with him, separated the combatants; and when Mr McCarthy, enraged by the blows he had received, pressed for renewal of the combat, they endeavoured to quiet him by telling him, what it seems he did not know, that his antagonist was the 'invincible pugilist Mendoza, the champion of England!' This information however, had a very different effect on Mr McCarthy, from what it was intended and expected to produce. With a fury it was impossible to restrain, he burst through the circle that surrounded him, and rushing upon Dan, in defiance of all his efforts of art, he seized him in his arms and carried him, struggling in vain to disengage himself, to the barrier of the entrance, over which he flung him with a force that astonished the beholders, to a considerable distance among the crowd, exclaiming all the time against his impudence for presuming to obtrude himself into a respectable place of amusement, and to insult gentlemen, and enforce quarrels with them when he did get in. Mendoza's friends, it may be supposed, did not complain of the chastisement he had received; nor were those who introduced him forward to resent or notice the animadversions made upon their conduct, not only by Mr McCarthy, but by the company in general. – Vauxhall has in consequence remained free from the annoyance of professed boxers ever since, although the science has so far spread in a general practice as to have become a nuisance in almost every other public place.[15]

Not written by an enthusiast for the sport, then, and allowance should be made for the hyperbole that naturally attaches to eulogy. Nonetheless, the account is very different from that given by Mendoza. If this was a different occasion it is equally indicative of the celebrity Mendoza enjoyed and under which he laboured: the comedian asked for a joke, the doctor approached for medical advice at a cocktail party, the fighter challenged – a price of fame.

His name entered common currency. A 'Mendoza' became a slang word for a 'good blow'[16], as described in John O'Keefe's play *The Young Quaker*, which evidently introduced topical elements with new productions, as it had first been performed seven years previously. Dan's was a name that would immediately be recognised by theatre-goers, and theatre of course, was a far more popular medium in the eighteenth century than it is now. Daniel Mendoza had become a metaphor.

Whatever the hoi polloi thought of the fighting Jew, he was welcome in aristocratic circles. He had become a familiar character around town, and while it is questionable whether he could have been called handsome, he was certainly striking. He was not brutish in appearance; he was full-lipped, long-lashed, his oval face framed by long, dark hair, tied in a bow. He dressed well; he was dapper.

At some point during that year he was persuaded to go foxhunting in Oxfordshire. He wasn't particularly interested, but 'in compliance with the solicitations of friends' he agreed to go. As appears so often in Daniel Mendoza's life there was an occurrence that promised violence.

> One day however I happened to follow this sport in a way that gave great displeasure to a gentleman, who rode up to me, and accusing me of riding among the hounds, and of other improper conduct, threatened to horsewhip me unless I altered my behaviour. I felt greatly irritated at this language, for though I perhaps deserved reproof, it might, I thought have been given in a milder way, and therefore warned him in a resolute manner, not to attempt anything of the sort, and declared, that if he even raised his whip for such a purpose, I would certainly strike him off his horse, be the consequence what it would. After some further altercation however, we each continued to follow the sport as it suited our inclination; but my surprise was greatly excited at learning, almost immediately afterwards, that the person I had offended was none other than his grace himself.
>
> When the hunt was over, the duke rode up to me again, and asked me how I liked the sport, upon which I told him I had enjoyed it much, and was happy that our previous altercation had terminated as it had; for that had his grace offered to raise his whip for the purpose of putting his threat into execution, I should undoubtedly have kept my word and knocked him off his horse, not knowing at the time who he was. His grace laughed at the circumstance, and observed that the impetuosity of his temper often drew him into an intemperance of behaviour by no means becoming.[17]

Mendoza, had he known himself better, might have made a similar confession. 'His Grace' was Henry Somerset, 5th Duke of Beaufort, about whom there is very little to say, other than that he seems to have been good-hearted if impetuous, and therefore not at all unlike Daniel Mendoza.

July saw the excitement building at the prospect of a contest. 'Mendoza and Humphries will certainly fight,' reported *The World*, 'nothing but the time and place being now to be resolved on. Some of Mr Humphries' friends proposed Steine at Brighthelmstone [Brighton] – but Mendoza rather preferred the field at Margate – as they would be sure of having plenty of backers among the descendants of Moses and Aaron.'[18]

The *Public Advertiser* agreed. 'Mendoza and Humphries are shortly to show striking proofs all their excellence in the arts – gymnastic – much support is expected – although the latter is the Goliath of the field – yet the little black bruiser is warmly patronised by the Broughtonian black legs.'[19] 'Black legs' was the phrase given to swindling bookmakers, who had multiplied with the rise of horse racing.

In August it was reported that William Warr (or possibly Ward) had challenged Mendoza, Humphries and Martin for 100 guineas each, the fights all to be had within 12 hours. It seems not much attention was paid. Other matches were rumoured: Mendoza was apparently to fight 'Death', so called for his pale complexion. His real name was Stephen Oliver. It was thought by the end of his career that he had fought 'more battles than any boxer in England'.[20] A 'noted bruiser' from Ireland was expected, sent for by a 'Noble Lord' expressly to fight Mendoza. On 14 August the *Morning Chronicle* reported that 'The boxing match between Humphries and Mendoza is off in consequence of the latter not having made good the deposit of 50 guineas.'[21] Quite what Dan Mendoza did with all his money has never been satisfactorily answered, though gambled it away is the commonest guess.

On 9 September, Mendoza and some friends set out to go to the annual Harlow Fair. At The Cock, a coaching inn in Epping, on the main road from London to Norwich (the building remains, but not as an inn) they came upon Richard Humphries and a gaggle of friends. *The World and Fashionable Advertiser* reported what occurred:

Mr Humphries gave that kind of defiance to the Jew, which among the French, produces what is called a rencontre en outrance.

In a word, Humphries put his fist upon the others face, which so exasperated Mendoza that though he had before declined the contest, they had an immediate set to in the inn yard, where they happened to meet; this continued for about three or four minutes, till the battle was put to an end by a constable.

In that small space of time, Mendoza put in two blows, and Humphries only one. The latter got a broken nose and a black eye; the blow that Mendoza received, was on the jawbone, and it brought him to the ground. Mendoza evinced wonderful agility in this, springing up and reaching over Humphries' guard.[22]

The constable, it seems, was later full of remorse to find what 'mischief' he had done in not letting the fight proceed. He had imagined the two men were pickpockets from London, wanting to 'take the usual advantage by raising a mob'. Had he known they were 'two such great men' he would 'never have put my staff between them'.[23]

According to Mendoza, the two men met again at Harlow, and Humphries offered to renew the fight 'but this I declined, telling him I wished not to take advantage ... when he was deprived of an eye; and advising him to take more care of the other'.[24] Mendoza himself wrote that at Epping he had 'succeeded in closing one of my opponent's eyes'.

The following month, at a fight between W. Savage and Dennis Kellyhorn in Epping Forest '... Humphries and Mendoza happened to be present – and the former challenged the champion of the Israelites. Mendoza agreed to accept ... provided that on weighing, there was no greater difference between them, than that allowed according to the give and take principles of Broughton.'[25] The difference turned out to be 7 lbs: Mendoza 10 stone 6 lbs (146 lbs), Humphries 10 stone 13 (153 lbs). Mendoza then objected to fighting on a stage, wanting to fight on grass. Humphries 'very properly' rejected this suggestion on the grounds, according to the newspaper, that 'it is a common practice with the Jews to break the ring, when they find their champion is in danger of being beaten.' This is said as though it were a commonplace, but given that there were very few other Jewish boxers at the time (Mendoza's success was to spawn many, indeed a tradition), it seems like a gratuitous slur against Dan himself. Humphries was to be saved by a similar action in the coming fight. According to the newspapers Mendoza further rejected Humphries' offer, put at the same meeting, to fight not for money but 'for love'. Mendoza also rejected fighting on a larger stage. One might reasonably gather that Mendoza was not ready to fight. However, his own account of the meeting is a little different: 'I challenged him to fight me for fifty guineas, and it was settled that we should meet in the evening at the Spread Eagle[26] to settle the conditions of the battle, and make the deposit.' At the pub another fight started when one of Dan's friends was hit with 'a whip loaded with lead'. Tempers eventually did cool down enough for the two men to agree on a date for the fight.

The newspapers did not communicate this information. Instead Mendoza's apparent prevarication elicited a subtly expressed belief that he was afraid. *The World* again:

> Tell it not in Gath, publish it not in the environs of Houndsditch, that Mendoza, after boasting he was a match for Humphries, declined meeting him on a stage!
>
> Mendoza is even more unreasonable than Shylock – for he [Shylock] only wanted a pound of Christian flesh – but he insists upon seven being taken from Humphries.[27]

Seven days later the same newspaper published the following:

> The following is a CHALLENGE sent by D. MENDOZA to R. HUMPHRIES, at Mr BRADDYLL's, Lancashire
>
> Mr Humphries
> Sir
> This will inform you, that I am ready to meet you on a stage twenty-four feet square, (which is agreeably with your own proposition) to adjust all differences that have existed between us – the time and place to be settled at a previous meeting.
>
> I remain
Yours, etc.
D. MENDOZA
19th October[28]

A week later, Humphries replied:

> Mr MENDOZA,
> I have received your challenge, and recollect that the terms proposed were, a twenty foot stage, allowing you to fall, or a twenty four foot not to fall without a blow. I perceive you have chosen the latter, which will give the gentlemen a better opinion of your courage than the cowardly method of tumbling down, which you have hitherto wanted, and which I certainly should have granted had you

preferred a twenty foot stage. I shall be in town shortly, when we will settle time, place and terms.

I am, yours etc.
RD HUMPHRIES
Lancaster, October 24 1787[29]

This discourteous letter from someone known as the 'Gentleman' boxer refers to one of Broughton's rules, those seven that loosely governed the sport. It permitted the fighter to drop to one knee ('fall') to begin a 30-second count at any time. Thus a fighter, realising he was in trouble, had an opportunity not only to recover, but to escape.

The fight, however, was on, and the anticipation grew more fevered by the day. Even those (perhaps especially those) who disapproved had something to say: 'I hear that Humphries and Mendoza are to have another bout at fisticuffs for the amusement of the polite and humane part of the public,' wrote someone calling himself or herself 'Serious' in the *St James's Chronicle*.[30]

On the day on which Humphries' acceptance of Mendoza's challenge was received, the publication was announced of *An Enquiry into the State of the Pugilatus, or art of bruising, among the ancients; with a very copious account of the cestus, or boxing glove, and an historical essay on bludgeons, proving them to be at least as ancient as the days of Hercules. By the Hon. George Hanger. With notes by Mendoza, Big Ben, Warr, Johnson and several other eminent professors.* Hanger was a friend of the Prince of Wales. He was 'irascible, violent, dissipated, extravagant, and individualistic sometimes to eccentricity'.[31] He was a soldier, a duellist, a writer, a gambler, a beau, a clubman. In August the year after the above was published – 1788 – he organised 'bludgeon men' for the Whigs at a Westminster by-election (the Whigs won). He married first a Gipsy, who ran away with a tinker, and then his housekeeper. He took boxing lessons from Sam Martin, the Bath Butcher, who had been defeated by both Humphries and Mendoza. In later life he was imprisoned for debt, became a coal merchant (as did Richard Humphries), inherited the title Lord Coleraine, and 'advocated public urinals with the state profiting from the sale of the urine as fertilizer, and taxes on cutlery and "absentee Scotchmen" who failed to reside six months a year in Scotland'.[32] His *Pugilatus* book was among the first of many to be written on the art in the following few years, but it is no longer to be referred to, as no copy seems to have survived. It would have been interesting to see Mendoza's 'notes' and to compare them with those in his own *The Art of Boxing*, published in 1789.

Boxing was in. Patronised by the wealthy, written about in the papers (the reports quoted above were reproduced in numerous local papers throughout the country). It was, according to a facetious piece in the *Daily Universal Register* (soon to become *The Times*) 'a polished amusement'. Mendoza and Humphries elicited as much praise, it suggested, as Mrs Siddons, the premier actress of the age. It concluded:

> If we judge from the present progression of this elegant accomplishment, we may venture to presage that black eyes and bloody noses will shortly succeed to patchou and dimples in all beautiful countenances, so that it may become a vulgarism to appear in public without some contusive mark of attachment to the gymnastic art.[33]

The guessing started as to where and when the fight would take place. The *Oxford Journal* reported that they would fight in Colchester: 'a convenient spot has already been marked out in that city, where they may "feed fat their ancient grudge".'[34] The *Daily Universal Register* was more circumspect: 'Hockerill, Newmarket and Colchester, are each mentioned as the place where the fight between Mendoza and Humphries is to be decided; but as the magistrates in different parts of the country have not shown a disposition to promote this species of fashionable diversion, it is not publicly known as yet.'[35]

Final arrangements were made between the two men at the beginning of December, Mendoza handing Humphries the following:

> Mendoza is ready to fight Mr Humphries on the ninth of January 1788, for fifty pounds, twenty-five pounds to be staked, upon a stage of twenty-four feet square, to fight without dropping unless by a blow, under penalty of forfeiting the whole fifty pounds.
>
> No quarrel between the seconds to be a hindrance to the fight, the party that may begin the quarrel to forfeit the money
>
> The door money to be equally shared
>
> No person to be admitted on the stage but seconds, bottle holders and umpires.

The place to be mutually agreed upon.

The remaining twenty-five pounds to be made good this day fortnight in the hands of the present stake-holder, who has received fifty pounds, or the deposit to be forfeited.

London, 5th December, 1787[36]

Mendoza and Humphries had one more meeting before their own fight, and this was at the bout featuring Tom Johnson, regarded as the Champion of England, and Michael Ryan, whose 'neatness in sparring was the equal of Mendoza's', no less. It took place at Wradisbury in Buckinghamshire on 19 December and was the cause of no little controversy, not least because of the actions of Humphries, who acted as Johnson's second. Mendoza was Ryan's bottle holder. What follows is Pierce Egan's description of the fight in *Boxiana*:

The set to was grand: fear was out of the question, and science was pre-eminent. It was like unto Pompey and Caesar, attended by their best generals to give advice upon the least disorder, in contending for the high honour of the purple. True courage was never finer displayed, and perfect heroism was seen upon both sides. The contest was doubtful in the extreme, though, at the commencement, the odds were in favour of Ryan. After the fight had continued for nearly twenty minutes, and at the close of a most tremendous round, Ryan put in a dreadful blow upon Johnson's temple, which so completely stunned him that his arms fell down as useless by his side, and was following up this advantage with another hit, which must have decided the contest, when Humphries ran in to save Johnson, and caught Ryan in his arms. The cries of 'foul! foul!' now resounded from all parts of the spectators, and the friends of Ryan instantly demanded the money, by observing that, as long as Johnson had not fallen, it was perfectly fair on the part of Ryan to strike him, and that the latter had won the battle. Here a general clamour took place, during which Ryan, with the warmth peculiar to his country, indignantly told his second, Dunn, that he had not done his duty by him as a man, in suffering such conduct to take place without resenting it, and, had he not been prevented, would have milled Dunn upon the spot, so great was his rage. Considerable time having now elapsed, Johnson was perfectly recovered, and challenged Ryan to renew the combat: the latter, like a man, notwithstanding it was considered there was no necessity for so doing, agreed to it, thinking he could beat Johnson. The battle was at length renewed; but it was soon perceived that Ryan's strength was exhausted by passion, and he now, in about ten minutes, became an easy conquest to Johnson, by giving away the chance. Ryan's conduct in the battle was so noble, and his manly courage and science so truly apparent, that the amateurs were still left in doubt to decide accurately which was the best man.[37]

The left-handed Ryan, though 'communicative and good-natured' had a quick temper, and was regarded in this respect as often 'an accessory to his own defeat'. As for Humphries helping out Johnson at a critical moment, we shall see that the favour was returned.

Towards the end of December Humphries went to Ipswich to start training. Daniel Mendoza closed up his school at Capel Court, presumably to concentrate on his own preparation, though he later claimed that he 'paid no more regard to training on this than on any former occasion, having sufficient confidence in my natural activity and the excellence of my constitution, and therefore passed the interval without varying in any way my usual mode of living'.

From the start of speculation, the odds had been very much in Humphries' favour. He was the heavier, more mature man (probably around twenty-seven years old), and, moreover, he was popular. Born in London around 1760, Humphries, according to one source, was the son of a servant of one of the Clapham Sect.[38] According to another, he was the son of a destitute army officer.[39] Whichever may be true, he clearly had a certain refinement of manner that made him attractive to those who regarded boxing as a genuinely healthy activity, both morally and physically, for individual and nation alike: 'a remarkably graceful boxer, and his attitudes were of the most elegant and impressive nature. He was about the middle size, strong, and well-limbed.' And it was Humphries' bout with Sam Martin at Newmarket that had once again brought boxing to the fore: 'he was so attractive as to revive pugilism, which had been on the decline for some time.'[40] After that fight Humphries had intended to call it a day. Shortly before Mendoza's own fight with Martin, *The World* informed its readers that 'Humphries fights no more. He now only teaches others to fight, in quality of a master.'

Humphries probably started teaching before Mendoza, from rooms in Panton Street, off the Haymarket in London. His pupils included the aforementioned George Hanger, and also Wilson Braddyll, his patron for most of his career. Braddyll was a Whig MP, an intimate of the Prince of Wales, and another 'great amateur of the pugilistic art'.

In his diary entry for 15 October 1796, Joseph Farington commented that Braddyl consumed his fortune not by gaming but by inattention to his expenses, such as spending time in taverns, and his 'profuseness of living', including his connection with the *cantatrice* Mrs Billington. It was Braddyll who had promoted the fight between Sam Martin and Mendoza and it was to Braddyll's establishment in Ipswich that Humphries retired to train (and to be fed):

> Hear thou, B – y– ll, well form'd for doughty deeds,
> Whose hospitable Beef thy Humphries feeds[41]

Humphries sparred with a man called Ripshaw, lifted weights, and ran every morning. Several sources suggest that Humphries, while the clear favourite, might in one respect be inferior to Mendoza, in 'wind'.

By 4 January, it was known that Odiham would host the fight. The *Gazetteer and New Daily Advertiser* carried a preview:

> The bets are now seven to four on Humphries; and if we consider the following circumstances, it is probable the odds will be still greater.
>
> Humphries, with infinitely more practice, is much stronger than his adversary, as was proved from his being able to second Johnson, while Mendoza could not act as second to Ryan, for want of strength to pick him up.
>
> Humphries is a grown up man, in the prime of strength – Mendoza is not yet arrived at his full growth, and is, besides, rather shorter and lighter than Humphries.
>
> Besides which, Humphries is the favourite, and those who generally contrive to constitute themselves umpires bet deeply upon him.
>
> Mendoza is indeed said to be in better wind – but Humphries has been for some time in training, for the express purpose of bringing himself into condition, at Ipswich, under the inspection of the man who prepared him for Martin at Newmarket – therefore this superiority of Mendoza cannot be relied on.[42]

The Times' 'Betting Room' gave odds of 2 to 1.

On Sunday 6 January, Daniel Mendoza set off from Houndsditch, with David Benjamin (a pastry chef) who would be his second, and a bottle holder by the name of Hestea (a fishmonger) but maybe Jacobs (the records differ – in Mendoza's own recalling his second was a Jacobs and his bottle holder an Isaacs). Humphries followed on the Monday. The fight was due to start on the Wednesday at 11am.

Doubtless the very wet weather[43] hampered the erection of a stage, 24 foot by 24 foot, in the Duke of Bolton's paddock at Odiham,[44] but it was duly accomplished without hindrance from the local magistrates and despite the objections of the Vicar of All Saints, the parish church.

The heavies of the ring – Tring, Ryan, Dunn, Sandler, Warr 'and many other noted bruisers' – were present as security. They looked like 'giants' and were armed with cudgels. Their chief duty was to ensure that only those with tickets gained entry. In the event they were overpowered by the hordes who had arrived, despite the rain and the cold, determined to witness the fight.

> In the town of Bagshot, more than three hundred persons slept in their way to the battle... At the little town of Hooke, seven fashionable gentlemen slept in the hayloft... Above twenty carriages returned to town, from the impossibility of getting horses, though any money was offered for them... Of the scenes on the road – some in beds, and some without – rooms with 20 people sleeping upon the carpets, and many gentlemen reduced to walk the last 14 miles.[45]

Those who paid their ½ guinea – some 400 – at least had seats on a raised terrace surrounding two sides of the stage. The take was later divided between the two fighters, who had each staked £25.

A little after 1pm, Richard Humphries entered the ring to 'huzzas and plaudits'. He bowed and then stripped down to 'a pair of fine flannel drawers, white silk stockings, the clocks of which were spangled with gold, and pumps tied with ribbon'. Years later Thomas Moore celebrated the occasion in his poem *Tom Cribb's Memorial*: 'When Humphries stood up to the Israelite's thumps / In gold-spangled stockings and touch-me-not pumps'. One of the items Humphries also removed was a pair of worsted socks.

Humphries was accompanied by Tom Johnson as his second and Tom Tring as bottle holder, two first-class boxers. Mendoza followed with his pastry chef and fishmonger. Mendoza himself was dressed 'plain and neat'.[46] A Mr Allen, a brewer, was umpire for Humphries, Mr Moravia ('a Jew merchant') for Mendoza.

MENDOZA v HUMPHRIES I
9 January 1788
Odiham, Hampshire

The two men come up to scratch in the middle of the ring. They shake hands. Mendoza smiles. Humphries does not. He appears to be full of implacable hate. He has treated Mendoza with complete indifference until this point.

Battle commences.

The early moments are cagey, neither boxer is inclined to strike. A feint or two, nothing more. Suddenly Mendoza advances, and catches Humphries the first blow 'near the eye', and promptly, with his own momentum, slips on the wet stage. More sawdust is added to the mix of sawdust, rosin (a kind of solid resin) and chalk that has already been laid down before the start of the fight.

Mendoza's second blow puts Humphries down, and draws blood from the gentleman's nose. Mendoza throws Humphries (i.e. pushes him to the ground, quite allowed). And so it continues for another 15 or 20 minutes, Mendoza forcing Humphries to 'every corner of the stage'.[47]

Dan ducks and dives, displaying 'as wonderful dexterity in stopping the blows of his adversary, as he did strength and firmness in the effect of them'.[48]

By this stage the betting has switched very much in favour of Mendoza. Humphries appears astonished at the onslaught.[49] Nevertheless, in the whispers and arguments among the crowd, one might hear the suggestion that Mendoza's superiority is not altogether due to his quality as a fighter, and that Humphries' footwear is to blame. Indeed, he is slipping constantly, so, he takes off his slippers and silk stockings, and exchanges them for a pair of worsted socks. Worsted (after the Norfolk village of that name) is a kind of wool yarn that is stronger than mere wool. They afford a grip.[50]

Many years later Mendoza is still angry about this.

It was expressly agreed between my opponent and myself, previous to the contest taking place, that there should be only half a minute allowed between each round, notwithstanding which at one time, when nearly exhausted, he complained of the tightness of his shoes, and was forty seconds beyond his time in changing them for a pair of socks, yet no advantage was taken or attempted to be taken on my part of this circumstance.[51]

Having dispensed with the finery, Humphries turns to Johnson, his second, and says, 'Now it will do.'

Humphries needs a rest after being relentlessly chased around the ring for a quarter of an hour. At the same time, once he has put on the worsted stockings, his ability to stand up to Mendoza improves; he is slipping less. Humphries manages to get back on terms, throwing Mendoza a 'cross-buttock' (a term for a throw over the hip – it makes an early appearance in Fielding's *Tom Jones*).[52] Mendoza falls on his face, cutting his forehead just above the right eye. His nose is bruised.[53] Mendoza recovers, and lands a few punches on Humphries' face but then takes a blow in the neck, below the left ear, and blood gushes from his mouth. Again he rallies but receives a big hit to the kidneys. It makes him throw up. At some point he slips and badly turns his ankle. The game is up.

Mendoza is described as 'fainting', of leaving the stage 'lifeless'. Certainly he was badly wounded. He had brought with him four pigeons, two dark and two light. The dark were released to fly back home to Duke's Place, carrying the sombre news of Daniel's defeat and the loss to Jewish backers of a colossal amount, estimated at £25,000.

There were suggestions that Mendoza had 'given in', but these may have been provoked by a sense of Christian moral superiority. Mendoza was certainly hurt quite badly. The *Gazetteer and New Daily Advertiser* of 14 January, less than a week after the fight reported that 'the blows [Mendoza] received were so very severe, and in particular about the kidneys, that he will not be able to stand up against any man for a considerable time.'

On his return to London, Mendoza was attended by a surgeon by the name of Henry Saffory. He was the author of the snappily entitled *The inefficacy of all mercurial preparations in the cure of venereal and scorbutic disorders, proved from reason and experience...* (it goes on, but suffice it to say that it was one of the first shots in what was to be the long-running 'Vegetable

Wars', fought over the virtues and vices of various cures for venereal disease, especially 'De Velnos's Syrup'). Of Dan's injuries, Saffory had no doubt 'that the excruciating pains he must have experienced, was sufficient to deprive him of the ability to stand'.[54]

In contrast, Humphries 'was so little hurt ... that in the afternoon on the same day on which he fought – he was walking about the town, and was introduced to different parties of gentlemen – who from want of horses were obliged to stay the whole night in Odiham'.[55] He returned to London the day after the fight and his carriage was cheered down Piccadilly.

Odiham itself was left in peace. No riots followed the fight. A Mr Price was pickpocketed of £25 but otherwise there seems to have been no sign of the feared criminality. The little town certainly benefitted. The local school took advantage of the publicity by advertising itself in the papers as a place where 'young gentlemen are genteelly boarded and tenderly treated, taught the Classics, English and Accompts, in all their branches; the use of the Globes, &c. &c.'[56]

The fight was regarded as exemplary. One report that did the rounds in newspapers up and down the country opined that 'a battle in which there was so much dexterity and skill, with such equality of strength and muscle, perhaps never was fought.'

But it was not without controversy, quite apart from the matter of the touch-me-not pumps and the worsted socks. Early in the bout, Mendoza had forced Humphries against the railing, possibly even breaking it – 'the back of Humphries was excoriated' – and was about to deliver a blow that, according to Mendoza, 'in all probability would have proved decisive', and actually have knocked Humphries from the stage, when Humphries' second, Tom Johnson, for whom Humphries had stepped in to stop Ryan, caught the punch. Strictly speaking this should have brought an end to the fight, but the umpires conferred, and it was decided that Humphries was to all intents and purposes already down when Mendoza went to hit him, and therefore the punch would have been illegal. Mendoza claimed in his memoirs that his own umpire had laid bets against him, and so was unlikely to disqualify Humphries. His choice of second had not been wise, either. Johnson was battle-hardened, experienced, and knew the tricks of the trade. David Benjamin was a pastry cook.

As against this, Humphries' supporters found Mendoza's attempts to gouge their man's eyes unsporting, to say the least, and his predilection for pulling Humphries' nose almost too much. These, Mendoza responded, were attempts to stop Humphries from 'closing' (what is now called 'clinching', to prevent your opponent from punching). More than one description of the fight has Mendoza laughing at Humphries' inability to hit him; the nose pulling may have been adding injury to insult.

It is worth examining here the very different ways that Humphries and Mendoza approached the technical business of boxing, for despite the former being the latter's master, Mendoza had developed his own quite different techniques (in a style the *Scots Magazine* described as 'nouvelle'). These would within a fairly short space of time become regarded as orthodox, but they were far from being so that wet January day in Hampshire.

The newspapers had a go: 'impetuosity of movement' and 'dexterity' has been already mentioned; Mendoza 'put in more blows than Humphries', 'Mendoza's blows were *straight*; those of Humphries were *round*'; 'Mendoza kept his guard closer to his body, and by that measure gave a greater momentum to the arm when struck out... Humphries held his arms more out at length'; 'superior quickness of striking, was soon seen to be in Mendoza'; 'he fought low, with cunning'; 'the general mode ... of Mendoza, is with the fists near each other, opposite the chin at some distance, the elbow bent, and the left hand propelled a little more forward than the right'; 'impetuous, animated, and active'.[57]

Despite defeat, Mendoza was now held in even higher regard. The rest of the month saw the two fighters in an epistolary debate as fierce as the physical one they'd just enjoyed. These letters represent the first example of the verbal sparring that has become part of the game of boxing.

4

WAR OF WORDS

No sooner was the fight at Odiham over than the adversaries set-to in print, principally in the pages of *The World*. This was despite the fact that Humphries had said he would retire if he won (and, as we have seen, he had already 'retired' once before). He didn't seem very retiring in his goading of Mendoza.

Newspapers were a phenomenon of the eighteenth century. At the time of Humphries' and Mendoza's battles, there were twenty-eight London newspapers, nine of them daily.[1] They spread both literacy and celebrity.

Edward Topham, man of letters, Horse Guard, and man about town, was known for his dramatic epilogues, and the celebrated actress and beauty, Mrs Wells, asked him for one such for a benefit night. Their association became intimate. On 1 January 1787, Topham launched *The World*, 'from a wish to assist Mrs Wells in her dramatic life'. It was a roaring success, not least because of its willingness to print gossip and scandal ('we will not cover our paper from top to bottom in Parliamentary debates,' the first editorial had declared). Much of the content was provided by Topham, while publisher John Bell, who had sold his shares in the *Morning Post*, was involved in the paper's management. (Bell is credited with removing the long 's', resembling an 'f', from English typography, bless him). *The World* thrived.

Sheridan and Mary Robinson were contributors. It was salacious with style. However, as Pierce Egan pointed out:

> ... it is a singular fact that the correspondence of two boxers, Humphries and Mendoza, raised the sale of the paper to a higher degree than all the contributions of the most ingenious writers. It was the fashion of that time for the pugilists to send open challenges to each other, and thus publicly announce their days of fighting. This they chose to do through *The World*, as considering it the most fashionable paper; and their writing beat Sheridan all to pieces.[2]

It has been suggested that the correspondence between the two men was rewritten, as the styles of the letter writers are similar.[3] It is not entirely unlikely that Topham himself did the work. However it may be, Mendoza put in the first blow, in a letter written the day after the fight and published on 12 January. Under the headline 'Mr MENDOZA's Letter in Vindication of his Behaviour at the late Contest between him and Mr HUMPHRIES', he wrote that he understood 'with no little degree of anxiety' that his conduct during the fight had been called into question. The criticism seems to have been that he was 'done' too easily. He insists that he lost by virtue of an 'untoward accident', by which he seems to mean being thrown on his head, hit in the kidneys and punched in the stomach. He at once challenges Humphries to a return. Included with this first letter is the surgeon Henry Saffory's affidavit that Mendoza is indeed badly hurt.

Humphries' response is swift. He agrees to a return within three months, on the same terms, but that the winner should take all the gate money. The stake should be 250 guineas each.

Mendoza responds that the size of the requested stake is actually 'conveying (in an oblique direction) a negative in the challenge'. In other words, it is an inconveniently large sum. He more or less makes the same point with regard to the time limit. Humphries knows that an injury to the kidneys can sometimes take a lifetime to heal: either he doesn't want the contest or he has 'want of feeling'. Dan 'cordially agrees' to the idea of the winner taking the gate. He then makes his own proposition, with this rider: 'I shall be indifferent to any answer he may convey; whether to meet me on the stage, or rather wear those laurels, with which *chance* has crowned him.' As to detail: very well, 250 guineas a side, on the same size stage as at Odiham. Yes, 'the victor shall have the door.' And yes, when he is fit, he will cheerfully fight. Unlike Humphries, who had demanded a response within the week, Mendoza 'shall *not* distress him for an immediate reply, but leave him to consult his friends, and his own feelings, and send an answer at his leisure'.

Not surprisingly, in his almost immediate response, Humphries takes umbrage at the idea that he is indebted to 'chance' for his victory. He points out truthfully that 'neither Mr Mendoza nor his friends seemed decided where they should fix this unlucky disaster.' Was it the ankle or the hit to the loins? Humphries has a fine line in facetiousness – his opponent's 'disorder … settled with excruciating pains, in his loins; where I am aware it may abide as long as he finds it convenient'. He accuses Dan of 'unmanly arts' such as gouging and closing (the very tactic Mendoza accuses Humphries of), which he describes as 'the effects of a defeated spirit'. Not content with casting aspersions on his manliness, Humphries attacks Mendoza's 'mode of reasoning', asks whether he is to wait forever for a new contest, and ends by repeating his challenge, with one additional condition.

> That should I be beaten through accident, he shall give me an opportunity of re-establishing my credit in another contest. It is clear, that should I accede to his ridiculous propositions, it would only be driving him to new straits – for the whole tenor of his letter only proves, that Parrying, not Fighting, is the end of his wishes.

The sardonic eighteenth-century tone that makes this correspondence so enjoyable [*see* Appendix B] continues in Mendoza's next letter (published on the day of his daughter Sarah's birth), which refutes Humphries paragraph by paragraph. He then grants his opponent a wish:

> … to prevent Mr Humphries the apology of wasting his prime of life in the expectation of my recovery, I will engage, at all hazards, to fight him by the meeting in October.

Next he ups the game by more or less calling Humphries a coward: '… the simple facts are there: Mr Humphries is afraid; he dare not meet me as a boxer.' Humphries' response is: 'tell me so personally' (at the same time accusing Mendoza of 'evasion, absurdity and falsehood').

This series of fighting letters ends with Mendoza (for whom, one suspects, it was important to have the last word) reiterating the challenge: 250 guineas a side, the victor to have the gate receipts, 'the man who first closes to be the loser', and the date for the fight to be October, at Newmarket. 'It would not be amiss,' he finishes, 'to have it well penned, neatly framed, and hung up in his *truly Scientific Academy*.'

So ended the first round of their epistolary mill. It had become, in itself, an entertainment.

> Mendoza and Humphries are not going, as some of the Daily Papers stated, the one to Oxford and the other to Cambridge, for the purpose of studying the Belles Lettres; as it was agreed, upon a consultation of their friends on the occasion, that their late epistolary correspondence has afforded a proof of their having arrived at the ne plus ultra of literary composition.[4]

The two men were making the most of the spectacle they had provided. Whether they knew they were buying publicity for themselves is, I think, doubtful. Mendoza was clearly upset at losing a fight he knew he had been winning. The point was, however, that the newspapers loved it. The letters were reprinted in sheets up and down the country. The fight at Odiham had brought boxing into full public glare, and the media hounds were onto it. Newspapers teemed with anecdotes concerning the boxers and their match, and pamphlets were published in favour of the sport. Prints of the action and portraits of the stars were everywhere.

> HUMPHRIES and MENDOZA were the rage ... they rose up like a NEW FEATURE OF THE TIMES! Boxing became fashionable, followed, patronized, and encouraged.[5]

Prints appeared, not least one by James Gillray, entitled 'Foul Play, or Humphries and Johnson a Match for Mendoza', portraying Johnson's intervention (*see* Appendix D). The picture is dedicated facetiously to Humphries' patron 'Wilson Braddyll, Esqr. Gymnastico Generalissimo'. A youngish John Hoppner, who was to become a very fashionable portraitist, had been present at the fight. The previous year Humphries had sat for Hoppner for a portrait commissioned by Braddyll. The picture had been engraved by John Young in a large folio mezzotint published on 3 January, six days before the fight. Also present was Robert Dighton, who specialised in both portraits and caricatures. The first issue of a new magazine *The Royal Magazine, or Universal Chronicle and Parliamentary Register* carried Dighton's 'striking likeness of Humphries and Mendoza on a stage, fighting at Odiham'.[6] *The Town and Country Magazine* for January 1788 featured 'A whole Length Figure of Humphries, the celebrated Boxer, in his most admired Attitude, taken at Odiham, during the Battle with Mendoza the Jew. (Price 6d)'. And the *Northampton Mercury* reported that 'The handmaids of fashion, the milliners at the West End of town, never fail to take advantage of the rage of the day, and to appropriate it to dress – a new muff has just been invented; it is of coloured silk, edged with fur, in imitation of a Jew's beard, and has been aptly named the Mendoza Muff.' There were mugs and cups and jugs and medals. In other words, 'merch' as it is referred to nowadays.

Debate, report and observation rumbled on. Many of the papers had emphasised, or at least had been amused by, the fact that the fight was between Jew and Christian. 'On Humphries being declared the victor, the Israelites retreated with gloomy countenances and lightened purses, from the exulting Philistines.' reported *The World*, adding that 'upwards of £25,000 of bets will be transferred from the Jews to the Christians.'[7]

The *Morning Herald* opined that 'Christianity and Juadism [sic] were actually set in opposition to each other, and those who never thought of religion in any other shape, were interested for those who were supposed to champion the cause of their respective creeds.'[8]

On finishing the fight Humphries himself had sent a note to his patron, Mr Braddyll, who had stayed in town, and was attending a concert when he received it: 'Sir, I have done the Jew, and am in good health at the present writing.'

It has been suggested that the general tenor of these reports was of an anti-Semitic nature, and some took a dim view of both the anti-Jewish feeling and, indeed, boxing itself. The *Morning Chronicle* would have none of it:

> It is illiberal, in some of the daily papers, to ridicule Mendoza for his religion. Every man has a right to entertain what religious sentiments appear most consonant to his understanding and belief, nor has the circumstance any probability of being dangerous in a public affair of such a nature as a boxing-match.[9]

Daniel Mendoza was far from being the only Jewish boxer, or the first. The first recorded bouts involving Jewish boxers were in 1769, when London plasterer Jack Lamb defeated first Abraham da Costa and then Isaac Mousha. However, up until then no Jew had had the temerity to challenge at the top of the sport. It was a curious period in British history. There was revolution in America, nationalism in Ireland, religious rioting in London, and corruption in India – the attempted impeachment of Warren Hastings, former Governor General of India, commenced with his arrest in May 1787, and was to continue for seven years. France was beginning to boil. Mendoza and Hastings shared the news for this period. Boxing was promoted as being good for English manhood in the face of questionings of British institutions and values. In his *Art of Boxing*, Mendoza equated boxing with fencing. It was, he wrote, 'a national mode of combat, and is as peculiar to the inhabitants of this country as fencing to the French'. That fights between women were far from unknown may simply have added to the defence of boxing as an expression of robust Englishness. The *Morning Post* remarked after the Martin–Humphries fight that such fights 'inspired the lower order of people with an ardour, intrepidity, and courage … in engagements more important to national honour'. Quite a claim. Of course, like horse racing, boxing also provided gamblers with another way of losing their money.

What is remarkable is the degree to which a young Jew had muscled his way into the common consciousness. The joke Jew was no longer a ragman or a seller of oranges – the joke Jew was a boxer, and the joke tended to be on his adversaries.

Mendoza probably had a lacerated kidney. He may also have had a fractured rib – the two often go together. There would have been blood in his urine, fairly severe abdominal pain, pain in the lower back. Nausea and vomiting are attendant symptoms. It was the kind of injury that could have been life-threatening. Treatment then, as now, was rest. Nowadays such an injury would probably take a couple of months to heal, but 250 years ago the likelihood of infection was much greater. There may have been delayed bleeding (usually within the first two weeks) and urine leakage outside the kidney. Hypertension was another possibility. Scarring caused by the damage might have caused urine to drain abnormally, causing the kidney to swell and stones to form. Whatever the precise problem, Dan's ailments were evidently ongoing through much of the year following the fight – and conceivably throughout his life.

His injuries were not enough to stop him going to the theatre, as in early February he was seen to shed tears watching *The Deserter of Naples* by Carlo Antonio Delpini, the pantomimist, who, like Mendoza, would later appear at Astley's amphitheatre.[10] It played successfully at the newly erected Royalty Theatre in Wellclose Square, Whitechapel. Daniel Mendoza, the 'little black bruiser' was a sentimentalist, as I suspect is the case for many boxers.

Nor did his incapacity stop other fighters issuing challenges, such as that of John Doyle, who, according to Pierce Egan, was 'not one of Fortune's favourites in receiving the smiles of victory often'.[11] He had recently been beaten by Savage, from which fight he reported himself recovered. His challenge was impertinent, and assumed that Dan had declined a second fight with Humphries, 'which at least is proof of your prudence'.

On 16 February, a poem, *The Odiad,* was published by Lowndes and Christie, price 1s 6d. This mock heroic poem relating the events at Odiham has not found its way into *The Oxford Companion to English Literature*, although it is, in its own way, a perfect example of the form. *The Critical Review* was impressed, judging it 'worthy of the celebrity of the battle'.[12] Unlike Gillray, the author of *The Odiad* has no doubt who is the better man, by virtue of his being Christian. But give the Jew his due:

MENDOZA, Mortal Foe to Christian light,
Aims his left fist against the opponent's sight.
Bold HUMPHRIES totters – foiled in every thwack –
Head, eyes, ears, nose, lips, teeth, loins, belly, back.
All smart alike, beneath the ruthless Jew,
Whose matchless blows the astonished vulgar view.

Odiham, it was clear, had fuelled the fire kindled by the two Martin fights – and arguably the Johnson–Ryan fight in February. Humphries and Mendoza were genuine celebrities, in celebrity's first great age (both 'celebrity' and 'publicity' are eighteenth-century words). Daniel Boorstin's famous definition, 'famous for being famous', describes a modern version of the phenomenon; the eighteenth-century French writer Nicholas Chamfort defined the state of celebrity as 'being known by those who do not know you'. In that sense it can be argued with some confidence that Daniel Mendoza was the first celebrated British Jew.

Although unfit to fight, Mendoza continued to run his school at Capel Court. He cut the price of entry to ½ a guinea. The same correspondent who had complained of anti-Jewish sentiments in reports of the Odiham fight wrote: 'Yet, surely, in its present state, half a guinea entrance, and, perhaps, two or three guineas more to learn the art, is but so much money squandered away, when it might be expended on books, music, drawing, or an hundred different purposes infinitely more useful as well as more laudable.' Well, quite. 'Twas ever thus.

That there should be a return fight was never really in doubt. It was a question of getting the two men to agree conditions and date. There had been more letters in May, and in June the two men met at Smitham Bottom near Croydon in Surrey, where they both had travelled to see John Jackson beat Thomas Fewtrell. It was Jackson's first fight, arranged by Colonel Harvey Aston.[13] It was a fairly one-sided affair, despite Jackson's ignorance of the science. Humphries attempted to goad Mendoza into the ring then and there, saying if the money could not be raised, then he would fight him for love. Mendoza merely agreed to meet, his health allowing, and as his letters had agreed, at Newmarket in October.

Mendoza's physical health actually deteriorated. His daughter died that same month, in June. In the *Memoirs* he describes himself as doubly distressed, as 'wounded', as 'one whose youth is only liable to render him fonder of his children'.[14] That Dan Mendoza was a highly sensitive man is suggested both by the quickness with which he took offence, and the tenderness of his response to those who were good to him. His temper was, I think, volatile. He could be very happy or very sad – or very, very cross. Many years after these events Mendoza was complimented on his conduct by magistrates to whom he had brought information concerning the cruel treatment of a child by its mother, a woman named Catherine Connor. Daniel Mendoza wasn't a very good father, but perhaps he would like to have been.

Soon, too soon following Sarah's death, Richard Humphries turned up at Mendoza's Capel Court academy. What transpired was noted down by a visiting journalist. The transcription of the two fighters' conversation appeared in many newspapers. It was, I suppose, a kind of scoop. It is worth reprinting in its entirety, for it gives not only a description of the school, but also a sense of the degree to which Mendoza was suffering, and the condescension and haughtiness of 'Gentleman' Richard Humphries. It has, too, the flavour of the age. The following transcription comes from the *Memoirs*, but is identical to that which appeared in newspapers.

Mendoza's academy assumed, on Saturday (July 5th, 1788), an entirely novel appearance. A stage was erected in the middle of the room, of about four feet in height, encompassed with a rail, on each side of which were placed several rows of benches.

Mendoza appeared in mourning. His illness, added to what he had suffered from the loss of his child, as stated in a former paper, had so much depressed him, as to make a total alteration in his looks and spirits.

After one or two sparrings were over, the company were agreeably surprised by the appearance of Humphries and many of his friends. The seats at one end of the stage were immediately vacated, when Humphries took his place in the centre of the front bench; upon which Mendoza walked over the stage to the other side, and sat opposite him in the middle of the first bench at the other end.

Some sparrings being over, Mendoza quitted his place for the purpose of sending some of his friends to give his compliments publicly to Mr Humphries, thank him for having honoured his academy with his company, and make an apology for his wanting strength and health enough to spar at all himself. Humphries made a very civil reply; and presently afterwards, leaping on the stage, asked for Mr Mendoza, who coming forward, likewise mounted the stage, when the following dialogue passed between them. As it is curious, the writer of this article has thought it worthy of being recorded, to the best of his recollection.

HUMPHRIES. I want to know, Mr Mendoza, whether you will fight me on the first of October?

MENDOZA. I am not at all, Sir, in a condition for fighting.

HUMPHRIES. I wish to know, that I may be certain at once, and not be told, that you will and you will not.

MENDOZA. I cannot help thinking, Sir, that your conduct in appearing here for this purpose, arises from envy. My intention in coming here is to entertain the public, and to teach the art of boxing, in which, I believe, the gentlemen present will allow few people excel me; nor did I expect the peace of the company to be thus disturbed.

HUMPHRIES: I came here because I did not know where else to find you, and because I wished to learn whether you would fight me.

MENDOZA. You had my address, and could not therefore be ignorant; when I am able to engage with you, I will. At present I am not only unable to raise the money, but am under a surgeon's hands.

HUMPHRIES. I am not in condition to fight you just now, and am under doctor somebody or other's hands. I do not know his name. But if you will fix a time, I will engage with you, whether well or ill. When shall you be well?

MENDOZA. It is impossible to reply. I am not my own keeper. You cannot suppose Mr Humphries, that I am afraid of you?

HUMPHRIES. Why, you seem to feel some palpitation.

MENDOZA. And you, Sir, seem, if not afraid, at least unwilling, to engage with several persons who wished to fight you. For example, there is MR _____ [Here he was proceeding to mention several names]

HUMPHRIES. That is not the question. I wish to fight no person but yourself, and as I am going into the country, I want first to learn, whether you will fight me or not?

MENDOZA. I will [Here the company gave great applause].

HUMPHRIES. When?

MENDOZA. As soon as I am well.

HUMPHRIES. How shall I know when that is?

MENDOZA. By its being thought by my friends that I am in proper condition: everybody must see at present I am very ill; not that I have received any harm from you, but from other causes.

HUMPHRIES. No. The harm you receive from me will be the next time we fight.

MENDOZA. I hope Sir, as you beat me, when last we fought, you will allow me time to get in health, that when we next fight, I may beat you.

HUMPHRIES. I will fight you next spring, which is almost a year.

MENDOZA. I cannot tell what will be the state of my health at that time [some hisses among the company] but if I am well in six months, I will fight you; and I will acquaint you a month before the time, in order that you be able to go down to Ipswich or any other place you please. [Much applause.]

HUMPHRIES. This is no determination: but I desire, Mr Mendoza, you will not take any liberties with my name.

MENDOZA. And I desire, Mr Humphries, you will not make too familiar with mine.

HUMPHRIES. I certainly shall if you give yourself airs about me; and when you are well, I shall take you by the collar, as I did once before.

MENDOZA. And I, Sir, shall not turn my back on you. [Here was much loud and general applause].

HUMPHRIES. Very well. I find, after all, I have come here for nothing.

MENDOZA. I am sorry that you have reason to complain. I hope you did not pay your shilling at the door.

HUMPHRIES. Yes, I did.

MENDOZA. Then it shall be returned to you. I thought you came here to see the exhibition, and of course meant that you should be welcome, as you always shall, whether on my private or public days. I am sorry that I could not box myself, though I hope I shall be able to entertain the company with a little specimen of boxing next Saturday.

Mendoza then retired, and Humphries resumed his seat, but shortly afterwards, stepping upon the stage, he asked again for Mendoza, who appeared, he then informed him that he might deposit any sum, however trivial, and that he would fight him for that; to which Mendoza replied, that before he ventured to deposit money, he thought it would be proper to consult his friends upon the subject. Many persons hissed, when several of Mendoza's friends exclaimed, he cannot say more. Mendoza then bowed to the company and retired. Presently afterwards Humphries appeared on the point of asking for him a third time; but on receiving a hint from one of his friends he sat down, when the rest of the sparring continued without interruption. None but the parties concerned interfered in the dispute, more than by signs of applause, or disapprobation, as before stated, except one man that intruded his opinion at the beginning, but was soon silenced by Humphries, who told him, that no seconds were necessary on the occasion. Indeed it is fortunate that no other interference happened, as it would have biased the dispute extremely unfairly, if not involved the whole company in a general quarrel.[15]

It is interesting how insistent Humphries was on the rematch, as though he took it badly that Mendoza seemed to have won as many garlands as himself for his performance at Odiham. Mendoza found it hard to understand why he had been bearded by Humphries in his own school, and assumed that perhaps Humphries had wanted to provoke a riot, which would have had the school closed down by city magistrates.

At the end of July Mendoza contacted Humphries through *The World*, stating that he would be ready to fight the following spring, at Newmarket. To hammer out the details the two men met at the Crown & Magpie Tavern in Aldgate on 6 August 1788. It is no great surprise to learn that they could not agree. Humphries asked Mendoza to keep their disagreement private – in other words out of the papers. The following morning this appeared in *The World*:

> Sir,
> I beg leave, through the public channel of your paper, to say, that I met Mr Mendoza. By mutual agreement the place was fixed on; and I meant, according to the tenor of his offer, to have embraced the challenge. But I found he would not be bound to stand up like a man, nor would he have any settled ring; of course he might shift as often as he wanted to get off; and in short, whenever he found himself beaten, he might escape without the battle being adjudged, or the bets being determined.
>
> I am therefore convinced that spite of all his pretensions, the man never meant to fight me, and I hereby declare him a coward!
> RICHARD HUMPHRIES

Naturally Mendoza responded with alacrity, and at length. He wasn't happy with the terms proposed by Humphries. That was within his rights. The idea that he would render himself 'perpetually ridiculous' and ruin his 'professional reputation' by running away was 'an insult to the understanding of the public'. It would be 'an act of positive madness'. He then goes on to counter the suggestion that he is a coward, by recounting the number of his fights (seventeen) and the fact that he has 'no need to fight again' and 'is willing to engage once more, merely as a point of honour'. (It is interesting to ponder the fact that it was a point of honour rather than money or glory that was to make Mendoza one of the most influential Jews of his time and ensure his immortal fame as a boxer.) The letter finishes with a restatement of the challenge, and a repeated declaration that he will fight Humphries at Newmarket in the spring.

Around this time Mendoza was invited by Thomas Harris, proprietor and manager of the Theatre Royal, Covent Garden, to 'exhibit the art of self-defence' for three nights. Harris had originally made his fortune in the manufacture of soap, but was known to have a fondness for literature and the company of actresses ('since the ladies have divided their time between cards and reading, a man, to be agreeable to them,' complains Lord Formal in Henry Fielding's play *Love in Several Masques*, 'must understand something of books'). Nevertheless, he also had a fondness for spectacle and exhibition, and was accused by highbrows of sacrificing serious drama, but this strategy of mixing the popular with the sophisticated made the theatre financially secure, which wasn't the case with Drury Lane. Mendoza, then, was one of these 'exhibitions'. He was engaged 'on very liberal terms' and received 'a most flattering reception from the audience'. His partner for this show was Henry Lee, known as 'an excellent sparrer', and whom we shall meet again in the next century.

In November Mendoza heard that Humphries was back in town, and wrote to him privately, proposing another meeting. They accordingly agreed to meet at the White Hart Tavern on 26 November. However, on the Saturday preceding the meeting, two City marshals entered Mendoza's Capel Court academy, arrested the two exhibitors then sparring and closed the place down. There seemed no good reason. Apparently charging to watch sparring on a public stage was illegal (unless, it seemed, it was done at the Theatre Royal, where both Humphries and Mendoza had exhibited). Mendoza took legal advice and came up with a clever solution. Instead of purchasing entry to the public exhibition days, punters were allowed in if they could show they had bought an engraved likeness of Mendoza, which Dan had had made by a city engraver of his acquaintance.

At the meeting with Humphries an agreement was drawn up and signed by both parties. Mendoza–Humphries II was on.

5

HUMPHRIES II

In August 1788 Mendoza took a lease on the Lyceum Theatre on the Strand, 'for the purpose of opening an academy for teaching the art of self-defence'. Whether this was because Capel Court had grown too small for the demand, or whether the Lyceum was in addition, perhaps better placed for the young men of the West End, isn't clear. Certainly it was a step up. Dan was also giving private lessons to characters 'of the highest respectability'.

One of these was Sir Thomas Apreece, recently made a baronet. He was actually a Londoner, born in Leicester Fields (now Leicester Square) and a firm supporter of boxing. Apreece became a kind of manager, inviting Mendoza to train at Cranham Hall in Essex. Cranham had been owned, and was perhaps still owned by his widow, by James Oglethorpe, who had founded the state of Georgia (there is a tiny city there that bears his name). The great Methodist preacher Charles Wesley had for a time been his secretary. Oglethorpe had died in 1785. Why Apreece had use of the house I don't know. It was demolished and rebuilt in 1795, presumably by Apreece. Sir Thomas was himself a fairly useful boxer of the amateur sort.

> Sir Thomas Apreece has lately had a pugilistic contest with a bruising ruffian in the street, who goes about with a woman, whom he strikes, and threatens to murder, in order to provoke gentlemen to interfere, who for their ill-directed humanity, are almost sure to get severely

thrashed, and to be plundered of their watch, clothes, etc, into the bargain – in the present instance, however, the ruffian met with his match, Sir Thomas coming off, after a violent conflict, with the honour of the victory, though with very little of his wearing apparel.

When local Essex gentlemen turned up to match themselves against Mendoza, Apreece told them he was unavailable and offered to fight them himself. Mendoza himself did not want to set any precedent, and refused to indulge anyone (except perhaps to spar with Sir Thomas himself).

So far as preparation went, he had – up to and including Odiham – relied on his youth and generally robust constitution to see him through. Now, having been severely injured, he took matters much more seriously. In his short sketch of Mendoza, published in *Boxing Reviewed* (1790), Thomas Fewtrell remarked that Mendoza took 'vast pains to prepare himself for action by proper training'.

The agreement between Mendoza and Humphries, made at the White Hart in November ran as follows:

Mr. Mendoza proposes to fight Mr. Humphries upon the turf, in a space of forty-eight feet square.

If either person falls without receiving a blow, he is to lose the battle, unless such a fall should be deemed by the Umpires accidental.

If the ring should be broke in upon, the man who leaves the field before the battle is decided by the Umpires, shall be deemed the loser.

Each party to deposit into the hands of a person, appointed by both, the sum of Twenty Pounds: the whole of which is to be given to the winner.

That no person be admitted to see the fight without paying.

The place of fighting to be enclosed in the strongest manner, at the joint expense of both parties.

That no person shall be admitted within the place of fighting but the Umpires and the Seconds.

That both the Seconds, immediately at the setting to of the parties, shall retire to one of the four corners of the enclosure till one of the combatants is down.

That the place shall be at the option of Mr. Humphries, who agrees to give one month's notice where it is to be to Mr. Mendoza; the time, the first Wednesday in the month of May, 1789, between the hours of twelve and two; and that the money collected from the spectators to be equally divided.

To all these propositions Mr Humphries accedes; and each party deposits Twenty Pounds in the hands of Mr. Hotchkins, who is hereby authorised to give the whole to either party, if the other refuses his performance to this agreement.

Signed by
D. Mendoza,
Richard Humphries.

The place decided upon was Stilton in Huntingdonshire (it is now in Cambridgeshire), on the Great North Road – the Roman Ermine Street – from London. Stilton is of course world famous for its cheese, but it was also a major coach stop, which at one time boasted fourteen inns (for a population of 500). Perhaps it was the ease of access that made it a good choice, though it is more likely because the fight's promoter, Henry Thornton, lived there. The fight took place in his park, presumably beyond the jurisdiction of any local magistrates who took a dim view of the manly arts. Thornton was a banker, an economist (his work won praise in the last century not only from Hayek but also from Keynes) and an MP (despite on principle refusing to bribe voters, he was MP for Southwark 1782–1800). He was in favour of the abolition of slavery (he was a cousin and associate of Wilberforce, indeed at one time they shared a house), and a philanthropist (he helped set up the first free school for deaf children). One of his great grandchildren was E. M. Forster. He was one of the founders of the Clapham Sect. (It has been suggested that Humphries' father was a servant to another member – maybe Thornton himself?) It seems he also liked boxing.

The park was big enough for an amphitheatre, octagonal in shape, accommodating 2,000 to 3,000 spectators, to be built around a 12 foot square turf ring. The highest seat was some 18 feet above the fighters. All this construction was paid for by the boxers themselves, at a cost of about £300.[1] A surveyor who happened to be present insisted that it be reinforced before people were allowed to take their seats. They were clearly well aware that the fight was going to attract a great deal of attention.

And so it did. The *Morning Post* reported that 'beds in and near Stilton, and the horses on the road, are all engaged for the ensuing combat.'[2] The number of carriages heading north from London was said to be 'beyond belief'.

Shortly after 1pm on 6 May, 1789, Richard Humphries arrived with his second, Tom Johnson, his bottle holder, Butcher (in the *Memoirs* Mendoza reckons 'Ford'), and his umpire, Alderman Harvey Christian Coombe. Coombe was himself a magistrate and a coming man. In the following years he was elected MP for the City of London and became Lord Mayor at the same time. Those opposing him in various elections often caricatured him as a pugilist, such was his known keenness for the sport. A Whig, opposed to the war with France, he was also known to be a gambler. He was said to possess 'a very warm heart and great kindness of disposition'.[3] Mendoza's umpire was Thomas Apreece. Mendoza arrived next, accompanied by Michael Ryan as his second and a Captain Brown as his bottle holder. Among the crowd were of course members of 'the Quality', such as Lord Delaware, Lord Tyrconnel, Major Hangar, Mr Braddyll (the list goes on). The start of the fight was delayed somewhat by Thomas Fewtrell – whose fight with Jackson both Humphries and Mendoza had seen – attempting to gain free ingress by climbing over a spiked railing.

At the start of the contest the odds were very much in favour of Humphries, and oddly stayed that way, at seven to four and two to one.

MENDOZA v HUMPHRIES II
6 May 1789
Stilton

The two men come to the mark, shake hands and set-to. The first punch is thrown by Humphries. Quick as you like, Mendoza parries and returns, knocking Humphries down. The second and third rounds go a similar way, Mendoza's speed too much for Humphries' aggression.

Half an hour in, in the twenty-second round, Mendoza aims a punch and misses. Humphries, however, falls, or evades the blow by falling. Dan turns, believing in victory. 'Won the money', he shouts to his friends. Falling without a blow, Humphries has forfeited the fight. The *General Evening Post* opines that Humphries, even before this controversial 'shift' has already, twice, 'dropped without being knocked down'. Humphries' corner insists he'd stopped a blow on his arm before going down. 'Foul' cries one set of supporters. 'Fair' cries the other. Tom Johnson and Captain Brown square up to one another. Johnson has said something

Brown doesn't like. Brown calls Johnson a 'liar and a blackguard'. Confusion reigns. Humphries, now recovered, keeps crossing the ring to Mendoza's corner, challenging him to continue. He throws his hat into the ring ('in token of defiance', as Humphries himself puts it). The hiatus lasts by some reports for an hour. The danger for Daniel is that if he does not resume, the fight would be called a draw. Eventually Harvey Aston, the third umpire, rules that the fall had appeared unavoidable, and that the fight should be resumed. By now it is almost 3 p.m. Eventually therefore, he agrees to continue. Twice more Mendoza knocks Humphries down. In due course Humphries again falls without being hit, and acknowledges Mendoza as the winner. Mendoza's fans, substantially outnumbered, erupt with joy. Strangely, the betting odds had continued to favour Humphries throughout the contest.

Woodfall's Register regarded Mendoza as having been far the more skilful fighter, and compared his coolness and resolution in this bout to his 'ardour and impetuosity of spirit' in the Odiham fight. Others remarked on 'the lightning of Mendoza's wrist'.[4] *Felix Farley's Bristol Journal* put the victory down to Mendoza's being 'very calm, very collected [and] from this possession of temper, and from much prior exercise'.[5] The *Public Advertiser* likewise referred to Mendoza's superior temper. Almost all the reports say that Mendoza fought on the defensive, but evaded most attacks while responding 'almost on the instant of defence', as the *Public Advertiser* put it. It is precisely the way that Anthony Joshua described the way he defeated Wladimir Klitschko, the speed of parry allowing him the room to strike. *The World* stated that Mendoza fought 'scientifically and coolly', and remarked on his 'lately acquired strength'.[6] The training with Sir Thomas had paid off. Mendoza was still growing. He would be twenty-four on his next birthday.

He was also reported, as in the first fight, to have mocked Humphries, pointing at him when knocked down, mimicking his words, dropping his guard, folding his arms, even patting him on the head 'with an air of mockery'.[7] Mendoza 'kept laughing at him, as if he had a schoolboy to deal with'.[8] Impossible not to think of Muhammed Ali baiting Joe Frazier.

Mendoza was comparatively unhurt. Humphries had one eye closed and a cut above the other. His lip was split. The *Morning Post* suggested he had been unwell for some time before the fight, and pointed out that at no time during the contest had the odds changed in favour of Mendoza. This was despite the fact that Humphries was knocked down, according to one estimate, forty-two times and Mendoza nine (a different report suggests Humphries was knocked down sixteen times – so much for eyewitnesses). It was agreed that he was knocked down repeatedly at the beginning of the fight.

Woodfall's Register alludes to Humphries' 'well known liberality', and assumed he would allow that Mendoza had fought 'with wonderful science and intrepidity'.[9] That wasn't to be the case.

The bad blood flowed: after Brown and Johnson's confrontation, a cousin of Mendoza's challenged Humphries' friend Ford, who had refused to pay him for his work at the gate. Ford was a much bigger man but it did not take long for him to acknowledge the fighting skills of Daniel's cousin.

Having picked up the box containing the gate money, which he would divide with Humphries the following day, Mendoza was carried on the shoulders of his friends to the Bell Inn. They had to negotiate a crowd chanting 'Mendoza forever', 'Mendoza *vekhayam'* (is alive and well). More friends waited at the inn, where they spent the rest of the day 'with the utmost conviviality'.[10] The Bell is still there. It offers 'charming accommodation with a stylish restaurant, bistro and cosy bar'. It is also regarded, quite seriously, as 'the birthplace of Stilton cheese'.

In the *Memoirs* Mendoza tells a characteristically farcical story of what happened on the night of the victory. He and a friend left the revels at around 2 a.m. They were heading for a Mr Newbury's house, which is where they were staying. It was a 2-mile walk, and the evening was 'exceedingly dark'. I think it is fair to suggest that they may have been suffering from a surfeit of conviviality. They missed the road and walked into a farmyard, or as Daniel, the Londoner put it: 'a pit full of dung and filth'. In response to their cries for help, the farmer and a hand appeared, and far from being put out, on hearing who was stuck in their mud, the farmer offered them beds and food. They declined, were put back on track and found their way eventually to the Newbury home.

The loss was a great embarrassment to Humphries, who had been favourite both with the bookies and in terms of popular support, so excuses had to be made. *The World* claimed that Humphries had 'lately had a paralytic stroke', which seems hardly likely. Humphries himself, in a letter to the papers a few days later claimed that he had been winning the fight when the controversial blow was thrown. Indeed, he suggested that Mendoza had had to be goaded in to continuing the fight by his bottle holder, Michael Ryan. Humphries explained that having stopped Mendoza's ferocious blow as he was stepping backwards, his balance was lost and he fell. Moreover, so long was Humphries kept waiting while Mendoza refused to return to the contest that he began to feel 'the effects of a rheumatic complaint'. He was as sore a loser as Mendoza. He issued a new challenge.

HUMPHRIES III

For Dicky, he stopped with his head
Was hit through his guard ev'ry round, sir
Was fonder of falling than fighting,
And therefore gave out on the ground, sir.

'Dicky' is of course Richard Humphries. 'Stopped' is sarcastic. In the *Memoirs* Mendoza quotes the entire song, from which this is the last verse. It was probably not the only one; *Boxiana* has a long appendix of boxing rhymes, songs and poems. If Daniel Mendoza had been a heroic failure after Odiham, he was now an exotic victor. And, once again, rich. It was reckoned that Mendoza made over £1,000 from this fight.

Shortly after the fight at Stilton, Mendoza's carriage, in which he was travelling with Sir Thomas Apreece, arrived in Peterborough, where it was mobbed and held up. Mendoza was obliged to stand on a bench in the marketplace, bowing and paying his respects to the crowd who wished to honour him. Wherever he went he was feted. Despite the reservations of one or two newspapers, it seems as though Mendoza was now no longer merely a Jewish hero, but getting on for a British one. Some weeks later, a genteel, gentile female, watching Mendoza spar, was reported to have declared aloud that she wished to become 'his pupil in the science'.[1]

'Few events', he wrote, 'ever attracted the attention of the public, in such a degree, as the contests between Mr Humphries and myself.'[2]

Not even the French Revolution. By 'the public' he meant not just those drawn by the noble science, not just gamblers or louche aristocrats, not just what came to be called 'The Fancy' (the term first committed to print by the poet Robert Southey, in 1814) but all sorts.

> Milling's all the go now. In London it occupies the heads and hands of dukes, lords, apprentices and blackguards, while at Cambridge it is not who is a senior wrangler, but who is the best boxer. The Lexicon is forsaken for the slang dictionary – we cut prize poems for prize fighters – Aristotle's logic for Mendoza's knock-down arguments...[3]

Indeed, 'Mendoza' had entered the language itself:

> In a funeral procession lately, in Rome, two priests who were to officiate, quarrelling about precedency, the procession was stopped, whilst the holy brothers, like true sons of the church militant, settled their dispute *a la* Mendoza, and the victor was left in full possession of the corpse, as his lawful spoil.

Of Lord George Gordon, it was said that 'his supplicant and prostrate knee is bent equally to Pius the Sixth and to Mendoza the First.'[4]

Whenever he returned to London, Mendoza found his fights 'were the general subject of conversation all over town'. Just as your grandmother knew who David Beckham was, so everyone knew the name Mendoza. It began turning up not just in songs and poems, but on the stage. Plays were rewritten in order to include reference to the man or to his abilities. Of course it was helpful to have a euphonious name, even if it did sound 'foreign' – 'Mendoza' has more sparkle than 'Humphries' or 'Johnson'.

As has already been seen, the stage and the ring shared a great deal. Spectacle and drama characterised both. Lord Barrymore 'seldom made a public appearance without a pugilistic or theatrical companion'.[5] As Brailsford further points out, 'The web of relationships around the stage and the ring was spun in many directions, with the Duke of Clarence producing ten children by his mistress, the actress Mrs Jordan, and General Tarleton marrying that other lady of the stage, Mary Robinson.'[6] William Oxberry, the author of *Pancratia, or a History of Pugilism*, was a fairly undistinguished comic actor-manager – he once played Shylock – of the Olympic Theatre on Drury Lane (built for the inventor of the circus, Philip Astley, of whom more later). In fact, beginning in the days of his glory, Daniel Mendoza was to spend far more time on the stages of theatres than in boxing rings. It is hardly surprising to learn that shortly after the Stilton fight Mendoza was invited to appear for three nights at the Manchester Theatre, earning 25 guineas on each sold-out night.

Other than a stay in Peterborough and his visit to Manchester, there is no record of what Mendoza did between May 1789 and January 1790. He ran his school, and it is tempting to think that he bought himself some new threads and enjoyed showing himself off in them. He was a natural performer, even if he couldn't sing. In the summer he was seen wearing a long shirt with large silver buttons inscribed with the word 'Stilton' (apparently a gift from an admirer). At the Royal Circus Theatre in St George's Fields, he sparred with Michael Ryan for the delectation of the public. He signed his letters 'PP', Professor of Pugilism, and so naturally he gave lectures at Oxford. As the rhyme went

> You must know that Mendoza has been in this town
> To manage the fists of the lads of the gown.

He even fought a cabinet maker there, a man 2–3 stones heavier than himself, with predictable results.[7] Perhaps it was just as a demonstration.

Shortly before the fight at Stilton, Mendoza published, at his own expense, *The Art of Boxing* (*see* Appendix A). It is a seminal work. Although there had been one or two previous instructional publications, Mendoza's was by far the most comprehensive. He presented boxing very much as a sport, seeking to render it 'equal to fencing, in point of neatness, activity, and grace'. He ends his Preface with a sideswipe at Humphries and his supporters:

> It will give me peculiar satisfaction and pleasure to understand, that I have attained my first object, by having taught any man an easy regular System of so useful an Art as that of Boxing; and that I have proved successful in my second, by having removed any prejudices which, from the misstatement of others, might have been unfavourable to my character.

Following a public exchange of brief letters, in mid-January 1790 Mendoza and Humphries met to discuss terms for a third fight.[8] They had planned to meet at the White Hart on Abchurch Lane in the City of London, but the publican, R. J. Hart, 'impressed with honest feelings for the cause of degraded humanity',[9] perhaps a white hart indeed, forbade them. Opposition to prize fighting was as vociferous as ever. Letters calling for boxing to be banned regularly appeared in the newspapers. The boxers went instead to the Crown, around the corner on Newgate Street. It may have been at this meeting that Mendoza offered Humphries 'a large sum of money', to help him in teaching at the Capel Court academy, to which Humphries' response was: 'What! Do you imagine I will consent to be an usher to you, who am able to be your monitor?' Despite this, there is a suggestion that the meeting was, for the two rivals, relatively peacable. Without too much fuss, the date agreed on was 12 May.

On the day Humphries and Mendoza met, they were both challenged by Bill Hooper, the 'Tinman', one of the great Bristol fighters (Bristol was second to London in its production of bruisers). Neither was inclined to accept. They were keen only to fight one another. Some years later Mendoza apparently first accepted another challenge from Hooper and then forfeited his deposit by withdrawing. 'Fear,' wrote Egan of the Tinman, 'never formed any part of his composition.' He was unfortunate enough to have as his patron the aforementioned 'volatile nobleman' Lord Barrymore, in whose company he became an alcoholic.[10] The following month Hooper fought and beat a fighter called Watson, before challenging 'Big' Ben Brain. They 'fought' in August. Pierce Egan regarded it as 'the most ridiculous match ... in the annals of pugilism', Hooper spending the bout shouting at Brain, squirting water in his face and falling over.[11] They jousted for three-and-a-half hours. Night fell. A draw. Ben drolly remarked that he would be happy to rise at 6 a.m. the next day, when they could have the whole day.

The agreement drawn up between Humphries and Mendoza for the third contest was practically the same as that made for the Stilton fight. There was an extra emphasis on accidental falling, reflecting the debate over Humphries' fall in the previous battle. Moreover, it was agreed that a third umpire would arbitrate. An interesting addendum was the fifth article. After making clear that the box office takings would be split fifty-fifty, the loser would be expected to pay 'the overseer of the parish where the battle shall be fought, 50 pounds for the poor'.

The date was originally set for 12 May, but in February the two men were summoned to the Bow Street magistrates' office and informed by Sir Sampson Wright 'that it was the determination of the magistrates to put an end to the shameful practice of prize-fighting'. He pointed out, in particular, the 'great injury it did to the lower class of people', by which presumably he was referring to gambling. Daniel Mendoza argued back, pointing out that more money was spent in the neighbourhoods where he fought than was lost; and, anyway, after this last fight against Humphries he intended to retire (his son Abraham was born on 12 February that year). To no avail. Both men were required to post bail of £400 for future good behaviour. Sir Sampson added that 'he did not mean to prevent ... resenting a personal insult, but to put a stop to public boxing matches'. The *London Chronicle* applauded the decision, ironic given that it was the newspaper that had published Samuel Johnson, a cheerleader for prize fighting.[12]

That it was only Humphries and Mendoza who were banned was complained of, given that they were really the ones anyone wanted to see. There was talk of the fight going to France or Ireland. Humphries apparently mentioned hiring a boat to transport all the principals. In May the *Public Advertiser* reported that the fight would take place in the private park of Sir Thomas Apreece, with no crowd, other than six friends of each combatant. This it was thought would prevent any 'offence to decorum'.

Whether Sir Sampson's ban was restricted to London and the Home Counties or by a period of time isn't clear. What is clear is that the fight was eventually rearranged for 29 September, at Doncaster, more than 150 miles north of London, far beyond Sir Sampson's easy reach. Humphries, as was his wont, went home to Ipswich to train. A horse called Mendoza, owned by a Mr Lumm, started to win races.

The impatience among the 'amateurs' (or 'the knowing ones' or 'the Fancy') for the fight, which had been brewing since the end of the previous bout, now began to reach a critical state. Mendoza and Humphries had burst the banks of boxing, of sport, and had reached the pulpits. A letter to the *St James's Chronicle* complained that 'The young Clergy now a-days, have nothing more to do than insult mankind, challenge Mendoza, ride over those ancient rights of manors, in spite of the Lord, after a pack of mongrel puppies like themselves.'[13] And Alan Bennett's simile-smitten priest is foreshadowed here in the *Whitehall Evening Post*:

> One of the low order of waddling preachers, on Sunday last, addressed his barn-assembled audience, not three miles from Chester, in the following, if not elegant, at least time-serving metaphor: – 'I daresay you'd all pay to see a boxing match between Humphries and Mendoza, yet you don't like to pay to see a pitched battle between me and Beelzebub; – oh! Many a hard knock, and many a cross buttock have I given the black bruiser for your sakes. Pull! Do pull off those gay garments of Mammon, strike a straight blow, and give the Devil a spiritual black eye! – I'll be your bottle holder – I ask nothing but the door money – which I hope you'll not forget as you go out.'[14]

Doncaster Racecourse is famous for the St Leger, a race founded in 1776 by Irish aristocrat Colonel Anthony St Leger, sometime MP for Grimsby, and latterly Governor of St Lucia. The final Mendoza–Humphries fight coincided with its running, so that, as *The World* reported, 'with boxers and jockeys, scarce a bed [was] to be had' in Doncaster. The bout took place not at the racecourse but in the courtyard of an inn, possibly what is now known as The Boat Inn (where, apparently, Walter Scott wrote the opening chapter of *Ivanhoe*, twenty-five years later). Five hundred tickets were issued at a ½ guinea each. Seated ticket holders were joined by another 2,000 standing. The courtyard was bound on one side by the backs of houses and on the other by a strong paling, behind which ran the River Don. It had been thought that the position would make it extremely difficult 'for any rabble to force their way into the enclosure'. However, on this occasion the Don flowed by no means quietly. Entrepreneurial river men brought two barges across the river, having charged a shilling a person for a perch on their masts.

The stage was 4 feet high and the regular 24 foot square. At 10 a.m. Humphries entered the arena, accompanied by William Warr, John Jackson and the Duke of Hamilton (who was to be Humphries' umpire). Mendoza followed soon after, with Humphries' former pair, Tom Johnson and Butcher, with the (if we are to believe Gillray's portraiture) diminutive Sir Thomas Apreece as umpire. Harvey Aston was the appointed referee. Both boxers were clearly up for the fight, both in good spirits and free of any sign of nerves or apprehension. What did get spectators muttering was the decided bulk that Mendoza had put on, not in fat but in muscle. For his part Humphries appeared to have slimmed down, in order, it was said, to be lighter of foot, to be more active against the knife-sharp Mendoza. The odds at the beginning of the fight narrowly favoured Mendoza, at five to four.

MENDOZA v HUMPHRIES III
29 September 1790
Doncaster

Richard Humphries begins vehemently. He is 'bold, rapid and vigorous', the idea being to overcome Mendoza's superior technical ability with a kind of chaos of violence. He has learned how to fight his opponent. For the first few rounds Humphries maintains this pace. Mendoza, as is his wont, fights on the defensive, using lightning-fast counter-attack. The chief technical difference between the two boxers is that Mendoza hits straight, while Humphries hits round (jab against swing). Not only is Mendoza faster, he is more economical with his breath and energy. Various moves, unknown to the modern fight game, such as throwing, are perfectly legal. Mendoza repeatedly leaps up in order to strike above Humphries' guard. (There is always this sense of bounce about Daniel Mendoza, and not just while boxing.)

Early in the fight Humphries twists his knee. In several accounts this more or less finishes the contest, though it continues at least another 45 minutes. Humphries apparently cannot put any weight on the damaged leg. Other reports however question the severity of the injury: 'the evil was no doubt magnified for the purpose of detracting from Mendoza's merit in gaining the victory.'[15]

It is clear long before the end of the fight that barring an unlikely accident Mendoza is going to win. Indeed so obvious is his superiority that he is obliged to show a degree of gallantry in refusing to finish Humphries when he has complete control over him, on several occasions helping his opponent down gently to the ground without striking him. But Humphries refuses to give in, despite the wishes of his friends. He afterwards acknowledged that the battle was 'entirely in Mendoza's favour' but continued in the hope of 'accident or the unexpected'.

The *London Chronicle* gave a detailed account of what the two men had done to each other:

> Mendoza was considerably cut between the right eye and the temple, and on the left ear. His head, likewise, was greatly swelled, and he received a gash upon his right ribs in consequence of a straightforward left-handed blow of his antagonist at his body, Humphries had several hits, which drew blood, under his left arm. His right eye was closed, and he received a severe wound over his left. His right cheek, and the left side of his nose, was cut as with a razor by one of Mendoza's springing straight blows; his upper lip was by the same stroke split, and when he attempted to ease his mouth, while on his second's knee, with water, the liquor mixed with the blood gushed through the incision.[16]

When Humphries had finally had enough Mendoza is said to have 'jumped about the stage' and to have 'hugged every man he came near, but particularly Sir Thomas Apreece', whom he apparently kissed. He then went to Humphries and shook his hand. He thanked the crowd and declared that he had no intention of ever fighting again. He then walked to the racecourse, no doubt followed by the crowd.

A by-incident during the fight, which may be emblematic of something more, involved 'Gentleman' John Jackson, Mendoza and Apreece. Jackson had 'addressed himself to Mendoza in a style of the lowest blackguardism' and Apreece at once demanded an apology, which was finally, perhaps reluctantly, forthcoming. Had Jackson insulted Mendoza for his faith or race? The *St James Chronicle* noted that 'the Jew gained another victory over the Gentile,' and suggested the fight might have been fixed. In a fine example of faux outrage the *Whitehall Evening Post* permitted itself to be 'stained' by mention of the fight. *The Argus,* a moderately radical newspaper owned by Sampson Perry (later to publish pieces by Tom Paine) carried the fullest description of the fight, and thought that the 'whole affair' had been described 'with a most shameful partiality'. In the final words of his account of the fight Pierce Egan expressed a similar thought (though written, it should be remembered, some years later):

> Mendoza, in conquering so noble and distinguished a competitor, added considerable fame to his pugilistic achievements; but the

greatest merit attached to the conquest was the manner in which it was obtained. Prejudice so frequently distorts the mind, that, unfortunately, good actions are passed over without even common respect; more especially when they appear in any person who may chance to be of a different country, persuasion, or colour. Mendoza, in being a Jew, did not stand in so favourable a point of view, respecting the wishes of the multitude towards his success, as his brave opponent... But truth riseth superior to all things, and the humanity of Mendoza was conspicuous throughout the above fight.

Most reports concentrated on Humphries' indomitable spirit, unconquerable obstinacy and so on. *The Argus* was a rare exception:

One of the amateurs present ... speaks with great rapture of Mendoza's superior generosity, as well as superior skill. Though Humphries had the advantage at the onset, yet soon finding his own inferiority, he made some desperate attempt, and even risked his own life, by violently aiming at his antagonist's heart.

Mendoza, soon perceiving the intention, cried out, 'Gentlemen, I will shew more humanity to my once master.' He kept his word; for at one time when they closed, he had the head of Humphries under his arm, and might then have easily decided the battle; but he let him loose without a blow.

Cowards are cruel, but the brave
Love mercy, and delight to save.

In the *Memoirs* Daniel Mendoza signs off from this great triptych, the greatest series of fights of the eighteenth century, with a handsome bow of respect to his great rival.

This being the last occasion I shall have ... to mention Mr Humphries, I avail myself of this opportunity of declaring, that with whatever reason I might conceive myself entitled to complain of his conduct towards me at different periods, his general conduct and demeanour were such as reflected great credit on him, and deservedly gained him the esteem of the public, by whom he was always considered and treated as a respectable member of society.

Richard Humphries, the 'favourite of the men of note', now retired and was set up by his patron, Braddyll, as a coal merchant at the

Adelphi wharf, off the Strand. Humphries made a success of the business and died in comfortable circumstances in 1827, at his home in Tudor Street, near Blackfriars bridge. Thanks to his rivalry with Daniel Mendoza, the oblivion the *London Packet* newspaper wished on him years before awaits him still. Mendoza, in the *Memoirs*, was in the end gracious about his old foe.

For Daniel Mendoza, now also apparently retired from prize fighting, it was time to cash in on his fame. He got to it straightaway.

SQUIRE FITZGERALD

One likes to think of the twenty-five-year-old Dan Mendoza basking in a little glory. 'The picture of Mendoza is, we hear, crowned with garlands in all the public houses in and about Duke's Place,' reported the ever-sympathetic *Argus*. Never shy of attention, he would surely have enjoyed this. His academy at the Lyceum on the Strand was more popular than ever. At the end of October it welcomed six distinguished visitors from abroad. They were Cherokee chiefs who had expressed a desire to witness the school in action. Already they had been shown grand pianos at Longman & Broderip in Cheapside, visited Covent Garden Theatre where they watched a comic opera called *The Poor Soldier,* and had been 'initiated into the mystery of the Royal Grand-Arch Constitutional Sols' in a masonic ceremony and celebration that had lasted until 5 a.m. They attended various debating societies.

The Cherokee had been allies of the British during the War of Independence. According to one newspaper the chiefs had come seeking support for a proposed conquest of Mexico, which is a little hard to believe. The government paid the chiefs a *per diem* of 1 guinea. One of the tour party was the son of a Scottish trader called Bowles, and was accordingly known as 'The Bowl'. He spoke English 'indifferently well' and was apparently 'decidedly Gaelic in appearance', having red hair and freckles. Dressed 'in the habit of their country, with their faces painted in an extraordinary manner', my hunch is that Dan Mendoza probably rather took to them. A yet-surviving belief (certainly as of 2001, and Beverley Baker Northup's, *We Are Not Yet Conquered*) is that the Cherokee are one of the ten lost tribes of Israel, survivors of Masada, the last refuge of the Jews as they were driven from Palestine by the Romans.

The Cherokee were not the only visitors. A curious and 'celebrated' French fencing master, drawn to the Lyceum and impressed by the deftness and speed of Mendoza's parrying, offered to give the boxer fencing lessons. 'Mendoza consented, and in a very short time acquired so much knowledge of the art of throwing aside a coming blow by a simple action of the arm, that he acknowledged, with gratitude, the benefit he had derived.'[1] Mendoza had very likely been under the tutelage of the 'Black Mozart', Joseph Bologne, Chevalier de Saint-Georges, a friend of the Prince of Wales's fencing (and boxing) teacher, Henry Angelo. Joseph Bologne, as well as being a gifted composer, was a renowned swordsman.

Much of 1791 was taken up with failure to set a date to fight William Warr. Mendoza didn't at first much want one. He had after all promised Esther privately and declared to the world publicly that his prize fighting days were over. His exhibitions and private instruction were bringing in enough money to pay for what was becoming a quite extravagant lifestyle. However, the Fancy wanted to see the contest. Several of the newspapers were under the impression that Joseph Ward was William Warr's brother, and so fuelled an impression of natural enmity between Mendoza and William Warr by reporting a bust up between Mendoza and Joe.

The previous May, Mendoza and Joe Ward, having been sparring in the Lyceum, made for Carpenter's coffee house at the east end of Covent Garden market. Carpenter's was better known as the notorious 'Finish' because it was 'open very early in the morning, and therefore resorted to by debauchees shut out of every other house'. According to John Bee, it would often mark the end of a 'round' which began at the 'Jump' with supper and wine, went on to the 'Go' for max (gin) or punch, 'with an intervening call at a Mrs Fubbs's' (brothel). The 'Finish' was at this time managed by Elizabeth Butler, who had run a successful business – 'seraglio' is the euphemism – in King Street, St James. The coffee at the 'Finish' was questionable but the beers and spirits and grog (rum and water) were popular. It was typically full of drunks, be they petty thieves or members of the gentry, and above. It was the sort of place where fights regularly broke out, popular with boxers and louche aristocrats, and given an odd sheen of gentility by the occasional presence of the Prince of Wales. One evening 'in a peaceable gutter in front of the "Finish", Richard Brinsley Sheridan, Esq., M.P., lay down overtaken in foreign wines, and told the guardian of the night that his name was Wilberforce. A wild place, that "Finish"'. Sheridan, the great playwright, author of *The School for Scandal* and *The Rivals*, the inventor of Mrs Malaprop, was a native Dubliner, whose family had left for London following a riot at the Smock Alley Theatre, of which Sheridan's father had been manager. As an MP he was described at around this period as 'in matters of sarcasm, repartee and witticism ... the acknowledged Mendoza of the House'.[2] As for William Wilberforce, the leader of the opposition to the slave trade, he was a deeply committed Christian and as likely to be found in such a 'peaceable' gutter as trading for slaves on the quay at Bristol.

The 'Finish' illustrates well the social fluidity of late eighteenth-century London. As indeed does the 'boximania' of the day. Revolution raged across the Channel; maybe it could not break out in a society in which footpads and princes shared tavern tables and sporting enthusiasms.

The fight broke out between Ward and Mendoza, by one report, 'in consequence of very ill language from the former'.[3] Mendoza's own story is slightly different.

> After dinner Mr Joseph Ward entered the room, and accosting me, demanded payment of two guineas, under the pretence of my having employed him to second Elisha Crabbe in a battle which a short time previous to this, took place between him and Tom Tyne. I was not a little surprised at such a demand being made upon me. Not having had any concern whatever with this battle, and having been present at it merely as a spectator, of course I refused payment, and on Ward's leaving the room, expected the affair would have ended, without any unpleasant consequences, but to my surprise, he re-entered a few minutes afterwards, and struck me a violent blow on the eye; and then endeavoured to effect his escape out of the room; this, however, I prevented by locking the door, and then gave him as severe a thrashing as ever he received. I had not, however, the satisfaction of inflicting this punishment upon him, without paying for it, for a looking glass, of some value, was broken in the course of the affray, which I was afterwards obliged to pay for.[4]

Mrs Butler, known for her jollity, had declined to step in. She complained of more breakages than a single looking glass: 'glasses, decanters and china', all were broken. The newspapers of the day confirm the brutality of the 'thrashing'. Ward's eyes were 'completely sealed up'.

Interesting in Mendoza's account is the suggestion that he was himself a promoter of fights. Ward clearly thought he was responsible for the Crabbe–Tyne meeting. This was not unlikely as Crabbe was a Jew who may very well have taken lessons from Mendoza. He had beaten 'Death' (as explained above, Stephen Oliver, the cognomen was applied for his pale complexion) but lost to both Watson and Tyne. He retired and became a policeman, and then a popular publican in Duke's Place. The passage further makes clear that seconds worked not for love but for money. Ward perhaps thought that Mendoza had somehow sub-let the position.

Joseph Ward was already a veteran in 1790. He was born in Billericay in 1750 and as a young man worked as an engraver at the Tower of London. He won many fights, but his reputation really was as the first among seconds. 'His judgement and discrimination ... has ever been looked upon by the Sporting World with considerable attention ... to recruit the exhausted – to gain wind – to infuse courage – to increase the offering...' Ward had often been second to Hooper, the Tinman. Hooper was understandably enraged to find that Ward was second to Tom Owen, to whom Hooper indeed lost. In later days Joe kept a pub called The Green Dragon near Swallow Street and filled it with prints and paintings of fights and boxers, both celebrated and less well-known. He commissioned portraits of those for whom he could not find and purchase pictures. The collection was broken up on his death and scattered to the four corners.

Relations between William Warr and Mendoza were soured when, at the beginning of 1791, Mendoza sacked Warr, having employed him for a while (he was nominally a partner) at the Lyceum. Mendoza had taken Warr on 'in order to relieve myself from some part of the fatigue attending the exercise of my profession'. Unfortunately, Warr's behaviour 'was by no means such as gave satisfaction' to Mendoza's subscribers. Having been fired, Warr at once challenged Mendoza to a fight, and a Mr Wiltshire, without mentioning to Mendoza that he had done so, made a match between the two fighters, paying Mendoza's 25-guinea deposit. The general feeling among what the press called 'the knowing ones' seemed to be that Warr would win such a battle, despite 'the dissolute manner of his living' (which may explain Mendoza's decision to sack his partner). Warr weighed in at 12½ stone, over a stone heavier than Mendoza. He was taller, too. At the end of January the *Morning Post* reported that the match had been made and the deposits put down. It was fixed for the second week in May. A fortnight before that report, however, the boxing world's attention was focused on a contest almost as celebrated as that between Humphries and Mendoza.

Tom Johnson (real name 'Jackling') was a corn porter, originally from Derby, but now a Londoner. He was recognised as the pre-eminent boxer of the day, a man credited by some for reviving in boxing 'the drooping taste for this most manly of British sports'. A cautious rather than a showy boxer, he had been fighting professionally certainly since 1783 and had defeated Stephen Oliver, William Warr, the mercurial Irishman Michael Ryan (twice, luckily), and, most notably, the choir leader, publican and 'perfect Hercules', Isaac Perrins.[5] Now he had been challenged by the veteran Bristol collier, Benjamin 'Big Ben' Brain. The men were of about the same height and weight (5 foot 9 inches and 14 stone) and were each undefeated. 'They seemed made for each other,' opined Pierce Egan in *Blackwood's Magazine*. Johnson was the slim favourite.

They fought on 17 January 1791, a fine sunny day, at Wrotham at the foot of the North Downs in Kent, some 25 miles to the south-east of London. It was to be a big year for Wrotham. One of the first trigonometric points for the Ordnance survey, which commenced later that same year, was on Wrotham Hill (in 1955 its transmitting station was the first in the country to carry FM). The fight had drawn some 2,000 spectators; 'upwards of one hundred and forty chaises and coaches' were lined up on each side of the road leading to the site of the fight. Entry to the ring was a ½ guinea, and the takings amounted to around £160. A flimsy scaffolding had been erected against a wall at the back of the enclosed field in which the fight took place, behind the Black Bull Inn (now known as The Bull). Half-way through the bout, the wall collapsed: 'bruises were received and limbs broken.' In the chaos many got to see the contest without paying.

Johnson was attended by Mendoza as bottle holder, and Joe Ward (yes, that Joe Ward) as his second. Big Ben's second was Will Warr, and his bottle holder none other than Richard Humphries.

The umpires were Colonel Tarleton and Major Hanger. Harvey Aston, as so often, was the arbitrator. Lord Barrymore (who arrived in a farm cart) and other 'notables' of the 'Fancy' were also present.

Mendoza and Humphries as bottle holders? It doesn't sound too glamorous, but that was the convention. Fighters would be supported by other fighters. Almost every description of a fight in the newspapers and journals of the time includes reference to second, bottle holder and referee. They were given far more status than their modern counterparts, and understandably so. Mendoza attending on Johnson would be equivalent to Joshua attending Fury.

So what exactly was the role of the second and bottle holder? Mendoza spent many years after he had more or less stopped fighting attending in these positions. He was understandably popular with the Jewish boxers, such as Aby Belasco and Dutch Sam, but with others too, who recognised his genius as a teacher.

The role of the 'second' had developed with the development of the 'science'. In an early fight, in 1776, a boxer named George Maddox was seconded by his sister, Grace. No aspersions are cast; women boxers were not unknown, but the fact was remarked upon.[6] Two husbands filled the position in a fight between their wives in Chelmsford in August 1793.

A working description of the role comes from *The Handbook to Boxing* by Owen Swift, published in 1840, a long time after Mendoza's day, but nonetheless concerned with bare-knuckle fighting. Swift was himself a boxer, adversary in a fight with – and one fatal to – 'Brighton Bill Phelps', after which new rules were introduced to the sport. Swift begins his chapter 'Of Seconding' with a paragraph expressing his 'unmitigated disgust at the system of *chaff*'. 'Chaff' was to prize fighting what sledging is to cricket. Tom Johnson, when seconding Humphries against Mendoza, had been guilty of chaff, trying to catch Mendoza's eye (and I daresay using language with reference to Mendoza's ethnicity) in order to distract him from the matter in hand. So too was 'Gentleman' Jackson, second to Warr in the battle with Mendoza, and taken to task for it by Sir Thomas Apreece. Nor was there any need, Swift insists, for seconds to respond to 'coarse jokes or flash patter'. According to the *Handbook*, the first duty of the seconds was to choose and agree upon referees and umpire, and then, if the sun was shining (a big if – it seemed to be raining during many of the Regency bouts)[7] to toss to see who might choose the shade (i.e.

attend to the mark with the sun behind him). The wind might also be a factor. Once that duty was performed, the second was expected to act as trainer. In the early years, and by the evidence of the prints, it seems that seconds could encourage and urge during the fighting, standing by their man. The new rules were emphatic that seconds and bottle holders should stay in their corners, other than to carry their man back there, should he fall (thereby ending a round). The fighter would then sit on his second's knee. The two men then had 30 seconds to repair any damage and offer advice before time was called for the next round. The bottle holder would sponge blood and sweat away, soak with cold water and provide refreshment, which was not always water. It was not unknown for seconds or bottle holders to drink themselves incapable while supposedly supporting their man. 'On the stage,' recommended a contributor to *The Modern Art of Boxing,* 'have your drink made of Holland's bitters, fine China orange juice, with some lump sugar to render it palatable.' A kind of alcopop. If in a fit state, the second might also make a decision as to whether his man should fight on. A sponge would be thrown in to indicate an end to the contest. Sometimes, instead of a sponge, a towel was thrown in – as a hat was thrown in to the ring to indicate a challenge.

Daniel Mendoza's experience with seconds suggest they were not always what they ought to have been. Apart from the chaffing of Johnson and Jackson, there was the behaviour of Tom Tring, nominally seconding Mendoza in his fight with Sam Martin. Tring 'twice supported Martin'; in the end Dan Mendoza had to knock his own second off the stage.

Johnson and Brain entered the ring, a 24-foot square stage, at or soon after noon, Johnson to a roar of approval, the Bristol challenger to a more muted murmur of appreciation. A hard fight was anticipated, and a hard fight is what the crowd got. About half-way through Johnson took Brain by the hair, until he was pulled off by Joe Ward, who proceeded to cut off his man's hair at the end of the round. Mendoza was watching, but did not learn. He wore his hair long, and it cost him dearly four years later, when 'Gentleman' Jackson employed Johnson's tactic.

'Ferocity was the order of the day,' wrote Egan. The newspaper reports bear him out. 'The combatants seemed to be inflamed by animosity, and to forget their trade. They fought sometimes with the utmost fury.'[8] Big Ben seems to have had the upper hand from the start. He forced Johnson into corners, and with his longer reach landed punch after punch. After half-an-hour Johnson gave in, exhausted, but also having fallen in such a way as to break a finger – 'the bone ran through the skin' as one correspondent vividly put it.[9] The crowd was silenced. There was no roar for the victor. The champion had been defeated.

Big Ben dressed himself on the stage, but he too was badly injured, so much so that he never fought again and died within the year, probably due to damage inflicted by Johnson. Colonel Tarleton, and many of his 'quality' friends, lost substantial amounts in bets, though the Prince of Wales, it was said, was 'a very considerable winner'.

After the fight Richard Humphries publicly challenged Dan Mendoza to yet another fight, in six months, for any sum. Mendoza replied that he'd fight for £500 within a month or two. Humphries declined this, saying his knee was not fully recovered after the last fight, and then made his challenge public, declaring that the two of them would meet again in six months' time. 'I would not wish for anything better,' Dan responded. The journalist who reported this added the following:

> The writer of this article regrets, as he has long since regretted, that two men whose manners are so superior to those of the common herd of boxers, as to render their respective friends uneasy at seeing either of them hurt, should always be at variance, when by their united abilities as teachers of the Art they might carry everything before them, and in a short time acquire a comfortable fortune.[10]

The newspapers were, anyway, scornful. One regarded a match with Humphries as providing Mendoza with an escape from 'the match he had the temerity to make with Warr'; another thought such a match couldn't be made 'with any intention of bringing it to a fair decision', so superior a boxer was Mendoza. Perhaps there is here a suggestion of possible fixing, a problem that bedevilled a sport that was more or less sustained by gambling.

Mendoza spent a good deal of time in the following months of 1791 going to and from Birmingham. He was, on the one hand, attempting to arrange a fight between Isaac Perrins and Big Ben, and on the other exhibiting himself. He and those with whom he was exhibiting, perhaps his brother-in-law Aaron and Fewtrell, were invited to join the cast of a theatrical adaptation of *Robinson Crusoe*, but were prevented by local constables 'prompted by the

Demon of Contradiction,' who turned up at the theatre wielding 'sticks, staves and other terrific weapons'.

As the year went on details of the Mendoza–Warr fight were in continual flux. Pleading ill-health, and a general disinclination to fight given the success of his teaching and exhibiting, Mendoza first declined to engage Warr. Mr Wiltshire, who had put up the deposit for a fight when Warr had challenged, was furious, and had Mendoza arrested on the grounds that he had advanced the money to him. At the trial Mendoza's friend and sparring partner Henry Lee was called on as a witness against Dan. Lee 'knew perfectly well that Mr Wiltshire was in the wrong', and yet appeared to substantiate Wiltshire's claim. The jury was unimpressed. Mendoza places the trial before his fight with Joe Ward but, as is so often the case, his memory is out of sync with newspaper reports.

So: Dan didn't want or need to fight – Dan couldn't raise the money – the fight was off and he had forfeited his deposit (or rather, Mr Wilshire's) – the fighters had met at the Garrick's Head in Bow Street and the fight was definitely on for 23 May – Mendoza deferred the fight to 15 June – the adversaries agreed to fight on 22 June, at Margate – Warr wanted to delay the fight so that the Duke of Hamilton could attend – Margate's magistrates forbade the fight – the fight was to take place at Wrotham – Mendoza and Warr would certainly fight on 'Wednesday next': at Sittingbourne – 'Mendoza, it is said, stakes a thousand pounds on himself' – 'the long expected fight between Warr and Mendoza which was to have taken place at Stokenchurch was prevented by … magistrates – 'it was agreed the fight should take place at Doncaster in September…'

The fight had actually very nearly happened at Stokenchurch. The Uxbridge road out of London was reported to have been crowded with 'carriages, horsemen and foot passengers', and it was at Uxbridge where Mendoza and his friends, Lee and George Ingleston ('the Brewer'), were informed that the fight was off. In Stokenchurch preparations had been made, when 'a worthy gentleman in the Commission of the Peace for the county of Middlesex made his appearance on a white pony, and gave a knock down blow to the business'. An attempt was made to move the show to a nearby cricket pitch, but there were objections on both sides. Mendoza and Warr and hundreds, if not thousands, of spectators all spent the night at Uxbridge. The newspapers thought it very unlikely that Warr and Mendoza would ever be able to fight.

At the end of June, Dan survived a mugging. Walking along the Strand, no doubt having been sparring at the Lyceum, but 'disguised as a gentleman' (the unexpected qualifier in the *Morning Post*'s report of the incident) on his way to see a patron, he was attacked by three 'full grown' pickpockets. He dealt with them one by one, and was given (or possibly volunteered) this departing line: 'Gentlemen, I found ye sharp, but I have made ye flat.' Does the odd 'disguised as a gentleman' remark mean he was more likely to be attacked? Or does it mean that he dressed up to visit the Duke of Hamilton or Sir Thomas Apreece? Or that, being a Jew, he had to disguise himself? Or perhaps he had got to a state of celebrity that required the same. He complained in the *Memoirs* that 'the favours I experienced from the public could not but fail of exciting the envy of a certain description of men, and drawing on me unmerited ill-treatment.'[11]

If the newspapers were mealy-mouthed about the Jewish triumph the previous September, the entertainment entrepreneurs certainly weren't. Returning to London, Mendoza had found himself inundated with invitations from theatres all over the country, asking him to exhibit. Most likely at the end of June 1791, he and Aaron travelled north, to Lancashire, which meant performances in Manchester, Liverpool, Bolton, Rochdale, Bury and so on. The population of Manchester and its surrounds was then around 250,000 and rapidly increasing as the Industrial Revolution got into full swing (the population of England was around 8 million). Then, as now, Lancashire, barring Surrey and Middlesex, the principal counties of London, was the most populous county in England. Dan was heading for the crowds.

And according to his own account, he wowed them. His success was 'unprecedented'. From Lancashire he moved on to Edinburgh, in the company of Mr Fewtrell, that same Birmingham native who had held things up at Stilton by trying to climb in without paying. Fewtrell – a man 'of great bulk and uncommon strength' – after many successful fights, had been beaten by John Jackson in 1788, at Smitham Bottom. He had remade himself as an expert of the fistic arts, publishing *Boxing Reviewed*, a collection of short portraits of famous fighters, in 1790. He had recently returned from Paris (in the throes of the French Revolution) where he had exhibited at Nicolet's Theatre to a large though unappreciative audience. The French continued to regard boxing as altogether too savage. Now he joined Mendoza for a tour of Scotland. The pair made a veritable caravan of pugilistic science.

In Edinburgh Mendoza gave private lessons, and sparred with members of the Gymnastic Society, including its president, the distinguished physician Dr Andrew Duncan. Naturally he bested them all. He was proud of a gold medal they presented to him.

From Edinburgh he and Fewtrell moved on to Glasgow. Here, again, he was well rewarded, but his chief memory is of a fight involving his friend.

> ... I was, I believe, the means of saving Fewtrell's life... Pugilistic men, when they have derived money from their exertions, seldom refrain from venturing it at cards, dice or some kind of gambling; and Fewtrell was not unlike his brethren in this respect; for having gained some money by our tour, he was never easy but when he was playing. One morning between two and three o'clock, I was awakened by dreadful shrieks of murder, and having opened my window, beheld five or six men assaulting Fewtrell with all the violence in their power; having called out to them to forbear and threatened to shoot them if they did not immediately desist, they refused to pay the least regard to me, but continued beating him in a most unmerciful manner; upon which I threw a table out of the window; this was a mode of attack they did not expect, and immediately dispersed, being apprehensive of having the whole contents of the room emptied upon them if they remained longer.[12]

I'm fairly sure Mendoza saw the comedy in this anecdote; at the same time the incident indicates the murderous fury of the times. It may also offer the merest hint of a clue as to how Mendoza managed to squander what were the undoubted riches he derived from his 'exertions'. He was a 'pugilistic man'.

From Scotland, Mendoza, with Aaron, and possibly Fewtrell or Lee, went to Dublin, invited by Philip Astley. Dublin was – and remains – a great Georgian city. Its inhabitants were proud of it. Handel's *Messiah* had its premiere there in 1742. Jonathan Swift had been Dean of St Patrick's Cathedral at the time. Sheridan and Oliver Goldsmith were natives. And Dubliners were proud. Mendoza was challenged to a duel merely for suggesting that large as Dublin was, it perhaps wasn't as large as London. It was a challenge in earnest. Pistols were produced. Mendoza dealt with the affair in a characteristically straightforward manner. Having been invited to meet his adversary at a nearby hotel, he 'requested to examine the pistols ... and having obtained them, immediately drew their contents and threw away the flints, and once more offered to settle the affair amicably'. To no avail, however, and Mendoza was forced to punish his adversary's conduct (scurrilous and insulting language had been used – a very unwise course of action in the hearing of the supersensitive Londoner) by giving him 'a severe caning' in the public room of the hotel.

Nonetheless, Dublin was indeed a fair city, and it was certainly grand enough a place for one of Astley's amphitheatres. Philip Astley is an important figure in the history of the theatrical, for he is generally acknowledged as being the inventor of – although his protégé Charles Hughes actually coined the term – the circus.

Astley had joined the army as a boy and distinguished himself as a cavalry trooper. He rose to the rank of sergeant major and was presented to George III. It is said that at his discharge his commanding officer gifted him a white stallion. Astley set up a riding school in Lambeth on the south bank of the Thames. As well as teaching, he laid on an equestrian show, in which he did his own tricks. His wife, Patty Jones, was also an accomplished rider and often stood in for her husband. The space in which these tricks were performed was circular, thereby increasing the centrifugal force on the horses and their riders and affording greater stability. One equestrian act called *le grand saut du Trampolin* featured 'The Great Devil' (an acrobatic rider by the name of James Lawrence) somersaulting over twelve horses. Another turn was that of clown Billy Buttons (played by Astley himself), a character that survived for over 100 years. Even now the name evokes ghost-like memories of clowns jumping on and off horses. Year by year the equestrian tricks were augmented by other spots and acts, by non-equestrian clowns and acrobats; by, say, French horn players, or the novel act of a performer named Carr, who stood on his head in the centre of a globe, and ascended 30 feet 'turning round in a most surprising manner, like a boy's top'. Nor should we forget the 'Grimacer' from Paris or indeed Toby the Sapient Pig. Eventually a stage was added to the ring, and Astley brought in actors to put on short sketches, often illustrative of current news items. It was this bringing together of diverse entertainments within one performance space, one ring, that made what Astley offered unique.

Philip Astley was tall and handsome and brave, and he was to prove a canny businessmen. By his death he had established no less than eighteen amphitheatres around the British Isles and Europe. In October 1783 he had opened in Paris, in the Rue du

Faubourg-du-Temple, under the patronage of Marie Antoinette; Philip's son John, who danced on horseback, had captivated her. John eventually married Hannah Waldo Smith, the niece of Adam Smith, the author of *The Wealth of Nations*. Whether the great economist ever attended a circus performance or what he thought of it if he did has sadly not been recorded.

Astley was also, it seems, a philosemite. His company contained many Jews. Chief among them was Jacob Decastro – a mimic and comedian, whose father had possibly been Daniel Mendoza's schoolteacher. He began working with Astley in 1786, leading a troupe that came to be known as 'Astley's Jews' and was likely known to Mendoza before they were in Dublin. One of the reasons we know they were together is a short anecdote from the *Memoirs* concerning 'the pugilistic exertions of one of [Mr Astley's] female performers':

> Returning home one evening in company with Mr. and Mrs. De Castro, we wished to pass through Dublin Castle, as being the nearest way to the part of the town where we resided, but were prevented by the sentinel on duty who refused to let us pass, declaring his orders were to admit no one through the castle after dusk. This refusal, however, gave great displeasure to Mrs. De Castro who immediately desired, or rather ordered her husband to knock the fellow down: this was no easy task for her husband to perform, who was by no means adapted for feats of this kind, being a remarkably slight man, not five feet in height, but upon his objecting to execute his wife's commands, and mentioning that he really thought the man had done no more than his duty, this high spirited lady (who is a native of Ireland) exclaimed with great indignation 'Now, by Jasus, if you don't knock him down, I'll knock you down.' And she kept her word, for immediately afterwards she attacked him with such force and quickness that the poor fellow was utterly unable to defend himself, and obliged to entreat for mercy, which was at length granted to him, after he had received two black eyes, and was otherwise severely bruised.[13]

The Dublin amphitheatre had been established in Peter Street in 1789, as Mendoza entered his period of greatest fame, and as the French commenced their revolution, an event first dramatised for the London stage at Astley's amphitheatre, and to have repercussions for his Dublin theatre.

Mendoza reports that he was 'recognised much sooner' in Dublin than he had expected. On entering town he was accosted by 'an honest Hibernian who, after fixing his eyes very steadfastly on me, exclaimed in a loud tone of voice, "Ah! By Jasus, Master Mendoza, to be sure I am very glad to see your honour safe arrived in Ireland. Pray let an old servant carry your portmanteau for you"'. It turned out that the old man had been engaged as a porter at the 'Finish' coffee house and had often seen Mendoza there.

Ireland contained a definitely oppressed majority in the form of Irish Catholics. In Dublin the Protestant ascendancy was in decline, and it had become a Catholic city once more. So far as the Jews were concerned, by 1791 the population had decreased to such an extent that the single synagogue, at Marlborough Green, had closed. Irish Dissenters also felt the weight of the English presence in Ireland and the Catholics and the Dissenters came together in October of 1791, some months after Mendoza had left the island, as 'The Society of United Irishmen'. Their aim was to abolish all religious distinctions, unite all Irishmen against the unjust influence of England, and to secure proper representation in a national parliament. Obviously, the influence of the American and French revolutions was prevailing. The leader of the United Irishmen, Wolfe Tone, a lawyer from County Kildare, was greatly influenced by the latter. Like so many young and idealistic men and women in the British Isles, he saw the French Revolution as 'the dawn of a new and perfect age'.

The Peter Street Amphitheatre was a staunchly Loyalist establishment (in 1793, at the age of fifty, Astley re-enlisted to fight the French) and anti-French scenes were re-enacted, often to the dislike of an audience broadly sympathetic to the Revolution – although it ought not to be forgotten that almost everyone was delighted to see the fall of the French monarchy. Barracking rising to the pitch of riot was common.

Mendoza reports that he himself was a tremendous success. As a Jew who had defeated the 'Gentleman' boxer, the perfect Christian Englishman, it is likely that he would have been seen as symbolically representative. 'I had the satisfaction of experiencing the most flattering reception during the whole of my engagement,' he wrote. Rioting only broke out when he did not perform:

My engagement with Mr Astley was for a certain number of nights ...
but he afterwards changed his mind, and wished a benefit for his

son to take place, on which occasion some new entertainments were to be brought forward ... and he therefore intimated to me his intention of dispensing with my performance for that night.

This new arrangement, however, was not approved of by the public ... indeed, such was the uproar and tumult that prevailed in the amphitheatre that his grace the Duke of Leinster, who was present, came behind the scenes and desired I might be permitted to appear on the stage and go through the usual performance, declaring at the same time, he was fully convinced that otherwise the house would be demolished.

The man who had stepped backstage was William Robert Fitzgerald, 2nd Duke of Leinster, Ireland's premier peer. He wasn't someone with whom you argued, even if you were Philip Astley. At the time of Mendoza's engagement he was recently out of government, having declared himself in favour of parliamentary reform and opposed to the war with revolutionary France. His brother was leading United Irishman Lord Edward Fitzgerald.

Leinster lived in a palace built by his father in the 1740s. It was grand enough to become the eventual seat of the Irish Republic's government, and is said to have been the model for the White House in Washington DC. He appears to have been a frequenter of Astley's, certainly while Mendoza was there, for following the near riot of the benefit night, he was witness to a more or less amicable spat between the boxer and the proto-Barnum:

Mr Astley seemed to imagine, like many other stout and athletic men, that the utmost art in boxing would not avail against superior strength, and would frequently express himself of this opinion. One evening, upon the duke of Leinster's entering our dressing room, he addressed his grace in the following curious manner: 'I can assure your grace, my house is not like a red cabbage, but like a variegated one; here now is horsemanship, dancing, and pugilism; all different, all variegated; here is Mendoza, the famous pugilist, whom I have brought down at a prodigious expense. He is received every night with great applause, and brings a great deal of money to the house, but Lord! What could he do against a man like myself – why he would never be able to strike a blow.' I happened to be present during these observations, and proposed to have a trial with him as we sat, to which he consented, and we accordingly drew our chairs near to each other, and set to, but I soon convinced Mr Astley that he was mistaken, for notwithstanding his superior length of arm I contrived to knock him off his chair in the course of five minutes: as he lay sprawling on the ground he exclaimed, 'Ah, Dan, this is too bad, did you do this for the purpose, aye, for the purpose, Dan?,' upon which I assured him if I had hurt him it was not intentionally; and having assisted him to rise, we shook hands, but he never afterwards proposed to renew the contest.

Despite or perhaps because of his popularity Mendoza was continually menaced while in Dublin, receiving threats by letter and imprecations in the street. He took to walking back to his lodgings in disguise because he was 'frequently laid wait for'. Whether he was despised as a Jew or distrusted as an Englishman or simply regarded as fair game, being a fighter, it is impossible to say, but he was certainly unimpressed by 'the ferocious conduct of the lower orders of the Irish'.[14] However, he was anxious not to be thought of as 'casting illiberal reflections on the Irish in general' and in fact took the opportunity in his *Memoirs* to gratefully acknowledge his 'generous reception … from numerous persons of all ranks'.

Another measure of his success was that (again by his own reckoning) he was a bigger draw than Mrs Billington, who was playing at the Smock Alley Theatre. This establishment had opened in 1662, and was, until the appearance of Astley's, the principal theatrical venue of the city. Elizabeth ('Betsy') Billington was a major star of the stage. She had been a child prodigy, playing piano at a concert in the Haymarket in 1774 at the age of nine, and before her twelfth birthday composing two sets of keyboard sonatas. However stressful this might have been, it was surely a relief from a childhood dogged by suggestions of illegitimacy and of incest, and the horrible reality of rape. In August 1777, aged twelve, she accused and had convicted of rape her own godfather, violinist James Agus. She married her teacher James Billington in 1783 and the couple went straight to Dublin where she commenced her operatic career as the principal in Gluck's *Orfeo ed Euridice*. By 1786 *The Times* could report that 'Mrs Billington is already established in the opinion of the public, as the first rate English singer, and taking her in comparison with Madam Mara, an ear, not exquisitely nice, would find it difficult to discover where the superiority lay, either in point of natural ability, or improved taste'. She went on to shine in Italy whither she went after the publication of scurrilous although possibly true revelations about her love life.

Leigh Hunt thought her 'a fat beauty' with 'more brilliancy of execution than depth of feeling'.

Her presence in Dublin at the same time as Daniel Mendoza was due to a falling-out with Covent Garden. *The Times* reported on 20 October 1790: 'At Covent Garden things are at what is called sixes and sevens – Penury at the close of last season, wanting to curtail her salary, lost Billington to the House – and an exorbitant demand of a hundred guineas per night, for a stated number of performances at the commencement of the present season, made her re-engagement impossible – She therefore decamped for Ireland on an engagement with Daly, for fifty pounds per night – out of which, in the usual Irish mode, she may probably receive one half.' The economics here are somewhat baffling, and how justified *The Times's* dig at Irish bookkeeping is is difficult to say, but there may have been other reasons anyway. She was having an affair at the time with Richard 'Dick the Dasher' Daly, the manager of the Smock Alley (among others) and 'infamous seducer of actresses'. But whatever the reason, Mrs Billington was a major draw, and while her acting (and apparently wardrobe) left something to be desired, 'listening angels would applaud' her singing. That is if they weren't watching Daniel Mendoza spar with his brother-in-law. Which, it seems, they were.

His contract with Astley did not allow him to exhibit 'the art of self-defence' in public anywhere other than at the amphitheatre, but he was not debarred from teaching in private. He conducted these lessons at his private address, at 7 Molesworth Street. One particular man, an experienced pugilist, almost 6 foot tall and as yet unbeaten, by the name of Squire Fitzgerald, insisted on a serious set-to. He was very likely a distant kinsman of the Duke of Leinster, who may have put him up to it. Mendoza would probably have had no choice but to reluctantly agree; the two men fought on 2 August, probably at Daly's Club, at 1–3 Dame Street, with predictable results.

Mendoza was not in Ireland for very long, a month at most, but, as usual, he managed to get himself into a number of scrapes and aggressive episodes: duelling, muggings, riots, fights. He seems to have had the ability to draw violent activity to himself while at the same time enjoying the most genteel of company. He was also obviously a natural performer, a presentable, proud man who enjoyed the limelight. He was evidently successful in Dublin, for on the strength of his appearances Astley engaged him for the following season, this time to perform at Liverpool. Despite all the aggravations, Dan seems to have liked Dublin. What is more, in introducing modern boxing into Ireland, the Jew from Aldgate may have been the progenitor of that fearsome pugilistic tribe who were to dominate boxing for almost a hundred years, the Fighting Irish.

Dublin had also been financially rewarding. He was said to have earned over £300 by his teaching alone. It was time to go back across the Irish Sea. Aaron Mendoza did not like the water, and so it was arranged they would exhibit in Belfast and sail the shorter route home. They travelled again to Edinburgh and then on to Hamilton, in Lanarkshire, where they were the guests of the Duke of Hamilton. Hamilton Palace was a quite incredibly grand house, all black marble, green porphyry, and treasures classical and contemporary, built under the instruction of Anne Hamilton, Duchess to the 2nd Duke, in 1695. Mendoza's Duke, the 8th, Douglas, was in his early thirties, and had scandalously married a beautiful commoner, Elizabeth Jane Burrell, before proceeding to become commitedly unfaithful (the Hamiltons divorced 'amicably' in 1794). He was, it is probably fair to say, a rake. It was, after all, the age of the rake.

Hamilton tried to bring William Warr and Daniel Mendoza together to settle finally on a place and date for their contest. Both men enjoyed his patronage. With the characteristic facetiousness of the eighteenth-century press, the *Morning Post and Daily Advertiser* announced that 'A convention has been agreed upon between Mendoza and Warr, by the mediation of the Noble Duke, their common patron. The Peace of Europe may, therefore, be considered as completely restored.'[15]

In October Daniel and Aaron Mendoza exhibited twice in Nottingham, where they earned 50 guineas a night. They proceeded eastwards to Bury St Edmunds, to start a tour of East Anglia. A few days before the boxers arrived, a 'troop of strolling comedians' had arrived in town. Mendoza made himself known to its manager, who hoped that the boxer would not set himself as a rival attraction. It so happened that the troop was short of a performer or two. The manager approached Mendoza, saying that he understood the boxer was 'no stranger to theatrical pursuits', something Dan found amusing, assuming that somehow the man had heard of his hungover exploits at the Purim show. That wasn't the case, but Mendoza had of course performed in theatres all over the country, often as part of a very broad revue type of entertainment. He regarded himself as a performer. Mendoza joined the company 'by way of frolic'.

How good it would be to know what pieces the troop performed, what parts Daniel Mendoza played. It was not, however, sufficiently remunerative – 'I could gain more pounds by the exercise of my own profession, than shillings by following that of a player' – and he left after three weeks and made his way to Norwich.

There he reports that a man claiming to be the brother of Richard Humphries challenged him to a fight: 'after about half an hour he gave in.'[16] Mendoza stayed in the city for much of November, exhibiting and teaching with Aaron and Henry Lee. He liked Norwich, and Norwich liked him. A pub in Chapelfield Road, still going, was named for him. It is called The Champion.

Daniel had written to William Warr from Bury St Edmunds, offering to fight him 'in twenty-four hours, or as many days, on any stage, in any manner he chose'. Warr set off immediately, only to find that Mendoza had left town, presumably with the strolling comedians, shortly after having posted the letter. Warr was furious, feeling he had been tricked. There is some element of mischief in Daniel Mendoza (and meat-headedness in Warr) that suggests Warr may have been right.

Then again, Mendoza wrote once more to Warr, from Norwich. He was, he wrote, 'very much surprised to hear you wished to demand the money, deposited by yourself and me, as forfeited, as you must be assured that the time was postponed by the desires of the Duke of Hamilton'.

He went on:

I have had the honour of writing to his grace this evening, informing him that my friends object to going so far as Scotland at this advanced season of the year, but will go anywhere within two hundred miles, if a proper place is procured: I have left it to his choice, if it should be postponed till he comes to town, when I will meet you in any of the fields near London at a day's notice; but if at a distance, shall expect a month, that my friends may be apprized.

The *Whitehall Evening Post,* in characteristically outraged disbelief, reproduced what it called a 'libel' that appeared in a country newspaper:

The long-depending match between Warr and Mendoza is expected to be determined early in January next, in Norfolk: the Jew has been some time in Norwich, and is in full health and regular exercise; he passed his time very agreeably, being admitted to the first tables, and is constantly hunting, shooting, and coursing, with all the principal gentlemen of the neighbourhood. His school is well frequented, his pupils numerous, and of respectable rank; he musters among them Aldermen, medical practitioners of the first eminence, young sprigs of divinity, and gentlemen of the army and law.

Following which, the newspaper thundered: 'Who can complain of restraints on the press when such monstrous insults are offered to public decency?'[17]

The *Morning Chronicle* reported that while in Norwich Mendoza had 'gained rather too much fat', though this doesn't seem to have adversely affected him too badly. There is a report of a sparring session that turned real when a 'tall dragoon' grew tired of the exercise and 'threw off his mufflers', demanding a real fight. Mendoza took off a single glove, and closed the dragoon's eyes within minutes.

Back in London at the end of the year, Mendoza and Tom Johnson 'joined their interests' in order to exhibit the art of boxing publicly with other celebrated pugilists at the Grand Saloon of the Lyceum in the Strand, tickets 1/6d in the saloon, a mere shilling in the gallery. The boxes, pits and galleries of London's theatres were thronged with audiences ardent for boxing.

> Let Humphries, Mendoza, George Brewer, Tring, Jones,
> And all that delight in the breaking of bones,
> Be thank'd and applauded, for shewing the town
> The genteelest method to knock a man down.[18]

The show rolled on.

8

WARR

At the beginning of 1792 the following appeared in newspapers:

Under the protection of the Right Hon. The Lord Mayor,
THE FIRST OF MENDOZA'S SIX NIGHTS
Will be on Monday next, 6th February, 1792

Mr Astley, Sen., most humbly craves permission to lay before the public the two following copies of letters:

Hotel, Liverpool, Jan 15, 1792
Mr ASTLEY
Sir,
Having exhibited at several theatres in England with general approbation, I hereby give you the preference to engage myself for Dublin, for six nights – terms invariable sixty guineas. I suppose you know I had twenty guineas per night at Covent Garden theatre. Your answer will much oblige,

Sir, your's etc
D. MENDOZA

Dublin, 31st January, 1792
Mr MENDOZA
Sir,
I have consulted some of my best friends here, and it is my duty as well as my inclination to let nothing escape that might afford

amusement – I agree to your terms, therefore please to embark by
the next packet.

I am, sir, your humble servant
P. ASTLEY

ROYAL AMPHITHEATRE
PETER-STREET
On Monday next, 6th of February, 1792
In addition to a variety of entertainments, will be exhibited,
A PEEP AT THE AMUSEMENTS
OF THE
LYCEUM, LONDON
Or the
SCIENTIFIC ART OF DEFENCE

By

D. MENDOZA

Habited in the same manner as he appeared at the Theatre Royal,
Covent Garden, in the presence of HIS ROYAL HIGHNESS THE
PRINCE OF WALES

Mr Mendoza respectfully informs the nobility, gentry, and others,
as well as the AMATEURS of this kingdom, that he humbly craves
their protection – it will be his study to merit the same; and he will
ever acknowledge their indulgence to a stranger.

Dan was back in Dublin, and as successful as he had been the year
before. 'No public performer drew more money than Mendoza has
to Peter street theatre,' the *Diary or Woodfall's Register* informed
its readers in February. Daniel and Aaron stayed until towards the
end of March. One of their pieces was 'a perfect representation'
of Mendoza's victory over Humphries at Doncaster. This was
the eighteenth-century version of YouTube. Back in London the
where and when of the Mendoza–Warr fight started up again.
The *Public Advertiser* of 27 March: 'Warr and Mendoza are
to meet in May next – This, we understand, is a settled thing –
their friend the duke has signified as much.' 'The duke' was of
course Hamilton, and this time, it looked as if the papers were
spot on, at least as to date. It would be fought at Wrotham – no!
Loughborough…

In the months since Mendoza's triumph over Humphries at
Doncaster, it seems that the popularity of the sport, in England

at any rate, had taken a dive. 'The rage for boxing has almost died away,' reported the *Diary or Woodfall's Register*. This was probably not unconnected to increasing friction between England and France, and the likelihood of war between the two countries. Mendoza the champion may also have been the wrong ethnicity at the wrong time. Boxing, which had been promoted as manly and British, in contrast to the effete and French insistence on fencing, was now represented by a Jew, a 'little black bruiser'. That wasn't quite the right image.

The intellectuals were quick to respond to the French Revolution, men like Edmund Burke whose *Reflections on the Revolution in France* was published in 1790, and Thomas Paine whose *Rights of Man* appeared the following year. By the summer of 1792 the 'froth of revolution poison' had seeped into every class. 'Citizens' squared up to supporters of 'Church and King'.[1] Crowds made the authorities nervous, and boxing attracted big crowds, especially if superstars such as Daniel Mendoza were involved. It was pointed out that horse racing too attracted big crowds, and suggestions were made that it seemed as though there was one law for the rich and another for the poor. This seems hardly fair because in fact all classes were attracted to both horse racing and boxing. Interestingly, the chief demographic difference between the crowds was that women were more attracted by the pugilism.

So perhaps the 'rage for boxing' had died away not because people did not want to watch (or fight) but because the authorities were suspicious of large groupings, and ready to read the Riot Act at the drop of a hat (an idiomatic expression, one of many, that came from boxing's rich argot). Whatever the reason for the decline, the boxing public remained as keen as ever to see Daniel Mendoza fight William Warr. With the defeat and retirement of Johnson and the ill health of Brain, the championship of England was vacant. It was not an official title, but it was generally agreed that whomsoever won this fight would be regarded as holding it. As John Bee put it in his dictionary of slang: 'no emolument ever arose from this honour, but casual presents often, and the acclaim of all the Fancy.'

Most people, including Mendoza's own friends, thought the fight a mismatch and that Warr would win easily. Certainly Mendoza had avoided his man until he felt up to it, but he was now in the best of health and was fairly sure he knew how to beat Warr.

In the articles of agreement between them he made sure to include a prohibition of 'dropping', one of Warr's favoured tactics. To 'drop' was to fall without being hit in order to bring a round to an end (the same tactic at which Martin had been so 'dextrous'). The idea was to try the patience of the opponent and perhaps draw a foul hit from him and hence a disqualification, and also, obviously, to grab some breathing time. In his fight with Johnson in January 1787, at which Mendoza had been present, Warr had 'dropped' again and again, to the extreme displeasure of the Fancy. Mendoza remembers the fight as having been a draw, but, according to Egan, it was the contest that made Johnson champion. Be that as it may, Mendoza, with his quick understanding, reckoned he could outbox the bigger man, despite the fears of his friends or the forecasts of the bookies.

They met finally at Smitham Bottom, some 5 miles south of Croydon, on the road from London to Brighton (fights were almost always organised on main roads, to ease access). Cricket was regularly played on Lion Green, looked over by the Red Lion pub, where the ring was almost certainly arranged. All that remains of pub and green is a car park and a supermarket. They paved paradise.

The actual spot was in a dip 'encompassed by eminences' that were packed with interested locals. Nearer the ring, coaches and horsemen from London milled about. No door or admission money was taken, but there had been a kind of toll of 1 guinea for anyone passing through Croydon. The *General Evening Post* proudly declared that 'the carriages and persons, that passed through Croydon, upon the day of the late battle between Mendoza and Warr, were exactly as follows: 54 coaches and pair; 36 coaches and four; 76 chaise carts; 127 post chaises; 182 single horse chaises; 531 horsemen; 592 foot passengers.' Top field reportage.

The ring was 24 foot square and was covered with turf. As was usual in prize-fights, the rain was incessant. The fighters mounted the stage at 2.45 by which time the turf must have been turned to mud, as there had already been one mediocre though long contest before the main event. Mendoza, it was remarked, was 'much increased in bulk since his last fight' (perhaps that was not 'fat' that he'd put on in Norwich), and in 'very high condition'. He was twenty-seven years old. His second was Tom Johnson, Butcher his bottle holder (they appear to have been a team). Warr was seconded by Jackson. The umpires were Harvey Aston and the Duke of Hamilton. The betting, as it had been as long as the fight had been mooted, was in favour of Warr: two to one against Mendoza. The correspondent of the *Evening Mail* described the fight in some detail and no little authority.

MENDOZA v WARR I
14 May 1792
Smitham Bottom, near Croydon

The first round was fought in a slovenly manner, in comparison with the others. After a few ineffectual blows, they closed, and Warr was thrown by Mendoza.

In all the succeeding rounds, there was more smart fighting, and a more equal display of skill, than had occurred in any boxing match for several years. Mendoza, however, showed infinitely greater dexterity in stopping, nor did he shift or break ground so much as Warr. For the first ten or twelve rounds he constantly kept the lead. Warr, after a set-to on both sides, generally tried to put in a strong blow; but this being stopped by Mendoza, they came to close fighting, when the latter always prevailed by his short straight-forward blows; Warr always using what boxers call a half-rounder.

In vain did Warr try the arts which had so well availed him in all his former fights. His feints were ineffectual to disconcert Mendoza, who fought with great presence of mind, and with excellent temper. Equally unsuccessful was he in attempting to beat down his guard. Mendoza, on the contrary, put in several chopping blows over Warr's guard; and by one of those dextrous strokes, had, early in the battle, nearly closed the right eye of his antagonist.

The advantage thus keeping on Mendoza's side, and with it the odds, shifting to the same quarter, Warr generally falling alone, or when they fell together being always undermost, about the twelfth round, the spirits of those who supported Warr revived by a fortunate blow which he put in under Mendoza's ear. It was the best knock-down blow given in the course of the fight, and, if well followed up, was then thought likely to turn the day in Warr's favour.

In the next round, however, Mendoza rallied with extraordinary spirit, and his strength appearing now as much superior as his skill had evidently been throughout the whole contest, Warr was obliged to try his last by a desperate body-blow. Failing in this by Mendoza's excellent stopping, he was thrown in every successive round; till, on the twentieth, receiving a violent knock-down blow, his seconds declared he had enough, after a contest of about 27 minutes.

Upon the whole, there did not appear to us the least doubt of the battle being fairly fought, though it terminated far differently from the general expectation. The truth is, that Mendoza, with infinitely more skill in stopping, was equal in quickness, and even force in hitting, with nearly the same weight, and with more strength in wrestling, has an advantage over Warr, which the greatest courage and bottom could not contend against; and it must be allowed, that in these qualities he did not support the good character, which he had hitherto maintained. Besides an eye closed up, Warr was severely cut in the face; Mendoza was very little hurt, and seemed perfectly fresh at the moment when he was declared the winner.

The fight had lasted about half-an-hour and twenty-four rounds. Mendoza himself recalls that he was deprived of his senses by the blow he received beneath his right ear. In a modern fight it may well have proven decisive, but there was no KO in 1792. The seconds jumped in and had half-a-minute to revive their man. Mendoza recovered ('with extraordinary spirit') and proceeded to win the next nine rounds, before, in a different account, in the twenty-fourth 'both combatants came to the ground – Mendoza, however, fell upon Warr', and Warr gave in.

Mendoza, it is said, took to the stage 'huzzaing to the audience with as much spirit and activity as if he had not been at all concerned in the contest'.[2] Warr was carried offstage by Wood, the coachman, whom Warr had defeated some time before.

The result was a shock, but quite unambiguous. It may well be considered Daniel Mendoza's greatest fight, though he himself gives it very little space in the *Memoirs*. He does however exult in the disappointment and chagrin of Warr's supporters. They had regarded Mendoza as presumptuous in daring to accept Warr's challenge, and had bet heavily on the Bristol man. Mendoza also mentions the words Warr whispered to him as they came up to the mark: 'Have you brought your coffin with you?' This brutal query referred back to an incident on the road to Stilton for the second Humphries–Mendoza fight, when Warr had killed a blacksmith called Edwin Swaine in a fight for a guinea. Warr was tried at the Old Bailey and found guilty of manslaughter. He was fined a shilling and imprisoned for three months. It was a good job he hadn't stolen the blacksmith's hammer or he might well have been transported to Van Diemen's Land for life.

The newspapers praised Mendoza, almost fulsomely. There was nothing grudging. The *Morning Chronicle* simply said that he was 'the better boxer'. The *Morning Herald* thought Mendoza 'fought in a most capital stile'. The *London Recorder* remarked that 'Mendoza, upon this occasion, has given Warr a lesson, that, had he received some time since, would have taught him that he ought not to have supposed himself the first boxer in the kingdom.' The *Diary or Woodfall's Register* reported: 'Mendoza stood up manfully during the whole fight; and fought on the offensive, showing wonderful skill, likewise in guarding his antagonist's blows. Warr on the contrary, frequently fell, or slipped down.' The same paper, in its next edition, printed this:

> Almost every person, those who lost by the event of the battle greatly, only excepted, rejoice that Mendoza has beaten Warr. A more consummate blackguard than the latter, a man more savage in manners or more vulgar and foul-mouthed, is not to be found perhaps in the whole catalogue of Pugilists.

In the passage above the *Evening Mail's* correspondent makes a distinction between the styles of the two boxers: 'they came to close fighting, when the latter always prevailed by his short straight-forward blows; Warr always using what boxers call a half-rounder.' It is worth looking in more detail at Mendoza's fighting technique. I am grateful to Martin Austwick, from whose video on Mendoza's fighting methods, the following is transcribed and edited.

> Mendoza had a square-on stance, his feet pointing forwards. The body is inclined forwards, the hands are brought up together and one hand is very slightly ahead of the other, which matches the lead leg. It's a very basic stance. As a small man, a middleweight at best, he gave up inches of reach, and a lot of weight to his opponents, yet he still managed to beat them. He was extremely skilled at in-fighting, at getting in close, and he was very good at deflecting blows. In *The Art of Boxing* he talks an awful lot about counter-punching, blocking then coming in with a strike. He talks about rising punches and counter-punching. It is all about getting inside that long-range point at which your opponent has the advantage because they're bigger than you. What Mendoza needed for that was a stance that allowed him to close in in the most stable way possible. He wants to be relatively square on, he doesn't want to

be at an angle, because if as he closes at an angle he's pushed or his arm is blocked it's going to turn him around, which is going to put him at a fairly significant disadvantage. What he's looking to do is to get inside and get some serious strikes in and use this short-range ability that he had to his advantage. Now the other thing that Mendoza is very clear about in his manual is that you have to be able to use each hand effectively; so most of the pugilists and pretty much everyone in England was famed for fighting with a left lead, and if you look at some of the other people's stances, people like Johnson's stance, people like Humphries, they're fighting in a much more side-on position, and that's exaggerated hugely when you start getting to the transitional pugilism of the period where the London prize ring became the Marquess of Queensberry Rules, but that's a long time after Mendoza. What Mendoza is looking for is being able to get inside, being able to strike you with a right or a left, being able to close distance, being able to deflect your blows off to the side, and to do all of that as effectively as possible; and to do that he needs to be relatively square on. So that's why you see pictures of Mendoza fighting square on with his chest out, his shoulders square, his hips square, his hands raised up in front. He's ducking his chin down, and he's arching his abdomen back away so that if there are any strikes coming out to the mark then he's able to slip away from them. But from that position he's also able to throw himself backwards, in order to avoid any strikes to the head, but keeping his feet where they are, which allows him to come forward again very quickly, and to enable him to then take advantage of that short-range technique that he's so good at. In a lot of modern pugilism people are recreating these systems of fighting, with chest on, hips square, both hands forward, hunched down, inclined forward position, because it's hugely effective at closing distance and getting to in-fighting. The modern boxer with whom Mendoza is often compared is Mike Tyson, who was noticeably shorter than all his opponents. The quality that most of Mendoza's contemporaries most often noted was his speed. And it was the speed of response. So: stop and hit, because that was when the opponent was most vulnerable.[3]

Despite the plaudits, Mendoza complained that he 'gained more honour than money' from his victory over Warr. His friends had bet very little, believing he would lose. The suggestion is that the friends of a winning fighter would contribute to the purse. Who took the Croydon toll money isn't clear. Mendoza won 'a small sum' from having bet on himself.

Within a week of the fight Warr had published his own account. Obviously some of 'the knowing ones' thought the fight had been thrown. Such contests were called 'crossed fights' – their increasing frequency was what brought the Pugilistic Club into being in 1814.

TO THE PUBLIC

Patronised as I have been, I feel it a duty incumbent to declare to a candid public, and more particularly those who were most interested in the event of my success with Mendoza, on Monday last, at Smitham Bottom, in contradiction of a report which now prevails, that I fought booty or otherwise across; therefore as the evident means I can adopt for the most obvious testimony of my justification, offer positively to swear an affidavit, that I did exert my utmost endeavour to win it; also, that a few days prior to the day of fighting, I was seized with a continual retching, loss of appetite, and total indisposition; in this situation and condition I was compelled to engage agreeable as the articles, or forfeit the sum betted, from the great change in my health, and no other possible cause which rendered me extremely weak, to which I attribute the loss of the battle. I have nothing so much at heart as to prove the sincerity and consistency of my conduct, and regret with much concern, losing a battle of such magnitude, possible in its extent and consequence, as great as ever came under the attention of betting; therefore I thus publicly challenge D. Mendoza to fight in four months time from this date.

W. Warr
Send an answer to the Black Bull, Grays Inn Lane.[4]

Mendoza's reply, reported by the *St James's Chronicle,* was that he had 'won the laurel, and meant to wear it'. Nonetheless, Warr was insistent. They did again meet, in November the following year, by which time boxing was at its lowest ebb since the pre-Mendoza days.

A month or so after the fight at Smitham Bottom, Mendoza reports that he began again to suffer from ill health, so much so that he could neither fight nor spar: 'I was unable to attend my scholars, and, at the same time was paying a very high rent for my house and living at a very great expense.' Prize fighters did not live long lives (Mendoza was an exception) and it is hardly surprising that they suffered illness or physical indisposition, but sickness seems to dot Mendoza's life as thoroughly as the measles. The age itself of course was not conducive to good health: the Industrial Revolution resulted in a population explosion and the herding together of large numbers of people. Mendoza may have been suffering from the ague – malaria – picked up in East Anglia. It sounds as though Warr, if he is to be believed (physical indisposition was the excuse of most losing fighters, including Mendoza after Odiham, and Humphries after Stilton) had suffered a bout of food poisoning.

Recovery required fresh air, and Mendoza sought it on the outskirts of London. He went to stay in Windsor for a few days, and

> ... during my stay in that town, had the honour of being introduced to a great personage. This happened one evening, on the terrace, where I was walking, and was suddenly surprised at being accosted by a nobleman, who, in a very abrupt manner [one wishes to say 'careful, my lord'], mentioned his intention of introducing me to His Majesty. He had scarcely spoken when the King, attended by some lords in waiting, approached the spot, upon which I was introduced, and had the honour of a long conversation with His Majesty, who made ingenious remarks on the pugilistic art, such as might naturally be expected to be made by a person of so comprehensive a mind and such transcendent abilities, as that illustrious personage is generally believed to possess! Before I quitted the terrace, the Princess Royal (now Queen of Wurttemberg) brought one of the younger branches of the Royal Family to me, and asked my permission (which I of course readily granted) for this young gentleman to strike me a blow, in order that he might have to boast at a subsequent opportunity of having at an earlier period of his life, struck a professed pugilist on Windsor terrace.[5]

Writers about Mendoza maintain that he was the first Jew George had met, but this seems unlikely, as Jewish elders had made representations to the King on various occasions. Still, the symbolism is powerful. Dan Mendoza was probably the first Jew to have had a 'long conversation' with the king.

It was possibly during this year, 1792, that Lord Barrymore proposed a match between his own man, Hooper, the Tinman, and the new champion. In the *Memoirs* Mendoza describes a visit Hooper made to the Lyceum:

> On one of my public days, just as the sparring was over, a person called and informed me that Hooper, the Tinman, had declared his intention of knocking me off the stage, in presence of my subscribers; upon which, I mentioned the circumstances to the gentlemen present, and requested the favour of them to wait Mr Hooper's

arrival, who soon afterwards made his appearance, and set to with me. He found, however, that so far from being able to keep his promise of knocking me off the stage, he came off himself, with the worst of the affair, for though we both had gloves on, we struck with considerable force, and as I was able to give him four or five blows for every one I received from him, he seemed convinced that the work which he had taken in hand was not to be accomplished so easily as he had at first imagined, and therefore gave in, after a contest of about half an hour.

It is worth a detour to look more closely at Hooper, who was the subject of a longer-than-usual biography in *Boxiana,* and his patron, Barrymore.

Pierce Egan tells a story very familiar to the modern reader, about the spoiling of a humble man. 'Where did it all go wrong?' was the famous question allegedly posed to George Best by a hotel bellboy delivering champagne to his room when confronted with a bed covered in cash won in the casino and occupied by Miss World. While Best admittedly never lost his humility, he is regarded as having been killed by success, by way of an addiction to alcohol. Tiger Woods fell from grace in a car crash that revealed his adultery. In boxing itself a recent example is Mike Tyson, jailed for rape and remembered for biting off Evander Holyfield's ear.

In the case of Bill Hooper, he was discovered while working as a 'tinman' in the Tottenham Court Road; he made saucepans. Following a number of successful fights, he was matched against a carpenter called Wright. The contest took place on 3 December 1789 at Wargrave Court, the home of Richard Barry, 7th Earl of Barrymore, who had recently celebrated his twentieth birthday. Barrymore was given the name 'Hellgate' by his friend the Prince of Wales. His brother Henry was known as 'Cripplegate' (for, like Byron, his club foot), brother Augustus as 'Newgate' (for the prison) and sister Caroline as 'Billingsgate' (for the foulness of her language). Barrymore lost prodigious sums on preposterous bets. He failed, for example, in his attempt to eat a living tomcat. He spent lavishly and generously on the theatre, building one in Wargrave, purchasing one in the Haymarket and part-funding the construction of the Royal Circus theatre in St George's Fields in London. What is more, he acted in them. He was also an inveterate prankster (he had 'a great propensity for *larking*'), often to the point of bullying. It was then he needed a bodyguard such as the Tinman at his side. It wasn't that he didn't fancy himself as a pugilist, he did (he married one, too, the daughter of a sedan carrier), but unwisely. For example, in September 1791, he had dined with the Prince of Wales at Lord's, and afterwards, driving his phaeton (the equivalent of a modern sports car), had 'thought proper to lay his whip across the shoulders of a gent who was driving a one-horse chaise'. Road rage: a fight ensued. Barrymore was getting the worst of it until his protégé Hooper stepped in.

Barrymore took Hooper on after the Wargrave fight (which he'd won). Several victories followed (though also the 'mockery' of the drawn mismatch with Big Ben) before a match with Mendoza was mooted. Egan reckons this was 1795, some three years after Mendoza's own record of the sparring match, but perhaps Hooper had already had visions above his station in '92. He finally lost to a fighter new on the scene called Tom Owen. Owen would fight Daniel Mendoza one day far in the future.

Hooper's deeds as a boxer were however overshadowed by the overweening character that he grew into in the company of Hellgate. Egan writes that prior to his association with Barrymore he was 'a civil, well-behaved, smart young man', but that association with the nobility made him proud, 'much attached to dress; and rather illiterate, his vanity was too conspicuous, and, not bearing in mind the real character in which he stood as a dependent, he considered himself of equal importance with his principal'. In other words Billy Hooper grew into an arrogant and presumptuous man, who acted as his master's enforcer in some of the less-than-popular larks that Barrymore inflicted on the people of Brighton, where Hellgate spent most of his time, often in the company of the Prince of Wales. According to Egan, Hooper's mind 'was not strong enough to sustain the sudden transition from obscurity to a more prominent situation in life'.

This then was perhaps an early example of the perils of celebrity, that new addition to social life that had come with the spread of newspapers, handbills, the appearance of impresarios such as Astley, and the increase in leisure time. Egan was fascinated by the Tinman, affording his story a long footnote in his introduction to *Boxiana*.

The Tinman's end was a sorry one. After Barrymore's early death in 1794 Hooper could find no equivalent patron, and took to drink full time.

... one evening, a few years since, he was found insensible on the step of a door in St Giles's [the worst stews in London], and conveyed to the watch-house; and, on inquiring who he was, he could very faintly articulate, 'Hoop – Hoop'; but, being recognised as the miserable remnant of that once powerful pugilistic hero, he was humanely taken to the workhouse, where he immediately expired.[6]

As for Barrymore, he shot himself in the head by accident while driving his phaeton and was killed almost immediately. He was twenty-four years old. Apart from this detour, we'll hear more about him in subsequent chapters.

Despite now being the champion boxer of England, Daniel Mendoza somehow managed to get himself into such financial difficulty that he was forced to open a shop selling snuff, in Dog Row, Bethnal Green, perhaps at Purim Place (Dog Row is now Cambridge Heath Road). The combination of illness, what he admitted was a lavish lifestyle, and the decline in the popularity of his profession – the *Morning Herald* spoke of its 'dying embers' in December 1792 – all contributed, but what that 'lavish' meant is not clear. Tiny bits of evidence suggest that he may have gambled away much of the substantial winnings he made. Those nobles, like the Duke of Hamilton, with whom he occasionally mingled were wont to bet on anything, and usually vast sums. As Mendoza put it himself: 'having, from the nature of my profession, formed connections with persons with larger incomes than myself, the consequence was, I had frequently been led into costly and extravagant pursuits.' One way or another Daniel Mendoza went bust aping his spendthrift patrons. The snuff shop did not last very long.

The following year, 1793, was not much better. January saw the passing into law of the Aliens Act, 'an act for regulating immigration', which was repealed after the war but which must have made anyone remotely other than Christian English feel a little uneasy. In February – the month France declared war on Great Britain – Mendoza was the second to his friend George the Brewer in a fight with Wood, the man who had carried Warr off the stage in Croydon. George was so badly injured his life was thought to be in danger.

Then in June Daniel Mendoza was charged with 'obtaining a quantity of goods, to the amount of seven pounds, under false pretences'. The 'goods' were 'a number of cambric handkerchiefs', and the story was unnecessarily complicated. The trial did not go ahead until late October, but in the meantime Mendoza published the following letter in the newspapers:

TO THE PUBLIC
A charge having been made against me, imputing to me an act of dishonesty, upon which charge the Grand Jury have found a Bill, and an indictment has been preferred, but cannot be tried before the next September sessions; I must request the public, and my friends, to suspend their judgment until the circumstances of the case come to be investigated in a court of justice. Having always experienced the most generous protection from the public, it has been my study not to be entirely unworthy of it. When the period of my trial comes on, I hope I shall be able clearly to prove my innocence, the strongest testimony of which is that my prosecutor has offered me to drop the prosecution, if I would give him a written engagement not to commence any action against him; this I positively refused, trusting my case to the laws of my country, against which I am conscious I have not offended.

DANIEL MENDOZA[7]

Whether he caused this to be published because he was worried about the effect of the charge on his school it is impossible to say, but in the event a woeful witness for the prosecution and the lack of any evidence led to a verdict of not guilty. Interestingly, the judge declared that 'when the character of a man publicly known had been so publicly called in question, he thought it his duty to call other evidence...'[8] The age of celebrity was now being enshrined in law.

Dan spent most of the year touring with Johnson and Lee. In October they were in Bath, exhibiting in a tennis court. You could buy tickets for 1/6d at the Three Cups Inn on Northgate Street.

December brought news that Mendoza and Warr were to fight again, in the not too distant future. The *London Evening Post* rather meanly remarked that 'during the present taste for more important contests, theirs, it may be hoped, will attract little notice.' There was a war on, after all. The *Morning Post* informed its readers that Warr was in training in Sutton, and wondered 'are these brutalities never to cease?' Even *The World* was fed up:

Mendoza and Warr, they say, are to fight on Monday next.
As some of the boxers, by ducal patronage are determined to insult public decency again, the attendance of a press-gang is

recommended; none can be so fit to go abroad to fight in a good cause, as those who are so ready to fight without any cause at all.

For good measure was added a line of ducal scandal:

The Duke of Hamilton and Mrs Esten parade together constantly the public walks of the metropolis – O Shame, where is thy blush!

There were cynical hints that the fight would be fixed; that the two men were 'crimps' (unlicensed recruiting officers); boxing, it was written, was 'a violation of all morality and decency' according to the *Oracle* of 11 January.

Still, the 'bruisers' were nonetheless celebrities, so well known that their names could be used for satirical purposes.

The House of Commons may be considered as the Stage for Intellectual Gladiators; and the Dramatis Personae may be ranked as follows:
  Big Ben – by Mr Fox
  Mendoza – by Mr Sheridan
  Perrins – by Mr Pitt
  Warr – by Mr Dundas
To continue the analogy, it must be admitted, that they frequently give and receive foul blows – sometimes trip up the heels of an assertion – and often give, with dexterity, the cross-buttock to an argument.[9]

The *Morning Post* compared the success at Covent Garden of 'Mendoza and the other bruisers... a few seasons ago' with what they might now manage: 'They would not now fill the front row of the upper galleries.'

And yet, and yet. In early January an estimated 10,000 people turned up at Hounslow Heath to watch the second Warr–Mendoza fight. They would have trudged or ridden or been conveyed out of London along the Great West Road, through Hammersmith, on the long road west towards Bath. In Hounslow itself new barracks were being built as part of the preparations to meet a French invasion. The stage for the fight had been built near the gunpowder mills that stood by the River Crane, perhaps on ground now occupied by Heathrow Airport.

The fight, however, did not go ahead. Middlesex magistrates were having none of it, and assisted by troops (perhaps stationed in the new barracks), had the stage broken up. On the whole, the newspapers, in their characteristically hypocritical way, seemed delighted. The *Whitehall Evening Press* rejoiced that Justices of the Peace had 'prevented these ruffians from exhibiting such a disgraceful spectacle'. *The World* was even more fulsome:

> We were in hopes that prize pugilism had fallen into such contempt, that we should no longer be disgraced by public notices of battles to be fought for money. The Magistrates who lately interposed to prevent the fight between Warr and Mendoza at Hounslow, are entitled to the thanks of the Public for their interference. Twere to be wished that they could have sent those fellows to Flanders, that they might learn to defend their country, instead of publicly insulting her laws.[10]

In November 1792 a coalition of European states had mobilised armies all along the frontiers of France with the intention of invading and suppressing the revolution and restoring the French monarchy. The new French Republic, with equal determination, was intent on spreading the revolution through the Continent, and was more than happy to fight. Most of that fighting took place in Flanders. In November 1793, a month or so before the proposed Warr–Mendoza fight, reinforcements from Britain had been sent to shore up Coalition defences. The campaign ended in Allied failure and the fall of the Dutch Republic. It did however blood Arthur Wellesley, the future Duke of Wellington, who had given up heavy gambling to concentrate on his profession. He is said to have learned much from the blunders of his superiors in Flanders.

There is very little information about Daniel Mendoza's doings for the rest of 1794. At some point around this period (the *Memoirs* give the year 1793, though that does not quite tally with newspaper reports) he was confined to the King's Bench debtor's prison. He probably surrendered himself in order to avoid forfeiting his home. He had a wife and at least two children, Abraham (born February 1790) and Sophia (born in 1792). With boxing at so low an ebb, he was certainly hard-pressed to pay his bills. His affairs were, in his own words 'in a very deranged state', and his creditors were insisting on settlement of their bills.

Of the 1,500 or so inmates of London prisons in 1779 almost 1,000 were debtors.[11] The King's Bench Prison was principally for better-off debtors and political prisoners. The novelist Tobias Smollett had spent time there for criminal libel, the reformer John Wilkes served time there for libel. George Hanger, prominent among the *bon ton*, went in for debt a few years after Mendoza. Emma, Lady Hamilton, fell into debt after the death of Nelson. 'Better-off' debtors were those who had friends who would support them, for prisons cost the State nothing. They were self-supporting institutions. The King's Bench 'rules' allowed certain prisoners, at the discretion of jailers, to live within 3 square miles of the building itself, so long as they had a job.

The prison had been rebuilt in 1758, following a parliamentary enquiry into the state of places of incarceration, and relative to other such institutions was recognised as comfortable. It was located on the south bank of the Thames, in Southwark, 'a veritable township of prisons', bang next-door to the Marshalsea, which catered for those in even more abject poverty, and a name familiar to fans of Dickens, whose novel *Little Dorrit* contains many scenes set there.[12]

However, it is not as if the Kings Bench was a place you wanted to be. The Reverend Richard Burgh certainly didn't, and he led a conspiracy in 1793 with the aim of burning the place down. It failed and the conspirators were tried. The attorney general

> ... lamented that five persons, all of education and respectable families, should, by their folly and imprudence, to call it by the softest name, bring themselves into such an unfortunate situation. One was a reverend divine, another an officer in the army, another had been in the profession of the law, and the others were of respectable parents, and with fair prospects of being honourable and useful members of the community.

They were sentenced to three years, which seems extraordinarily lenient, and surely can only be understood in terms of class.

One of the conditions to which Mendoza had to conform was that he would avoid getting into fights. This, of course, especially in a prison, was like asking a horse not to stamp or a dog not to bark. From the *Memoirs*:

> There are circumstances and situations however, which would make any man not devoid of the feelings of human nature, lose sight

of prudence at the moment, and, at all risks stand forward to punish barbarity, and protect, if he were able, the infirm and defenceless against the attacks they are sometimes compelled to suffer from those, who, on account of their superior strength, seem to imagine they have a right to conduct themselves with as much brutality as they please.

One of these deserving of punishment was another 'ruler', a man called Hadlam, a soldier who had once fought Big Ben. He had, writes Mendoza, 'an insolent manner', something, as we have seen, Daniel Mendoza could not abide. The inevitable fight came about as follows: Mendoza had been sitting on a bench at the door of a pub when an old, rather infirm man stopped 'to take some refreshment'. The two got chatting, and the man happened to mention that he had a son in the army, in a regiment stationed abroad, probably Flanders. The old man, presumably not having heard from his son for a while, wondered how to get any information about him. Mendoza pointed to Hadlam, who was sitting nearby, saying that he was a sergeant in the army and more likely to be able to help. The old man shuffled over and repeated his enquiry, but got short shrift and 'infamous language', at which he remonstrated, and was rewarded with a blow on the face. Mendoza 'could not forbear reproving' the sergeant, got told not to interfere, interfered further, and finally challenged Hadlam to a fight. Challenge accepted: 'our contest was not of long duration.'

This story is pure Mendoza. The chat in the first place, the advice given, the outrage felt, the battle won. He is chatty, natural, impetuous, confident and always ready to settle an argument by force, *a la* Mendoza.

Characteristic, too, is the failure of Mendoza's next attempt to make money outside boxing. With the help of friends he raised enough to take premises in London Road, which connects St George's Circus to the Elephant and Castle. Here he opened 'a shop in the oil trade'. The house was large, and he had to pay a commensurate rent for it, but he had very few customers, and those he did have bought small amounts. He did not make enough to keep the shop open. His memory of the short-lived scheme is wry, to say the least:

I was frequently without many of the most necessary articles in my trade, and obliged to put off customers with the best excuses in my power: for instance, if sweet oil was wanted and I happened to be without it (no unusual case with me) my answer perhaps was 'I had just returned the last that was sent me, not being quite of the prime sort, and expected some of the most excellent kind in a day or two, and in the meantime had plenty of rape oil, if that would serve the purpose'. If mould candles were asked for, my answer was probably 'I had none left, having just completed an extensive order that was given to me only hours before, but had common candles, if they would do'. In short, nine times out of ten, I had not the most common articles that were asked for, and my shop, though denominated an oil shop, was, in reality, little more than a depository for empty jars and boxes.[13]

It is impossible not to be a little charmed by Mendoza's honest dishonesty, the Del Boy excuses, the frank admission of abject failure: 'Before a few months had elapsed I found myself in a worse condition than when I commenced business.'

London was famous throughout Europe for its shops. Both their number and their splendour astounded visitors. But Daniel Mendoza was not a shopkeeper, he was a boxer.

Deciding against a life in retail, he chose to become a 'serjeant of the recruiting service', and this, one must assume, procured his freedom from the rules of the King's Bench. It is possible that it was also a means of avoiding being conscripted into the army. This apparently was the method employed by what the *Morning Post* described as 'the pugilists and Light-Fingered Tribe'.[14]

Regiments of the British army all did their own recruiting. And in time of war new regiments were raised. One such was the Fifeshire Regiment of Fencibles, which was formed in 1794. Fencible (from 'defencible') regiments were raised for home defence only (though this did include Ireland, which was friable with revolutionary unease). It is impossible to say how Mendoza came by the job. Perhaps his favourable standing among aristocratic Scotsmen played some part.

Despite the general disapprobation that adhered to the sport at this time, the second fight with William Warr did go ahead, in November 1794. It took place on Bexley Heath, in Kent, accessed by Watling Street. There wasn't much there other than a windmill. The newspapers did not seem all that interested. The fullest report appeared in John Bell's short-lived *Oracle*.

MENDOZA *v* WARR II
12 November 1794
Bexley

The long-expected battle took place yesterday between these well-known Pugilists.

They met at Bexley in Kent, where a stage was admirably adapted for the combat.

For the first two or three rounds, Warr was the favourite. He gave his antagonist one or two severe blows; but the disaster seemed to increase rather than to diminish the manly efforts of the Jew, who, in the course of ten minutes, conquered the Christian.

Mendoza's courage and capacity were infinitely superior to those of Warr. The stops and hits of the former were equal to his best exhibitions; and we never saw his set-to, or put in his blows, with greater dexterity. Warr displayed, comparatively, little or no skill in his movements; and the knowing ones thought that, after the first three rounds, he betrayed symptoms of fear, and a want of real bottom.

When victory was declared for the Jew, in the plenitude of his joy, he bounded several feet from the stage and was loudly applauded by the numerous spectators.

Mendoza was to include an imitation of Warr's boxing style in his touring show. Presumably it entertained audiences outside London, but it went down badly at the Fives Court years later, the newspapers calling it 'ridiculous' and 'malicious'. It probably was.

The contest at Bexley had lasted about 15 minutes.[15] Later Peirce Egan wrote:

In his contests with Bill Warr [Mendoza's] excellence was so superior, that it was like a diamond in contact with paste, contending for brilliancy or value; the scientific Bill, who knew how to win better than any other man in the kingdom, from his perfect acquaintance with the manoeuvres of shifting and dropping from the prowess of his antagonist, when necessary – with Mendoza was put to a stand-still – the perfections of the master stared him so strongly in the face, that the impression proved too weighty upon his mind, particularly in the second contest, that he stood no chance, and his inferiority was glaring.

There was no doubt as to who was champion.

JACKSON

January, 1795. Not only a date, but also a poem, by Mary Robinson, the Prince of Wales's first mistress. It is worth reprinting entire, so good a description does it give of the nation, still at war with France and destined to continue to be, more or less, for the next twenty years.

JANUARY, 1795

Pavement slipp'ry, people sneezing,
Lords in ermine, beggars freezing;
Titled gluttons dainties carving,
Genius in a garret starving.

Lofty mansions, warm and spacious;
Courtiers cringing and voracious;
Misers scarce the wretched heeding;
Gallant soldiers fighting, bleeding.

Wives who laugh at passive spouses;
Theatres, and meeting-houses;
Balls, where simp'ring misses languish;
Hospitals, and groans of anguish.

Arts and sciences bewailing;
Commerce drooping, credit failing;

Placemen mocking subjects loyal;
Separations, weddings royal.

Authors who can't earn a dinner;
Many a subtle rogue a winner;
Fugitives for shelter seeking;
Misers hoarding, tradesmen breaking.

Taste and talents quite deserted;
All the laws of truth perverted;
Arrogance o'er merit soaring;
Merit silently deploring.

Ladies gambling night and morning;
Fools the works of genius scorning;
Ancient dames for girls mistaken,
Youthful damsels quite forsaken.

Some in luxury delighting;
More in talking than in fighting;
Lovers old, and beaux decrepid;
Lordlings empty and insipid.

Poets, painters, and musicians;
Lawyers, doctors, politicians:
Pamphlets, newspapers, and odes,
Seeking fame by diff'rent roads.

Gallant souls with empty purses;
Gen'rals only fit for nurses;
School-boys, smit with martial spirit,
Taking place of vet'ran merit.

Honest men who can't get places,
Knaves who shew unblushing faces;
Ruin hasten'd, peace retarded;
Candor spurn'd, and art rewarded.

Plus ça change!

Daniel Mendoza was by now a Sergeant Major in the Aberdeen Highland Regiment, a fencible regiment also known as the Princess of Wales's. It had been raised in October the previous year. One of Mendoza's jobs was to hunt down deserters. Travelling from Birmingham to Wolverhampton in early April, 1795, he was doing just that when he got into an argument with an 'insolent' turnpike keeper, who was foolish enough to knock Mendoza off his horse. Dan's foot got caught in the stirrup. He might have been quite seriously hurt. Disentangling himself, he went straight for the unsuspecting bully and inflicted 'a most severe and deserved punishment on him'. It may have been the only training he did for the fight he had been lured out of retirement to contest a few days later, on 15 April 1795.

Mendoza had by now absolutely decided no longer to fight for money. He simply had not made enough from it. The fights with Warr that had made him more or less champion of England had brought in surprisingly little, and ill health had prevented him from maintaining his teaching, and by the time he was healthy again the 'rage' for the sport was in considerable abeyance. He was winkled out of this retirement by the promise of decent remuneration from a fight with a relative novice, John Jackson. The stakes were 200 guineas a piece.

Jackson was four years younger than Daniel Mendoza. He was born in London to parents who had come to the capital from Worcestershire. His father was a builder, responsible for the arching of the Fleet ditch at St Pancras in 1766. Jackson likely learned to box at a sparring school rather than on the streets, possibly Humphries'.[1] He was introduced to professional prize fighting by Harvey Aston, that inveterate umpire, who arranged for him, at nineteen years old, to fight Mendoza's friend Fewtrell in June 1788. In a little over an hour, Jackson emerged the winner. The Prince of Wales was present, and impressed. Jackson's next fight was against another friend of Mendoza, a big, rather slow fighter, 'of undaunted resolution and sound bottom', named George Inglestone, known as 'the Brewer'. They fought in Essex in March 1789. Jackson had much the better of the fight, being quicker and stronger, and the betting swung decisively in his favour. As usual, it was raining. Jackson slipped, dislocated his ankle and broke a bone in his leg. He wanted to go on with the fight, sitting in a chair, but he was very likely the only person not to regard this as a ridiculous suggestion.

He made his living first as proprietor of a pub in Surrey, and then as a publican in Gray's Inn Lane, perhaps at the Blue Lion. Occasionally he served as a second in high-profile fights. As a younger man he had held the bottle for Humphries at Doncaster. He had seconded Warr against Mendoza in Croydon. The two men were not then unknown to each other. It is conceivable that there was a degree of enmity.

The extent of Jackson's professional fighting experience, then, was not great. He was being matched with the reigning champion, a veteran of over thirty fights.

Jackson's chief quality as a boxer appears to have been a natural athleticism. He was good at sport. He was also tall (5 foot 11 inches) and strong (14 stone, and it was said that he could write his own name with an 84lb weight attached to his little finger – strange times).[2] 'His symmetry of form is attractive in the extreme,' gushed Pierce Egan in a welter of hyperbolic praise in *Boxiana*.[3] However, as far as the *Morning Chronicle* was concerned, Jackson had 'never much distinguished himself before either for skill or courage'.[4]

What kind of shape Mendoza was in we don't know, except that he had been recruiting rather than sparring. He was, however, the favourite, unbeaten since Odiham (and Humphries' victory there had been of a Pyrrhic nature), almost seven years before.

They met at Hornchurch in Essex. Everyone was there: the Duke of Hamilton, Lord Delaval, Sir Thomas Apreece, Sir John Phillipson, Mr Clark, Mr Bullock, Mr Fawcett, Joe Ward, George Ingleston (the Brewer), Tom Tyne, plus about 3,000 spectators around a ring of 24 foot square 'so excellently adapted that no one could claim a superiority of station'.

Dan Mendoza entered at around 1 p.m. with second Henry Lee and bottle holder Symonds (known as 'The Ruffian', and possibly to be the husband or father of the husband of Mendoza's daughter Matilda). Jackson followed, seconded by Tom Johnson, with Bill Wood ('The Coachman'), as bottle holder.

MENDOZA v JACKSON
15 April 1795
Hornchurch

The two fighters shake hands, and set-to. The difference in stature is striking. Jackson is much the bigger man, 3 stones heavier and 4–5 inches taller. It looks a mismatch. Nevertheless, it is a cagey start from both men. The first round goes to Jackson, Mendoza falling from the first hit of the contest. The second round is fairer, Mendoza defends cleverly, stopping and avoiding, and returning with his old quickness. In the third round Mendoza seems to be gaining the upper hand and the odds return in his favour but the round finishes with his falling again. The fourth round sees Jackson take the ascendancy – he has badly cut Mendoza above the eye. The bleeding is profuse, but Lee and Symonds patch up their man, and back to the mark he goes. The odds had switched decisively in favour of Jackson.

There follows a round of boxing containing one of the most infamous incidents in the sport's history. Already winning, Jackson takes Mendoza by his long hair, holds him down and punches and punches until Dan is punched into the very ground. Mendoza's seconds and supporters cry foul. The umpires are resorted to, but apparently such action is perfectly consistent with the rules. Broughton would not have approved: a second edition of his 'rules' has added the offence. As Alex Joanides suggests in his extensive footnote to the bout in his edition of the *Memoirs*, had Mendoza been pulling Jackson's hair, there is little doubt he would have been disqualified. Joanides further points out that the last time an opponent's hair had been pulled in a fight for the championship was when Tom Johnson – Jackson's second – had pulled Big Ben's.[5] As we have seen, in that instance Joe Ward, Big Ben's experienced second, a man of practical common sense, cut his man's hair off and the fight was won. Joanides further brings to witness against Jackson the Old Bailey itself. In the case against William Warr for killing Swaine the blacksmith, it was pointed out that Warr had been infuriated by Swaine's having pulled out chunks of his hair, and had exclaimed 'You blackguard! I never had my hair pulled in my life.' The pulling of the hair led to a charge of manslaughter rather than murder. So clearly, it was regarded as unacceptable even if not proscribed by the rules.

Mendoza gamely continues, but the battering has exhausted him, and in the ninth round he concedes defeat. The fight has lasted just over 10 minutes. The result is a shock.

Some thought it must have been fixed. The *St James's Chronicle* certainly thought so. The fight, it decided, 'had no doubt been previously settled'. Opined the *Morning Chronicle*:

> It is to be observed, that when more money is to be got among the fraternity and their patrons by a champion's losing than by his winning a battle, it almost always happens that he loses.[6]

The Times was equally cynical: 'As had no doubt been previously settled, the Jew appeared overpowered by the strength of the Christian.' The same paper also thought it 'worthy of the notice of the magistracy to consider whether a man who breaks the peace should be a fit person to have a licence as a publican'. Of course this demonstrates astounding unworldliness. Everybody knows – or knew at any rate – that sportsmen, when they retire, invariably buy a pub.

If it wasn't a fix, then surely it was a cheat. *The Star* put it down to the hair.

> Several erroneous accounts having appeared in the public prints, respecting the late contest between Jackson and Mendoza; and being present during the whole of the fight ... I beg leave to state the following particulars... Jackson has greatly the advantage of Mendoza, both in size and strength, being six feet high; weighs fifteen stone, and is remarkable stout made. Mendoza on the contrary is only five feet seven inches high and only weighs 11 stone, but far exceeds Jackson in the scientific art ... notwithstanding the size and strength of Jackson, I have no doubt but he [Mendoza] would have won, if Jackson has not fastened on his hair for a considerable time, when he received more blows, than he otherwise did during the whole of the fight... I would advise Mendoza, if he again fights with a man so superior in size and strength, to have his hair cut off...

John Jackson never fought again. He had spent less than 90 minutes of his life in the prize ring. He went on to become 'Commander-in-Chief' of the sport as it gradually recovered a certain respectability, to the extent that Jackson was recognised as a 'gentleman', and referred to as 'Mr Jackson'. Only champion-in-waiting John Gully, of all these generations of prize fighters, was also known thus, having become a Member of Parliament after his fighting days.

It seems unlikely that the fight was thrown. Apart from the fact that Mendoza was not that kind of man – he valued honour and was as proud as Lucifer – he never forgave Jackson, and Jackson in turn kept Mendoza out of his magic circle, but then it is human nature to hate those you have wronged. (An aperçu from Tacitus, not me). It should be remembered that Jackson had behaved abominably at Doncaster, and had been remonstrated with by Sir Thomas Apreece. There is a niggling thought that 'Gentleman Jackson' may have had something against Jews.

A couple of months after their fight the two men met again, this time as seconds, Jackson to Mary Ann Fielding, and Mendoza to 'a noted Jewess' from Petticoat Lane. The Christian won that fight too.

> Everything having been properly arranged, the combatants set to, and for some time each displayed great intrepidity and astonishingly well-concerted manoeuvres in the art of boxing. Fielding fought with great coolness and singularity of temper, and by well-directed hits knocked down her adversary upwards of 70 times. After the battle had lasted one hour and twenty minutes, with much alternate dexterity, Fielding was declared the conqueror. [7]

In Jackson, boxing now had a leader who fitted the required image (Byron said Jackson had the finest physique in Europe). Yet he did not truly impose himself on the sport until after Nelson's victory at Trafalgar, almost as if he was awaiting the appropriate moment, the moment when the French Revolution no longer had any serious attraction as it transformed into an imperial undertaking, and the British had a proper enemy in Bonaparte. Jackson retired as champion and was succeeded by good fighters Tom Owen and Jack Bartholomew, but not until the emergence of Jem Belcher in 1800 did a fighter appear who might be mentioned in the same breath as Mendoza, and the sport remained in the doldrums.

It was at this point, with the emergence of Belcher and noises suggesting a fight between Mendoza and the young Bristol genius be set up that Mendoza's bitterness at the manner of his defeat to Jackson first expressed itself in print. Daniel Mendoza's indication in the *Morning Post* that he would fight no one but Jackson echoed his promise to Esther, years before, that the only person he would fight after they married would be Richard Humphries. It was as if Mendoza needed a personal reason to fight. It is not hard to imagine William Warr insulting him, and he had already had to face Jackson's insults at Doncaster. As boxing's biggest draw he turned down challenges all the time (there had been a possible match with Tom Johnson's brother earlier in the year). However, it is extremely doubtful that Mendoza meant to suggest anything other than his being hard done by.

That was not how the *Oracle* chose to see it. Unlike other newspapers, Mendoza's remarks were repeated as a formal challenge. Jackson responded with alacrity. Most interesting is Mendoza's assertion that he had challenged Jackson within a month of the Hornchurch fight, and that Jackson had declined to fight for less than 500 guineas.

> NB We are further authorised to assert that Mendoza is ready to fight Jackson for 100 guineas down, whenever the latter pleases, provided Jackson promises to stand manly up, and fight fairly without availing himself of the sinister art of pulling or holding his antagonist by the hair.[8]

This was Jackson's response:

Wednesday, Dec. 1, 1801.
TO THE EDITOR.

Sir, I was somewhat astonished, on my return to town on Saturday, to learn that a challenge was inserted in your paper of Thursday last, as if from Mr. Mendoza. Should I be right in my conclusion, by believing that it comes from that celebrated pugilist, I beg you will inform the public, through the medium of your paper, that for some years I have entirely withdrawn from a public life, and am more and more convinced of the propriety of my conduct, by the happiness which I enjoy in private, among many friends of great respectability, with whom it is my pride to be received on terms of familiarity and friendship: goaded, however, as I am to a petty conflict, I hope that it will not be considered as too much arrogance on my part, simply to observe, that, after waiting for more than three years to accept the challenge of any pugilist, however dexterous in the science, and however highly flattered by his friends, I think it rather extraordinary that Mr. Mendoza should add a silence of four years to those three, it being nearly seven years since I had the satisfaction of chastising him for his insolence; but Mr. Mendoza derived one great good from the issue of that contest —he was taught to be less hasty in forming his resolutions, and more slow in carrying them into effect. This cautious and wise principle of action deserves much commendation; and having served an apprenticeship of seven years to learn a certain portion of artificial courage, he now comes forward with a stock of impudence (the only capital which during that time he seems to have acquired) to force me to appear once more in that situation, which I have for years cheerfully avoided. Reluctant, however, as I am, to attract again, even for a moment, the public attention, I shall have no objection to vindicate my character, by a meeting with Mr. Mendoza, when and where he pleases, provided he'll promise to fight, and provided he'll also promise not to give previous information to the magistrates of Bow-street, or elsewhere. Flattering myself that your readers and the public will pardon this intrusion on their more precious time, I am, Sir, Your's and their's, most respectfully,

JOHN JACKSON[9]

Mendoza answered this pompous, condescending and generally disagreeable letter:

Mr. Editor,
It was with inexpressible concern that, in your paper of Wednesday last, I observed a letter, signed, 'John Jackson,' purporting to be an answer to a supposed challenge from me, inserted in your detailed account of the recent pugilistic contest at Maidenhead. Mistake me not, Sir, I was not concerned at the contents of Mr. Jackson's elegant effusion, nor in the least affected or surprized at the opprobrious falsity, brazen impudence, or malignant calumny of his assertions, which I deny *In Toto*; but felt particularly hurt at the idea that I was compelled either to sit down tamely under injury, or incur the risk of offending my best friends, and particularly the respectable magistrates of this division, by resuming a profession which, both from principle and conviction, I had wholly relinquished. In order satisfactorily to refute Mr. Jackson's allegations, it is only necessary to observe, that a month after our battle at Hornchurch I waited on him, upbraided him with his unmanly conduct, by laying hold of my hair, and offered to fight him for two hundred guineas—Jackson proposed to fight for one hundred guineas; and upon that sum being procured, declined fighting under five hundred guineas. Here was courage! Here was consistency! Here was bottom and yet Mr. Jackson is a man of honour, And Of His Word!!! – Mr. Editor, after this I left London for five years, which may easily account to Mr. Jackson for the interval of silence. I have fought thirty-two pitched battles—four with Humphries (three of which I won) and two with Will Warr, in both of which I was victorious: these two men were both game, and good fighters, and of course, having received so many blows, my only motive for wishing again to fight Mr. Jackson must be that spirit of honour and retaliation ever inherent in the breast of man., Mr. Editor, I again repeat, that I am delicately situated; that I wish to fight Mr. Jackson, and intend it; but that, from a dread of injuring my

family, by offending the magistrates as a challenger in a newspaper (which would be indecorous in a publican), I can only observe, that I should be very happy to see, as soon as possible, either Mr. Jackson or his friends, at my house, where they shall receive every attention from me, as I wish most earnestly to convince the world what a deep and just sense I entertain of all Mr. Jackson's favours conferred upon

DANIEL MENDOZA
Admiral Nelson, Whitechapel

P. S. Allow me to thank you for your liberal impartiality; and, through the medium of your valuable paper, to return my acknowledgements to the public for the many flattering marks I have experienced of their partiality.

Nothing came of these challenges and counter challenges. Neither man had fought since Hornchurch and they were probably both, for different reasons, disinclined. Mendoza was just about making a living as a publican, Jackson was enjoying, 'in private', the company of friends 'of great respectability'.

Great respectability was not something conferred on Dan Mendoza by a disturbing incident earlier in the year, in February 1795, well before the Jackson fight. He was arrested for assaulting two women, Rachel Joel and Rebecca Marcella. The trial, in the City sessions at the Guildhall, was not held until October. It caused quite a stir within the Jewish community: 'the court, together with the avenues leading to it, were very much crowded with persons of the Hebrew sect.'

Rachel Joel, the 'prosecutrix', was a washerwoman, 'a small, thin and delicate woman', who had done some washing for Esther Mendoza. Joel was probably not a servant as such, but clearly the Mendoza household was used to sending its washing out to be done, saving Esther the chore (for substantial chore it was, requiring a lot of water to be boiled, then the cottons and linens to be washed with lye soap, which burnt the skin, then rinsed and hung to dry in the hope it wouldn't rain or get besmirched by London soot and grime). Joel was owed 1/6d for the work and on 15 February called on Esther to collect it. She was referred by Mrs Mendoza to her husband, whom Joel found in Duke's Place, and 'requested him to discharge the bill'. According to Joel, Mendoza, 'instead of complying with the just demand, poured on her a torrent of foul language and disgraceful epithets'. He then struck her on the face and head. The woman ran away, but was pursued by Mendoza, who caught her and threw her to the ground. He proceeded to kick her (it was pointed out by Joel's counsel that Mendoza had been wearing his Aberdeen Fencibles regimental boots at the time). She said that she had to confine herself indoors and could not, 'by means of the hurt done to her, sit with any ease for some months afterwards'. Joel's counsel called as witnesses Benjamin Nathan, Rebecca Marcella, and Hannah Solomon. They all agreed that the story she told was broadly accurate.

It is a horrific tale, and there was no attempt to deny the assault, only to explain it. It was maintained that Mendoza had been provoked. The witnesses for the defence, Henry Isaacs, Nathan Levi, and Gabriel Jonas said that Joel had called Mendoza a 'crimp', had called his wife an 'adulterous woman', and that the first assault had been committed by Joel who snapped her fingers in Mendoza's face, and aimed a blow, which he warded off with his arm. A 'crimp' was essentially an unlicensed recruiting officer, and a term of opprobrium, analogous in terms of offence with the modern 'snitch' or 'scab'. John Bee's definition of 'crimps' reveals the casual anti-Semitism of the age: 'persons employed in procuring seamen for the merchants during war: mostly Jews, and invariably cheats. None employed for the army since 1796'. It is quite possible that among the general populace recruiting officers, albeit commissioned, were not much distinguished from those who were not commissioned, so the accusations – of both accuser and defendant – are quite plausible. As for Esther's adultery, it is of course impossible to know. Mendoza was often on tour, it is true, and Esther was often pregnant.

The judge thought the defence inadequate, and more or less told the jury that it should find Mendoza guilty, which it did 'without any manner of hesitation'. As for Rebecca Marcella, who had been a witness for the prosecution, the judge charged that the same evidences applied and that the parties should 'settle it amicably', while recognising Mendoza's guilt in that case as well.[10] The trial took place in October, and sentence was handed down in November. In one account the *Free Mason* magazine took great pleasure in recounting the whole episode as though it had been a boxing match that Mendoza had lost, reporting that 'the Jew was obliged to give it in after a most severe dressing, which the Judges have pronounced will confine him to his room for the space of three months'. Rather less sardonic reports say he was charged 50s for each offence, paid to the Sheriff's office.

An irony was that Mendoza had been made a sheriff's officer just days before his trial. Nevertheless, one way and another, the glory days were well and truly over.

10

MRS JORDAN

It was the age of gin, and one of the great gin distilleries of London was S. D. Liptrap & Son in Whitechapel. The 'Son' was John Liptrap. Born a year after Daniel Mendoza, and within shouting distance, he, like Mendoza, had found success at a young age. He was a magistrate, a philanthropist, a patron of the arts and sciences. In 1795 he was elected, at the age of twenty-nine, to serve as one of London's two Sheriffs. He was a man who clearly stood firm upon his own dignity: he had once chased the Prince of Wales out of his house, having discovered the heir to the throne in Mrs Liptrap's bedchamber. In mid-October 1795 Daniel Mendoza was appointed a Sheriff's officer, seconded by Sheriff Liptrap, 'though strongly opposed by the whole neighbourhood', according to the *St James's Chronicle*. Henry Downes Miles, in his history of boxing, *Pugilistica* (published 1866), remarks that the job was 'a favourite Jewish calling in the days of arrest on mesne process and of sponging-houses'.[1] A sponging house was a house kept by a bailiff or sheriff's officer, as a place of preliminary confinement for debtors. Mesne process was 'the process employed in a lawsuit and authorised by the court to ensure the initial appearance of a defendant' (OED); a writ.

Daniel Mendoza hadn't much liked being a recruiting officer, though apparently he was very good at the job. It required much travelling and what Mendoza describes mysteriously as 'harassing exertions'. He may have been referring obliquely to an incident in June when he was viciously attacked, beaten up and robbed by a gang on the outskirts of Coventry. 'They were supposed to be a gang of disappointed bruisers who went down from London on this brutal errand,' reported the *Morning Post*. Whether this incident (added to the punishment he had received at the hands of Jackson) accounted for another bout of ill health is impossible to say, but once again he felt himself weakened and unwell. He needed a job that would keep him close to home. As a sheriff's officer he could not operate outside the area of his commission, Middlesex, which suited him better (though, vicissitudes of health or not, he was never averse to a tour of the provinces).

What then were his duties? A sheriff's officer was employed to carry out the orders of the courts, serving writs and so forth, with the power to arrest.[2] At first, it seems, he enjoyed the theatrical element – or at least, he enjoyed giving it a theatrical element. As we have seen, he enjoyed dressing up, relished being on stage, had acted with a professional theatre troupe and his own touring show included imitations of other boxers. In his *Memoirs* Mendoza tells two anecdotes of his time as a sheriff's officer, one involving a threat to his life possibly more dangerous than any he had encountered in the ring, the other the mistress of the future king, William IV.

Mendoza, who gave, in his book, a mere twenty-five words to his fight with John Jackson, gave over a thousand to his account of the arrest of a Mr S****. This subject, a gentleman, but 'long in very embarrassed circumstances', had proven difficult to apprehend, not least because he seemed prepared to defend himself to the very death. After 'almost every sheriff's officer in the county of Middlesex had made unsuccessful attempts at gaining access to him', Mendoza was 'resorted to'. He was promised a 'liberal remuneration' if he succeeded. Perhaps Sheriff Liptrap thought Mendoza's reputation would be enough to bring Mr S**** out of hiding. However, Dan had a plan, more devious, maybe more enjoyable, less ruffianly, certainly thoroughly characteristic. He would disguise himself as servant to a tradesman. To this end he staked out Mr S****'s home, and determined that the best bet was the milkman. For a 'small gratuity' he borrowed the milkman's jacket, apron, and took charge of his milk pails. He proceeded from house to house down the street, supplying each with milk, until he arrived at Mr S****'s address. The door was opened by a servant girl, to whom Mendoza explained that the regular milkman had been taken ill. He asked if her master had risen. 'No, he has not,' she replied. Having determined that he was indeed at home, Mendoza closed the door behind him and told her that he would wait as he had 'something very material to communicate to him'. The young servant now became alarmed, and declared that her master was in the country. Mendoza told her that 'all attempts at deception were in vain', and insisted again that he would not leave the house without seeing her master. At this point the mistress of the house, aware of the altercation, made her appearance, and 'assuming an air of great importance' (which tended to be a costly error with Daniel Mendoza), asked what his motive was for 'daring to disturb the house, and refusing to go about my business', having been told that her husband was not in. Mendoza, in some dudgeon, told her that he would *go about (his) business*', once he had concluded it with her husband, and that it might be an idea for her to find him, otherwise he would search the house for him himself. She clearly had no intention of doing any such thing, and so Mendoza pushed her aside and made his way upstairs. On reaching the second floor, he heard the door of one of the rooms lock from the inside. He knocked, demanding admission. Mr S**** refused, saying that if Mendoza attempted to force his way in, he would be putting his life in danger.

> Conceiving, however, that having proceeded so far, it would be disgraceful to recede, and knowing that threats of this kind are often made only to serve the immediate purpose of exciting alarm without being intended to be put into execution, I determined to do my duty notwithstanding the menaces held out to me, and therefore burst open the door. On my entering the room Mr S**** instantly came forward and presented a blunderbuss at my head; upon which, I immediately knocked this dreadful weapon of destruction out of his hands, and took possession of it myself.[3]

The Sheriff's officer now produced the warrant and handed it over, but Mr S**** was not done yet. He went for a pair of pistols that lay on the mantelpiece. Mendoza cocked the blunderbuss and pointed it. He said clearly that he would not hesitate to shoot. Mr S****'s game was up. Mendoza took his prisoner to his own home and locked him up. Eventually the man's brother arrived and paid the bail, and apologised that Dan's life should have been in danger, when all he was trying to do was to 'discharge an unpleasant duty'.

The manner in which Mendoza tackled this task tells us that the skills he brought to the ring were useful in other pursuits: cunning, directness, swiftness of thought, and bravery; but he found the 'profession' of being a Sheriff's officer deeply unpleasant, even 'odious'. He was, according to his own words, given 'great credit for assiduity and diligence', and stood to do very well by the business but 'no pecuniary gains could make amends for the scenes of distress at which it was frequently my task to be present.'

> For instance, what gain could make me amends for being compelled to call, in the way of my profession, on an old friend and patron; this disagreeable task often fell to my lot, and what could make amends to a person possessing any feelings of humanity for being sometimes obliged to tear the husband from the wife, or the father from his children, or to seize with unrelenting hand the small stock of furniture, nay, perhaps the only bed of a worthy but unfortunate family, and thereby reduce them to beggary and wretchedness; to hear at every turn the curses of the unfortunate, and to be everywhere shunned as a nuisance to society.

Daniel Mendoza no doubt hated being called names, as we have seen, and he was of a convivial nature, but his emphasis on the degrading nature of the job (to all parties) is heartfelt, and was born of personal experience. It would take another seventy years for the punishment for debt to become remotely civilised. 'Arrest for debt has been truly described as having its origins in a refined state of barbarism,' wrote a relatively (he is not free of an anti-Semitic trope) fair-minded solicitor, J. Bowditch, in a pamphlet published in 1837 intended as a guide to the Law of Arrest, aimed specifically at merchants and tradesman who might find themselves in debt. He goes on: 'Is there no way of satisfying the heartless and mercenary creditor, but the inside of a prison? No way of interdicting between the ravenous Jew, who must have the penalty of his bond or the pound of flesh, but that of dragging a man from his business, his connexions, and his family, and putting him under control of a Sheriff's officer?'[4] While Dan Mendoza of course gives the lie to the ravenous Jew, his own words seem to ask the same questions as do the lawyer's.

The fate of Mr S**** is one of two anecdotes Mendoza tells about his work as a Sheriff's Officer. The other is about a much more celebrated figure, who just so happened to be connected to both the theatre and the royal family. Mrs Jordan, real name Dorothy Bland – she compared the Irish Sea, which she had crossed at sixteen to make her way in London, to the River Jordan – was, from 1791, mistress of the Duke of Clarence, brother of the Prince of Wales and later King William IV. She bore him ten children. One would have thought the duke would have kept her sufficiently in funds, but in fact the roles in reality were reversed, for she made more as an actress than he did as a duke. It was very likely his profligacy (which was prodigious) rather than hers that brought Mendoza to her door. She would almost certainly have been pregnant. The date was likely towards the end of 1796. In December Mrs Jordan was in court for non-payment of a bill sent by a woman in Richmond who had done some sewing for her, and who was owed £18 12s 6d.

Once again, Dan had staked out the joint. He decided that ingress was best achieved by presenting himself as a person 'of rank and fortune'. He therefore dressed himself up as 'a colonel in the army' and hired a hackney coach to drop him at the house in Jermyn Street. He was at once admitted and shown into a 'very handsome apartment' and asked to wait a few minutes. Mrs Jordan, witty, intelligent, recognised immediately that Mendoza was not a colonel in the army. Upon his

> ... mentioning I had a letter for her, she shook her head, and replied 'she rather feared it was a writ, for she well knew me and my profession, and consequently was aware of the probable object of my visit'.[5]

He was pleased no explanations were required, and that the famous actress willingly accompanied him home, 'where two of her friends were so kind as to attend shortly afterwards and become bail for her'.

NOT BELCHER

For the next decade or so Daniel Mendoza spent his time touring, exhibiting, sparring, except, that is, for the time he spent in prison for debt. Given that more than half the population of England's prisons in the 18th and early 19th centuries was in jail for debt, often trifling, Mendoza's not infrequent stays are not out of the ordinary. Some 10,000 people were imprisoned for debt each year. The overcrowding of local prisons with debtors was dealt with every few years by Parliament, which would pass an Insolvency Act to discharge them on certain conditions. There were thirty-two such Acts between 1700 and 1800.[1]

Just as there was no shortage of jails, so there was no shortage of theatres. The eighteenth century had seen a huge increase, and by 1800 there were almost 300 places of regular theatrical entertainment in England. Mendoza played in many of them. His exhibitions took the form, on the one hand, of sparring in order to demonstrate the art and science of pugilism, on the other of imitating the styles of other famous boxers. This was always successful with audiences. He was clearly a good mimic.

Having left the Sheriff's employ, he made first for the West Country, commencing in Exeter, where he put on a show with a comedian by the name of Barrett. Mendoza and Barrett would alternate their turns. This seemed to be working well until Barrett, who 'like most of his profession, had a very high opinion of himself', decided that their success depended more wholly on his part of the show, and that pugilism was an art easily acquired. In fact, he went so far as to maintain he had been taught by Richard Humphries, and suggested that perhaps one evening he should be Mendoza's sparring partner on stage. Accordingly, they exhibited the following evening. Mr Barrett had made a mistake, and, according to Mendoza, made himself also 'perfectly ridiculous'. 'Laughter and hissing' followed, and as it did, so Barrett grew angrier, and his hitting more violent. Mendoza retaliated. 'Mr Barrett received a pair of black eyes, and at the termination of the contest had every appearance of having engaged in an encounter of a more serious nature.'[2]

That, one must assume, brought to an end that particular relationship. Mendoza made for Teignmouth, from where he wrote to an 'S. Foote', manager of the Plymouth theatre, and presumably playwright, satirist and actor-manager Samuel Foote's nephew. S. Foote seemed glad to have him. There were contractual complications, but they appeared to have been ironed out when Mendoza started his five nights (on the first four nights, after 12 guineas were taken, takings would be shared; on the fifth everything above 10 guineas would go to Mendoza).

According to Mendoza, Foote reneged on the agreement. Dan made his feelings clear, as was his wont, and Foote immediately challenged him. Not to a boxing match, but to a duel. With pistols. Mendoza's contempt for duels with pistols or swords was well known, and the boxer thought Foote imagined he would refuse to settle an argument that way (thereby losing it). Mendoza decided to call the Devon man's bluff, and accepted the challenge, believing, in turn, that Foote would probably not have the courage to go through with it. Now Foote stuck literally to his guns. Mendoza, his own bluff called, left and returned with a pair of pistols, which he had made sure were unloaded. He presented them to Foote, telling the theatre manager that he had loaded the weapons and that they should set-to right away. Foote 'quitted the room, in terror and dismay'. The two men compromised on the difference between them, and Mendoza moved on.

He played Devonport (then known as Plymouth Dock) and travelled on to Liskeard in Cornwall. Cornwall was home to a small but thriving Jewish community, not least the descendants of the German Jewish merchant Abraham Hart, who settled in Penzance in 1720, and whose grandson Lehman, known as Lemon, was to found a rum distillery that thrives in Penzance to this day.

Needless to say, Mendoza got himself into trouble. On the last night of his Liskeard run he managed, while demonstrating Johnson's mode of fighting, to throw an exhibition punch that failed to be parried by his partner, who walked off the stage in pain and indignation. He was finally persuaded to come back, but when Mendoza informed the audience that his 'Johnson' demonstration was not yet finished, his partner exclaimed 'What? More of Johnson? I think we have had enough of him – I'll have no more of him, by God!'

After Liskeard Mendoza went on to Penzance, where he struck up a friendship with John Wolcot, better known as the satirist Peter Pindar, who was then at the height of his fame. Though he was often caustic in print, he was a mild-mannered man in person, aware of social injustice and fond of the theatre. Mendoza reports that Wolcot attended 'every night of my performance'. A full house at Penrhyn followed at the end of the year. Mendoza, it is evident, would and could talk engagingly with anyone, king, huntsman, journalist, comic, impresario, satirist.

The *Memoirs* maintain that he spent the first four months of 1797 in Wales, but newspaper reports place him in London in February.

> Among many other eminent endowments which Mr Gibbs ascribed yesterday to the Duke of Hamilton, was that of superior education. Had my Lord on the bench doubted this, Mendoza was in court to hear the learned council out.[3]

This referred to a suit against Mendoza's patron the Duke of Hamilton, brought by a Mr Esten, represented by Mr Gibbs, for reparations due him for the duke's 'criminal intercourse' with his wife, Harriet Esten. It seems that in 1790 Mr Esten had sailed for a job in the West Indies, leaving behind his actress wife. Returning six years later, he discovered that Harriot and the Duke had been living 'as man and wife'. Such was his grief at this discovery, said Mr Gibbs, that 'it was not in his power to describe its extent and severity.' However, it turned out that the duke's counsel, Mr Erskine, had a paper – a sort of post-nuptial agreement between Mr and Mrs Esten – in which Mr Esten, on departing for the Caribbean, 'relinquished all claims whatever over her person and property', and thus he was not in a position to commence an action for adultery. Mrs Esten was, indeed, 'at liberty to become the property of another'. Lord Kenyon, who was presiding, took a dim view of the morals of all parties, but threw the case out.[4]

That Mendoza was present suggests loyalty but also curiosity, and perhaps even a personal knowledge of Harriet Esten. Harriet was an accomplished actress, and for a period the manager of the Theatre Royal in Edinburgh. After Hamilton's death she married, in 1812, Sir John Scott-Waring, Warren Hastings' political agent. It is thought she lived to over a hundred.[5]

By May, Daniel Mendoza was back on the road, performing at Hereford and Wrexham. At Chester he was invited to perform in the Town Hall due to his kindness to the Mayor's daughter when she had been taken ill years before during a coach journey. Mendoza thanked her for her 'kind interference' with her father. From Chester he moved on to Lancaster, 'some intermediate places' and then Manchester, where he reports receiving 'the highest applause'. In August he was in Preston, 'exhibiting his scientific skill'. He was akin to the modern rock musician, constantly on the road, travelling from town to town. He was again in the north at the beginning of 1798. From Rochdale he went to Halifax, where he performed for three nights, and where he received written plaudits that he obviously kept, because he reprinted them in full in the *Memoirs*. He was, for example, entitled to be 'well-spoken of', he was a model of 'propriety and decorum', eminently 'respectable'. Daniel Mendoza's career was based on an idea of boxing as an art, as damn near genteel. And while his fame as a boxer was prodigious, it was his reputation as a master and his abilities as a mimic that kept him – insofar as it was able – financially stable. As Egan wrote, 'No man united the theory of sparring with the practice of boxing to greater advantage than Daniel Mendoza.'

Halifax had been at the end of February. He moved on to York. Some were none too pleased.

> The merited oblivion, to which the names of Mendoza, Humphries, and other celebrated heroes of the fist have long been consigned, induced us to hope, that this dishonourable profession was abandoned: but from a paragraph in the York Paper, we find, that the inhabitants of that town are still capable of receiving amusement from the scientific attitudes of Big Ben, Johnson, Perrins, Warr, etc, as exhibited by Mendoza.[6]

On he went, to Hedon, Peterborough and Leicester ... and despite the suggestion in some quarters of his 'oblivion', Mendoza's name was kept alive in the phrase '*a la* Mendoza', used whenever an argument descended into physical combat. Here are three of many examples:

> Johnstone and Rees, of Covent Garden, have had an affair behind the curtain. The former took offence, because the latter asked him to sing for his Benefit. After invectives, the contest terminated to the advantage of Johnstone, *a la* Mendoza.[7]

> The house was well-filled ... though the Gallery gods were very riotous ... and a scene *a la* Mendoza was forced to take place before tranquillity could be restored...[8]

> Two of the fair sex, a few days ago, at Stratford, having an affair of honour to decide, on the subject of a sweetheart, agreed to settle it *a la* Mendoza. The place of action was very eligible – a pin fold; where they partially stripped, and (soaping their hair to prevent foul play) to it they went with the meekness of tygeresses (as Lingo would say) *ad fistum-scratchum-tearum-plugum* etc etc, when after Roxana and Statira had amused themselves at least half an hour in this rational way, the civilized spectators separated them – and the termination of the battle between these Stretford Amazonians was postponed *sine die*.[9]

The man himself was now in the Midlands with a Mr Stretton, who sang songs by Charles Dibdin, the outstanding singer-songwriter of the age (he wrote over 600 songs). The two performers alternated over the course of the evening. The playbill contained whatever is the opposite of a trigger warning:

> The ladies are respectfully informed, there is neither violence or indecency in this spectacle, that can offend the most delicate of their sex; as an affirmation of which, Mr Mendoza has, by repeated desire, performed before their Majesties and the Royal Family.

This is another piece of ephemera kept by Mendoza. He had a sense of his own importance.

Stretton and Mendoza started in Stafford and then visited Nottingham, Leek, Stone, Uttoxeter, Belper, Hanley, and what are now outlying suburbs of Stoke, such as Lane End. In the last he was nearly arrested. While taking a morning stroll on the day of the exhibition, he bumped into a man who told him he had a writ against that notorious pugilist, Daniel Mendoza. Mendoza, taking an interest, suggested that he wait until after the performance, otherwise he might cause some 'tumult' in the audience. The man agreed. Mendoza determined to make a speedy exit – to 'decamp directly', as he put it – at the show's end, but the officer had twigged, and was waiting at his door. Mendoza said that he would not go quietly, and suggested that a little forbearance on the part of the officer might be rewarded.

> Whether this proposal was what he was waiting for, I know not, but after some little hesitation he yielded, and consented to act, as greater men have not scrupled to act, upon more important occasions, – he accepted a small bribe, and departed without giving me any further trouble.[10]

Having escaped complications in Lane End, he then found there was another writ out for his arrest in Congleton, a little further north, towards Macclesfield. Again, he decamped directly and made for Lancashire. He eventually found himself in Hull in the north-east where, perhaps still on the run from his creditors, he took a job as a sutler, providing goods to the Nottingham militia. As was usual with any occupation that had not to do with boxing, Mendoza made a hash of this and was soon 'considerably in debt'. He meant considerably more in debt.

Summer came, and he returned to exhibiting, in Lincolnshire and then in Liverpool, where the magistrates restricted him to a limited run. Needless to say, he overstayed his welcome, and his performance was shut down by a company of constables. He and his brother spent the night in a 'miserable dungeon, but having made up an excellent fire, and sent for some wine to regale ourselves, we passed the time very well until the morning', when they were released, on condition that they agree not to perform any more in public.

Following a private subscription night, Mendoza commended 'the liberality of the people of Liverpool', and in particular a gentleman amateur who sparred with him wearing spectacles. From Liverpool he went north again, finding himself by September in Carlisle, 'where unfortunately I was arrested for a debt contracted with a wine merchant at Hull'. This doubtless dated from his attempts at sutlering in that city.

Daniel Mendoza therefore spent the turn of the century incarcerated in Carlisle Prison. By 1815 the prison had fallen into disuse, which rather suggests it wasn't the most salubrious of gaols, even by eighteenth-century standards. Still, it seems that the keeper, though not his wife, was a fan of the boxer.

> The first night I passed in Carlisle Prison I overheard the keeper's wife ... express her opinion of me ... in the following manner: 'So, here's a pretty guest we have got! I am very sorry this Mendoza has come here. I hope you will contrive to put him in close confinement, otherwise he will be nagging everyone that comes in his way'... Her husband's sentiments were not in unison with hers. For in reply ... he answered, 'I believe you need not be under any apprehensions concerning him. I have known him many years, and can assure you, you are mistaken in his character. I am sure he will conduct himself peaceably, and he shall want no convenience with which it is in my power to accommodate him.'[11]

While incarcerated, Mendoza attempted to pay his debts by issuing signed 'bank' notes printed with his features, selling, in effect, his signature, for tuppence a time. In this he was following a trend to 'ridicule and burlesque' the Bank of England for issuing notes for 'the small sums of one and two pounds'. This scheme was to compensate for the shortage of gold coins brought on as a consequence of the war with France – hitherto the lowest denomination banknote had been for £20. Had he been forging Bank of England notes, and been discovered, he would have been hanged (over 300 people were hanged for forgery of bank notes between 1797 and 1821). Mendoza may have been playing a dangerous game: 'I sometimes jocosely told my customers, these notes would pass for their value at all public houses and chandler shops in the neighbourhood.'

Mendoza was in Carlisle Prison for six months before coming to an arrangement with his creditors, whereby he promised to pay back his debt at 2 guineas a month. On release Mendoza, who must have been at least somewhat malnourished after his incarceration, walked at once to Hexham – a little under 40 miles – and took a room at the Golden Lion in Allendale. He found out from the landlord that there was a company of players in town. The boxer wanted to know how they conducted themselves. The landlord told him 'Why, sir, they be good company enough on some respects;

they make people laugh; but the worst of it is, they pay nobody.' However, he must have taken something to drink, for he joined the troupe and performed at the theatre that night. Newcastle and North Shields, followed, and thence to Scotland, returning to Dumfries, where the magistrates objected to his performance but allowed private 'subscription' shows. He travelled back to Edinburgh, and there met Fletcher Reid.

Fletcher Reid, 'always actively alive', was one of the leading 'amateurs', and most famously a backer of the Belcher brothers.[12] He now proposed a contest between Mendoza and Jem Belcher, perhaps the two greatest fighters of the bare-knuckle era, representing old and new schools. Daniel refused without hesitation, but when approached again, having 'taken my wine pretty freely', he assented. Mendoza maintains that the idea was that the fight should take place in Scotland, within three months, for the sum of 600 guineas. Well, it might have amounted eventually to 600; certainly, 250 were already subscribed.

The sum must have been irresistible to a man always on the run from – 'harassed by' was Mendoza's phrase – creditors. He used various acts of deception to avoid the bailiffs and sheriffs' officers who pursued him, such as printing bills for performances he never gave, while exhibiting secretly elsewhere. In his *Memoirs* he is quite frank about his reasons for accepting Reid's proposal, despite his oft-repeated resolution not to fight any more 'pitched battles'. The money would have allowed him to relieve his family of the 'great distress' in which they found themselves. He does add: 'Perhaps, also, the hopes of closing my pugilistic career with a successful engagement with the Champion of the day, might have operated in some degree upon my mind.'[13]

Jem Belcher, 'good natured in the extreme', was a strong, coming boxer. He was the grandson of John Slack, who had defeated the great Broughton fifty years before. His sister was married to Bill Watson, another good fighter (who had challenged Mendoza after the first Humphries fight). When Belcher moved to London at the age of seventeen, he took instruction from Bill Warr in Covent Garden. In April of 1800 he beat the useful Paddington Jones and the following month the even more accomplished Jack Bartholomew, who was, admittedly, thirty-seven years old.

It was proposed that to avoid charges against Mendoza that would lose him the landlordship he had recently acquired of a pub in London, and in order that the contest would go ahead uninterrupted, the fight would take place in Scotland. The papers were disapproving but, in their hypocritical way, excited at the prospect. Mendoza and Belcher were probably the two finest boxers of the age. But in September the Civil Powers in Scotland made clear that they too did not approve the fight, and it was called off.

The difference in age was one thing (Mendoza was thirty-five), but there was a weight difference too. Belcher was reckoned by two sources to be 12 stone 12 lbs, Mendoza, on one reckoning 12 stone, on another no more than 11 stone 4 lbs. Belcher was also taller at 5 foot 11 inches. The *Oracle* reported that the bets were very much in favour of Belcher, but that the fight was 'expected to be the most severe and scientific contest recorded in the annals of Pugilism'. The *Whitehall Evening Post* noted that the betting was at five to four in favour 'of the Jew'. The *London Packet*, also known as *New Lloyds Evening Post*, reported that 'bets are nearly equal, though it reckoned that 'from Belcher's dexterity at the fatal cross buttock, it is supposed the Jew will be vanquished.' The *Sun* merely remarked that it had hoped that this 'barbarous species of amusement was fallen into fashionable contempt' and hoped that 'magistrates would bring the combatants into field with "old father Antic, the Law"'.

Which is precisely what happened. After making the agreement with Fletcher Reid to fight Belcher, Mendoza had moved on, from Edinburgh, to Dundee, to Glasgow, one step ahead of the officers. When he finally returned to London, he found his house 'stripped of almost every article of furniture' and a writ of execution placed upon it (the house is in Paradise Row, in Bethnal Green, and it is still there; current average value of houses in the street a cool £1 million). On his second morning back home, he was woken by two police officers who hauled him off to Bow Street to face Richard Ford JP.

Again, as with the proposed fight with Warr, the magistrates were out for Mendoza in particular. He was 'brought' to the Public Office in Bow Street, and told to keep the peace by promising not to fight Belcher 'or any other person'. He explained that it had not been he but Belcher who had issued the challenge, and that the fight was planned for Scotland, and therefore out of a London magistrate's jurisdiction. Richard Ford, the said magistrate, would, he said, write to Scottish magistrates on the matter. He must have known that Mendoza had not fought since having had his hair pulled by Gentleman John Jackson five years previously, and was not known as a regular disturber of the peace. When asked again if he had made the challenge:

> Mendoza: He has challenged not only me, but everyone else.
> Ford: Indeed! Then why has he not challenged me?
> Mendoza: Because you cannot fight, sir. I know no better reason.

It is hard to avoid the idea that the powers-that-be rather resented Mendoza's popularity and perhaps influence as a celebrity and a Jew. But Joanides in his edition of the *Memoirs* raises the possibility of a personal antagonism between Ford and Mendoza, certainly a dislike for the boxer on Ford's part. Richard Ford, it seems, was until 1790 the lover of Mrs Jordan, later the Duke of Clarence's mistress. Ford and Jordan had three children. As we have seen, Mrs Jordan was one of Mendoza's victims when he worked for the Sheriff, following his defeat by Jackson in 1795. This probably did not sit well with Ford, who at that time was already a magistrate with the Home Office and secretary to the Duke of Portland. In 1795 he was sent to Dover to oversee immigration under the Aliens Act. He may well have had a hand in forestalling the Warr fight as well as preventing the Belcher proposal.

It should also be remembered that England was in its seventh year of war against 'egalitarian' revolutionary France, now ruled by First Consul Bonaparte, and where Jews had been given the same rights as all other Frenchmen (though Jewish life was far more regulated than in England. Liberty means different things, depending on context.)

Then again, for all this, it is likely that Mendoza was relieved, that despite the hope mentioned above, he knew he would lose. Robbed of a rich payday, and bound now not to fight, Mendoza, harassed and persecuted by his creditors, took again to private teaching. He also applied almost immediately to Philip Astley's son, John, by way of the newspapers, in which the following letter, response and advertisement appeared:

To JOHN ASTLEY, Esq
PROPRIETOR of the ROYAL AMPHITHEATRE
WESTMINSTER BRIDGE

Sir, in making application to you on a subject of a pecuniary nature, I shall, no doubt, have to encounter (should such a request prove successful) with the censure, not to say malignity, of certain individuals, whose reprobation can only arise against the art or profession of Pugilism. My conduct, however, as a man, both in public and private life, I hope I may say, has ever been found both peaceable and orderly, and to such I attribute the possession of a numerous and respectable body of friends, more than to any peculiar merit of my own. In speaking of the laws of my country, I hope I never offended them; at least I can truly say, I never did so intentionally; and, in regard to a late engagement between myself and Mr Belcher, the Magistrates thought proper to interfere and forbid its taking place, and, to such an authority, I bow obedience. And now, sir, let me say, that if you will grant your theatre, for one night, towards the support and relief of a numerous family, that humanity which has at all times proved the characteristic of Mr Astley, Jun. will particularly, in this instance, prove the means, with the assistance of a generous public, of contributing towards the happiness of,

Sir, you much obliged humble servant,
DANIEL MENDOZA

To MR MENDOZA

Mr Mendoza, your application to me, relative to the grant of the use of the Royal Amphytheatre, for one night, for the purpose of a Benefit, I have turned in my mind, and although not in the habit of granting the use of the house to any person or persons but my own Company, and certain Charitable Institutions; yet, in consideration of your claiming it, in behalf of a numerous and distressed family, your application shall be attended to, by my compliance with your request, and, with wishing you every success, remain your humble servant,

JOHN ASTLEY

In consequence of the above answer, Mr Mendoza most respectfully begs leave to inform his friends and the public that this BENEFIT at the ROYAL AMPHITHEATRE, is fixed for Monday next, the 13th of October, when will be presented a variety of new and splendid ENTERTAINMENTS, particulars of which will be expressed in the bills and newspapers of the day on which evening (and for that night only) Mr Mendoza will spar with a Gentleman and several celebrated Pugilists, being his first appearance there seven years, and the last night but two of the Company's performing this season.

How much this raised, we do not know, but Mendoza was to rely on such 'benefits' for much of the rest of his life. He would also have been paid for acting as a second, as he did for the Irish fighter Gamble in his fight with Jem Belcher on Wimbledon Common in December 1800.

'It seemed as if all the inhabitants of London were on the alert,' wrote Egan. There was an estimated crowd of 30,000. 'The number of light carts, horsemen and pedestrians were, as a French general observes, incalculable,' reported the *Star*. The fight was delayed by the late arrival of Daniel Mendoza, doubtless held up by the throng. The fight could not start without him as he was Gamble's second. For all the anticipation, the fight itself was a damp squib, lasting a mere 9 minutes. Belcher hit Gamble in the kidneys in the fifth round, and (Egan again) 'they swelled as big as a twopenny loaf,' and that was it. Afterwards, Belcher, tying his shoes, had words with Mendoza. They were reported by the *Oracle:*

BELCHER: Dan Mendoza!
MENDOZA: Well, what do you want?
BELCHER: I say, these were the shoes I bought to give you a thrashing in Scotland.
MENDOZA: Well! Well! The time may come.
BELCHER: I wish you'd do it now.[14]

But Daniel Mendoza could not risk it.

He was introduced around this time to a character who, even in a period of outrageous characters, was infamously unhinged. Thomas Pitt, Lord Camelford (described by the Dictionary of National Biography as 'naval officer and rake') was brave, foolhardy, violent, compassionate, irritable, brilliant, foolish, both pro- and anti-revolutionary France, and with the death of his father, tremendously wealthy. Mendoza in the *Memoirs* refers to Camelford's 'impetuosity of temper' and goes on to tell the following story, worth repeating in the boxer's own words:

When I attended his lordship, he requested me to spar with him, which I accordingly did, and he professed to feel highly gratified at my exertions, and intimated that he would show me an original attitude of his own, in which he had attained a degree of perfection

Above left: James Figg, a pugilist. *Line engraving by R. Graves, after J. Ellys. Courtesy of Wellcome Collection.*

Above right: Jack Broughton, the Boxer. *Oil painting by John Hamilton Mortimer,* c.1767. *Courtesy of Yale Center for British Art, Paul Mellon Collection.*

Mendoza. *James Gillray. Courtesy of Library of Congress.*

Above: The London Docks. *Engraving, artist unknown. Courtesy of Library of Congress.*

Below left: The Jew's Progress. *A Jewish boy selling oranges; a Jewish man in a top hat and coat selling bonds; representing the advancement of Jews from street-selling to high finance. Wood engraving. Courtesy of Wellcome Collection.*

Below right: A Highwayman Tries to Sell Stolen Articles to a Group of Jewish Receivers. *Mezzotint, 1777. Courtesy of Wellcome Collection.*

The Prize Fight. *Possibly Humphries v Martin, Watercolour by Thomas Rowlandson, 1787. Courtesy of Yale Center for British Art, Paul Mellon Collection.*

Above left: A Jockey Holding a Race Horse by its Reins. *Line engraving by J. Tookey after J. C. Ibbetson, 1797. Courtesy of Wellcome Collection.*

Above right: The Thunderer. *Banastre Tarleton boasting of his exploits to the Prince of Wales outside a brothel labelled 'The Whirligig.' Etching, James Gillray, 1782. Courtesy of Library of Congress.*

Vauxhall Gardens. *Aquatint by John Bluck. Courtesy of Yale Center for British Art, Paul Mellon Collection.*

Above: A Game of Cricket
(*The Royal Academy Club
in Marylebone Fields, now
Regent's Park*). Oil on panel,
unknown artist, between 1790
and 1799. Courtesy of Yale
Center for British Art, Paul
Mellon Collection.

Right: *Richard Humphries,
from* Boxiana.

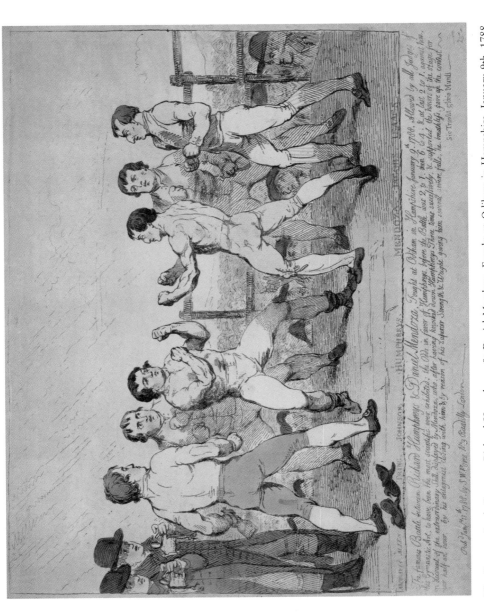

The Famous Battle Between Richard Humphreys & Daniel Mendoza, Fought at Odiham in Hampshire, January 9th, 1788.
Etching by James Gillray, 1788. Courtesy of the Lewis Walpole Library, Yale University.

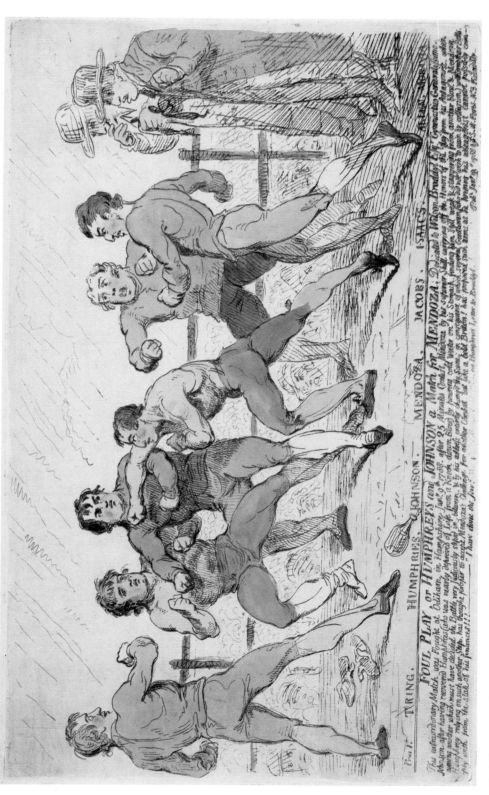

Foul Play, or Humphreys and Johnson A Match For Mendoza. *Etching by James Gillray, 1788. Courtesy of the Lewis Walpole Library, Yale University.*

Above: Polite
Amusement of
Brute Beasts at the
Lyceum. *Drawing
and watercolour by
Samuel Collings.
Courtesy of Yale
Center for British
Art, Paul Mellon
Collection.*

Right: The Moment
of Imagination.
*Captain Topham,
founder of* The
World. *Engraving,
artist unknown,
1785. Courtesy
of Library of
Congress.*

A Pugilistick Club.
*Portraits of Humphries
and Mendoza are
on the back wall.
Etching by J. Barlow,
after S. Collings,
1789. Courtesy of
Wellcome Collection.*

Duelling in Phoenix
Park, Dublin.
*Engraving by unknown
artist, 1834. Courtesy
of Wellcome Collection.*

Joe Ward, from Boxiana.

Above left: George III. *Stipple engraving and etching by George Siegmund Facius & Johann G. Facius, after William Berczy the Elder, 1791. Courtesy of Yale Center for British Art, Paul Mellon Collection.*

Above right: A Voluptuary Under the Horrors of Digestion. *Caricature of the Prince of Wales. Engraving by James Gillray, 1792. Courtesy of Library of Congress.*

The Fall of Phaeton: '*The Prince of Wales falls headlong, but gracefully, from his high phaeton, and is about to land on Mrs. Fitzherbert, who lies face downwards on the ground, on hands and knees, her petticoats over her head, leaving her posteriors bare...' Engraving by James Gillray, 1788. Courtesy of Library of Congress.*

Left: *William Warr, from* Boxiana.

Below: Dan Beating the Philistines. *Daniel Mendoza defeats William Warr. Engraving by George Cruikshank, 1792. Courtesy of The Jewish Museum.*

Above left: Mrs. Jordan in the Character of Hypolita. *Mezzotint by John Jones after John Hoppner.* *1791. Courtesy of Yale Center for British Art, Paul Mellon Collection.*

Above right: Mr John Jackson. *Engraving from the portrait by Benjamin Marshall from* Boxiana.

Women Fighting in Duke's Place. *Etching by unknown artist. Courtesy of Wellcome Collection.*

Above left: *Dutch Sam, from* Boxiana.

Above right: *Tom Belcher, from* Boxiana.

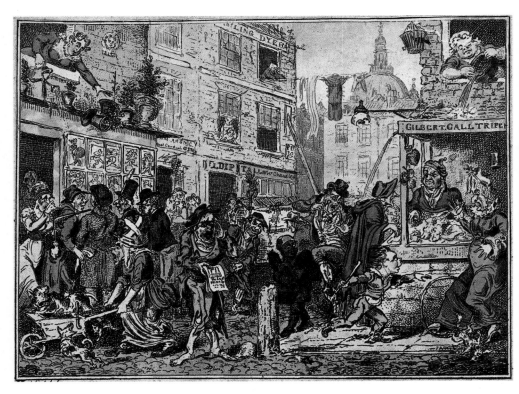

Grievances of London. A Crowded Street in London, 1812. *Etching by George Cruikshank. Courtesy of Wellcome Collection.*

Killing no murder. As performing at the Grand National Theatre. Satire on the Old Price Riots when theatre goers rioted for a return to previous prices and a number of boxers, including Daniel Mendoza, were hired to keep the peace. People being attacked by gangs of ruffians in the pit of the theatre. Mendoza holds his victim by the throat is saying 'Down to H–l with all O.P.s and say t'was Dan that sent thee there'. Engraved by Cruikshank and published 1809. Courtesy of The Jewish Museum.

The set-to between Old Price and Spangle Jack the Shewman – fought with unabated vigour for nine rounds & yet undecided. *John Philip Kemble, tall and muscular, and 'Old Price' a much smaller and weaker opponent, October 1809. Hand-coloured etching. Courtesy of Library of Congress.*

Above left: *Aby Belasco, from* Boxiana.

Above right: *Daniel Mendoza, circa 1820. Stipple engraving by Isaac Cruikshank. Courtesy of The Jewish Museum.*

that would counteract any assault that could be made on him. At his request, therefore, I aimed several blows at him, one of which took place, and in consequence of his lordship's throwing back his head with great violence, he thrust it through the glazed door of a book-case. This accident irritated him greatly, and as soon as he was extricated, which was not done without great difficulty, he asked, whether I had ever played at the game of single-stick? On my answering I was not entirely unacquainted with the sport, he insisted on my engaging with him; and having procured a pair of weapons from an adjoining room, we set to. At this game I found his lordship a better proficient than myself; he struck with great force as well as skill, and I speedily received a violent blow over the ear, which caused great pain at the time. However, I was resolved not to yield, and therefore continued till he was tired, when he again proposed to change the amusement to fencing, and though I candidly told him, I knew nothing of this art, he insisted upon my engaging with him, to which I was with reluctance induced to consent. On one of the foils happening to break, he very coolly observed, we might as well change them for a pair of small swords, with which, he said, if we took proper care, we could not possibly injure each other. To this proposal I at first strongly objected, and declared my determination not to engage with weapons of such a dangerous nature; upon which my noble antagonist appeared highly irritated, and I began to apprehend the violent effects of his anger; therefore with the view of appeasing his wrath, I pretended to assent to his proposal, merely expressing a wish that he would take care of my family, in case of any accident happening to me. This he promised to do, and left me for the purpose of fetching the swords. As soon as the coast was clear, I rushed out of the room, and flew down stairs, with all the rapidity in my power: such was my impatience to depart, that I never stopped till I had reached the bottom of the stair-case, when I found I had descended too low, and had got to the cellar door; consequently I was obliged to return, and having, at last, reached the street-door, departed abruptly from the house, and, as may readily be imagined, never felt the least inclination to re-enter it.[15]

Daniel Mendoza's readiness to laugh at himself and to express it is an attractive quality, and one of the pleasures of his *Memoirs*. At the same time, he is a stranger to false modesty. I suppose the best word to describe this combination is candour.

In July 1801 Belcher and Mendoza found themselves in opposite corners as seconds for a fight between Paddington Jones, who was Mendoza's age and had been a protégé of Johnson, and Isaac Bitton, a Jewish boxer, born in Holland and trained by Mendoza. The fight took place on Wimbledon Common, and Mendoza's man won. Following the fight there was a set-to between a drunken Joe Berks, an ox of a man, and Jem Belcher. Camelford, present, and probably watching from the top of his carriage, was captivated by Belcher's swift destruction of a man so much bigger (and drunker) than himself. He was fairly sure, however, that with the right training Berks could beat Belcher. He paid Mendoza to train the Irishman, who was put on a strict diet of raw eggs and raw meat. He responded well and Camelford was sure that Mendoza's science added to Berks's strength would be more than enough for Belcher.

In November 1801, at Hurley Bottom near Maidenhead, Jem Belcher defeated Joe Berks again, and afterwards once more challenged Mendoza to fight for 300 as against 200 guineas. Mendoza replied that he had relinquished the trade, and was satisfied being a publican in Whitechapel, thereby supporting his family. The pub had originally been called The Children in the Wood. This was hardly a name with which a pugilist might wish to be associated, so he changed it to The Lord Nelson. ('Before this time tomorrow, I shall have gained a peerage or Westminster Abbey,' Nelson had said before the Battle of the Nile, in 1798, three years before). Mendoza relinquished the licence in 1812 and the pub was rebuilt in 1876, lost its skittles to the railway, a storey to a fire, and closed for good in 1903. The premises are now a clothes shop popular with Muslim women.

Esther had by now borne Dan at least four living children: Abraham and Sophia, as previously mentioned, plus Isabella, born 1796 and Jesse, born 1801. There was usually another on the way; the next would be Louisa in 1803.

Although he would not fight Belcher, there was, however, so the *Morning Post* reported, one man he would fight 'and that was Jackson, who, in consequence of his having behaved unhandsomely and unfairly in their former context, had aroused Mendoza to satisfaction, if not to vengeance'.[16] This led eventually to the short epistolary sparrings of the previous chapter, and came to nothing. And this was despite the serious debt in which Dan now found himself.

Mendoza was fairly sure that given the time, and with patience on the part of his creditors, he would have been able to pay off his debts easily through his tremendous abilities as a publican. Knowing of his previous attempts to make money in any way but by his fists, it is hard not to be sceptical, as those creditors seemingly were. He struggled on, not helped by various criminal incidents, one involving a woman called Margaret Lowe who tried to pass off a bad shilling at the pub (she got three months for that), and the theft of substantial amounts of liquor in October 1802 by a servant at the request of one Isaac Hardy, a soldier of the Guards, who lodged at the pub.

However, not for the first or last time, Mendoza was his own worst enemy. His principal creditors were the brewers who had leased him the pub, Stottard, Hewson & Co. Mendoza had approached them in August 1801 saying that he had retired from fighting and wished to settle down. They agreed to set him up at The Children in the Wood and lent him a generous £150. Mendoza had asked the magistrates to change the name, and that was done – the pub was now The Admiral Nelson. The business, initially at any rate, was a great success. But Dan couldn't keep away from the game: 'instead of being always at the tap, he was constantly frequenting his old sport of boxing matches.' The rent fell into arrears. Mendoza insisted that he owned enough in the way of plate, furniture and so forth to cover any debts. Indeed, he valued his own property at £400. He showed the brewers' collector, a George Pollard, a 'vast quantity' of such stuff. Mendoza explained to Pollard that he was 'in the habit of entertaining bankers' sons and other gentlemen, which obliged him to have all those accommodations for them'. The brewers were persuaded not to serve process for the rent. When they did, it turned out that the 'vast quantity of goods' belonged to Mendoza's neighbour. On 8 February 1803, Dan Mendoza was 'transferred to his new apartments in Surrey', once more becoming an inmate of the Kings Bench Prison, where he remained until released under one of the frequent Insolvency Acts in October 1805.

It had not been a straightforward process, though. His first application had been refused, due, according to Dan, to those chief creditors' determination 'to persecute me to the last'. At the session the magistrate, an admirer of the prisoner's pugilistic art, felt he had no choice but to 'oppose [his] liberation'. The whole sorry tale was played out. At the end Mendoza was asked what had become of the £50 he had received for lease of his house. 'Ask my children,' he replied. In the *Memoirs* Mendoza then refers to *The Merchant of Venice*, pointing out that in his case the roles of Antonio and Shylock are reversed: 'The Christian is the unfeeling persecutor, the Jew the unfortunate debtor'.[17] The session took place in September 1805. He was released the following month.

While Mendoza had been trying to be a landlord, a new boxing star had been welcomed by the Fancy. A new Jewish star.

For reasons unknown, Sam Elias's parents had fled to London from Holland in March 1771 and found refuge with Abraham and Esther Mendoza in their house 'near Bishopsgate Street' (almost certainly Petticoat Lane). Sam was born within a fortnight of their arrival, on 4 April 1775. By the age of fourteen he had established a reputation as a local tough around Whitechapel and Aldgate, but he came to the full notice of the Fancy only in 1801, at which point Mendoza and Lee attempted to take him properly in hand.

Dutch Sam was not known as a dedicated trainer, to put it mildly. He was, rather, a dedicated drinker, often to be found 'in the stews of St George's Fields, usually drunk and sometimes diseased; full of sprees, of lark, and ribaldry'. His life was dominated by gin, late hours and that elegant euphemism, 'Paphian sacrifices' (whoring). The following anecdote comes from the pages of a short-lived periodical *The Fancy*:

One example of Sam's impropriety, while under the tutelage of Mendoza, may be taken as a type of his usual mode of no-training: they were at Sutton, and Dan found himself constrained to allow a little latitude of indulgence to Sam – a double quantity of negus, an hour's relaxation at night, and an occasional absence, were not enough. Sam also found a means to get drunk in the daytime. This irregularity happened invariably when, running across the downs, the two friends visited Epsom. Here an old female cottager had been induced to provide him with a bottle of Max at each call; and in his avidity to taste the forbidden fluid, would the infatuated man drain it to the very dregs. But Dan, having procured the assistance of a trusty person, nosed out Sam's misdoings; and leaving his inebriated protégé at the Spread Eagle, he went over and persuaded the old woman, that Sam belonged to the Excise and only meant to have her up. Probably the Reader needs not be told, that at his next visit the old matron fell a-board him with such abuse that Sam repaired to his old friend with a sheepish aspect.

For all this, Mendoza does seem to have imparted a good deal of his own style to Sam, who is best known to boxing historians as – if not the inventor – the first effective user of the right-hand upper cut.

Dutch Sam's first serious pitched battle was in Highgate, in August 1804, with the hitherto undefeated Caleb Baldwin. The following year at Shepperton Common, he fought a Bristol boxer called Bill Britton. He won, according to the *Hampshire Chronicle*, 'in such a style as has not been equalled since the fighting days of Dan Mendoza'. Whether this was a nuanced reference to his ethnicity or the considered remark of a pugilistic 'knowing one', we cannot judge, but Dutch Sam was now, emphatically, Mendoza's successor as a champion of the Jews.

Once restored to liberty, but perhaps neglecting his land-lording, Mendoza continued to attend fights, either as a spectator or as a second. Despite supposed incarceration in the King's Bench Prison, we are told he was present, along with Lords Craven and Albemarle, Fletcher Reid, Jackson and Bill Warr, to see Tom Belcher defeat Ryan at Daleham Barrows in June 1805. The following month Dutch Sam was due to fight Belcher, with Mendoza as his second, but Elias was injured in a traffic accident: 'As Dutch Sam and a friend were driving down a hill in full canter, they pulled the reins tight to keep the horse's head up – the traces broke, the horse plunged, broke the shafts, and overturned the chaise.' The fight was rescheduled for the following February. It was the first of a three-fight series that would stir memories of the great rivalry between Mendoza and Humphries, and indeed of the popularity the sport had previously enjoyed.

* * *

In 1802 the Fives Court in Little St Martin's Street, which nowadays runs from the south-east corner of Leicester Square to the back of the new Sainsbury wing of the National Gallery, became more or less British boxing's headquarters (or 'high change' in Regency vernacular). It was baptised as such with a sparring session put on by Daniel Mendoza and William Warr. The street at that time ran on into what is now Trafalgar Square (the Fives Court itself was demolished in 1826 to make way for Nelson and his lions, not to mention the National Gallery). Sparring at the Fives Court was superintended by John Jackson (now known by the cognomen 'Commander-in-Chief'), and drew the Fancy in great numbers. According to Pierce Egan, 'the most refined and fastidious person may attend these exhibitions of sparring with pleasure; as they are conducted with all the neatness, elegance and science of fencing.' The Fives Court became the place for new fighters to show themselves and seek patronage. The sell-out occasions were benefit nights, for which boxers would rent out the space in the hope of first recouping their expenses and then making a handsome profit. Sometimes the place was 'crowded to suffocation', and takings could reach up to £200. Reportedly on Bill Richmond's recommendation, a stage was erected in the centre of the court on which the ring was set. Fighters were matched as to weight, experience, skill and so forth. Richmond's other suggestion was that the boxers – and remember this was sparring, with gloves, not prize fighting – strip to the waist, so that, in the words of *Fistiana*, 'the full development of their muscular powers was perceptible, and every movement could be accurately appreciated.'

Here challenges were made and accepted, the details drawn up in local pubs, many of which were either owned or run by pugilists or ex-pugilists. One, on Panton Street, yards from the Fives Court, then called The Union, was what is now called The Tom Cribb after the champion boxer who once owned it (and where Bill Richmond, Cribb's great rival and friend, downed his last drink an hour before he died).

There were other sparring venues, such as the Tennis Court in Windmill Street (Mendoza had many benefits there), and further east the Minerva Rooms,in Leadenhall Street, preferred by Jewish fighters in particular, though Mendoza seems to have as often as possible chosen the West End venues. With the arrival of John Jackson, 'gentleman', at the head of the sport, it was perhaps no longer disgraceful to appear in public with a black eye or a broken nose. Boxing was getting on for respectable. Perhaps a memoir might sell?

In July of that year, 1805, a 'proposal' appeared in the *Morning Post*, for the publication by subscription of 'Memoirs of the Life of D. Mendoza, P.P. – containing an impartial account of all the pitched battles he ever fought, with observations on each, and a distinct chapter, in which the pugilistic science is reduced to a few rules that may be easily attained, and practiced with success. Interspersed with humorous and original anecdotes'. There follows a rhyme:

By art directed o'er the foaming tide,
Secure from rocks, the painted vessels glide,
By art the courser scours the dusty plain,
Springs at the whip, and feels the strait'ning rein,
To art our bodies must obedient yield,
Should Pugilistic Science, keep the field.

The work would be printed in two volumes, on 'superior' paper, with 'neat' type, and the price to subscribers would be 14s. This could be deposited with a Mr J. Jackson (surely not that one) in Pimlico, a Mr Lumley at St James's, or with the author at the Swan Tavern, Fish Street Hill (it runs, still, from Eastcheap to Lower Thames Street, by way of the Monument, and was home – at very different times – to the Black Prince and Oliver Goldsmith).

The 'New Edition' of this work was published eleven years later. No copy of this first two-volume edition appears to have survived. Possibly it never existed. It is worth noting, however, that the book we now have ends in 1806, with what Mendoza thought would be his last 'pitched battle'. It was, sadly, with an old friend.

12

LEE

Henry 'Harry' Lee had a long and sometimes fractious relationship with Daniel Mendoza. They first publicly sparred together at Covent Garden in 1788. Over thirty years later, Lee was his bottle holder in Mendoza's last contest, against Tom Owen.

Back in early 1791, a Mr Wiltshire had claimed he was owed money by Daniel Mendoza and went to court to retrieve it. Mendoza, who was denying any such thing, was surprised by Lee's appearance as a witness on behalf of the plaintiff.

> We had, for some time previous to this been on terms of intimacy; and Mr Lee had won considerable sums of money on many of the contests in which I had engaged; he knew perfectly well that Mr Wiltshire was in the wrong; but he never heard me acknowledge that the money was advanced at my request; notwithstanding which he came forward in the manner before stated, and endeavoured by his testimony to substantiate Mr Wiltshire's claim: this evidence, however, was not sufficiently satisfactory to the minds of the jury, to establish the demand of the plaintiff, who was consequently non-suited [i.e. the plaintiff had failed to make his case].

Despite what Mendoza must have seen as an act of treachery, in June we find them together again, in company with George Inglestone (the 'Brewer') at the Old Hats (now, not inappropriately, a sports bar) on the Uxbridge Road in Ealing. It was here Mendoza learned his fight with William Warr had been banned by the Stokenchurch magistrates. Very likely Lee would have been Mendoza's second at that contest. Then, in the autumn, along with Daniel's brother-in-law Aaron, the little band toured East Anglia, sparring and exhibiting in Bury St Edmunds and 'instructing the bucks' in Norwich.

Like many a boxer before and since, Lee was also a publican. The pub he ran was called The Antigallican, in Shire Lane, Temple Bar, and it was a favourite of the Fancy (or as the Victorian human geographer Walter Thornbury put it, 'low sporting men').[1] Very likely it was there that Richard 'Hellgate' Barry, 7th Lord Barrymore (whom we met earlier) and who is known to have frequented it, proposed a meeting between Hooper, the Tinman, and Mendoza. Hellgate's brother, Cripplegate (the 8th Lord), also drank at The Antigallican. He it was who first employed Harry Lee's son, George Alexander Lee (born 1802), as the first 'tiger', a mobile groom, so called for the yellow and black waistcoat he – and subsequent tigers – wore. The boy born in 1802 grew up to become a composer, singer, and musical director, sometime co-leasee of Drury Lane, owner of a music shop in Regent Street, and author of *A Complete Course of Instructions for Singing*. Cripplegate Barrymore, although no less eccentric than his brother, was known to have a fine singing voice. Hellgate not only built a theatre in his garden, he acted in it. It seems likely that, one way or another, it was through the Barrymores by way of Lee that Mendoza met John Kemble, by whom he was going to be employed so disastrously a few years later.

There was also a young fighter named Lee, who was known as the 'Whitechapel Butcher', with whom Harry Lee was sometimes confused, who fought with 'bottom' but with 'little knowledge of the principles of the science'.[2]

Our Lee, by contrast, knew all about the science but little about the practice. He was not in fact a professional boxer. His chief claim to fame was his 'discovery' of Dutch Sam, whom he saw fighting a much larger man named Baker by the roadside in Enfield in October 1801. And it was perhaps the case that Lee had a trainer's eye. He had seconded often: for Crabbe in his fight with Tyne, at Horton Moor in March 1790; for Burke against Belcher at Hurley Bottom near Maidenhead in November 1801, at the end of which fight Belcher challenged Mendoza again, 'who observed that he had done with pugilism'. Lee had been bottle holder to Mendoza's second, for Gamble against Belcher at Wimbledon.

Lee fought only one 'pitched battle', that against his friend and sparring partner Mendoza. In early 1806, the following letter from Daniel Mendoza was sent to the *Daily Advertiser,* the *Oracle* and the *True Briton*. Lee, it seemed, was disrespecting his mentor. (The following 'epistolary effusions' appear also in *Boxiana*.)

After my frequent resolution never again to appear before the public in the character of a fighter on the stage, and which resolution I have for years carefully and rigidly persevered in, it may perhaps be incumbent upon me to state to that public, whose partiality I have so often experienced, the cause of my acceptance of a challenge from a person by no means entitled to the smallest lenity. Some weeks ago, I unfortunately visited Harry Lee, then in temporary lodgings under the roof of a Sheriff's Officer; he was then in DURANCE VILE [a long prison sentence] on two actions; he told me a long and piteous tale about his hardships, and the injustice and cruelty of his creditors; he assured me, that if I would become one of his bail, he would then be enabled to obtain his liberty, and that he would take special care that I should not suffer, as he would settle, or discharge, both actions as soon as he got out of his present confinement.

Notwithstanding I am not now very apt to act the part of a fool on such an occasion, having already sustained at various times considerable losses by former acts of credulity, and consequently become wiser by dear-bought experience, I listened to his statements, and gave an implicit belief to all his declarations. It being found that my bail alone would not give legal satisfaction, I persuaded my brother, and another friend, to join the bail-bond, giving them, like gentlemen in a certain great house, a bill of indemnity. I was induced to go this length to serve him, because Harry Lee assured me that he had no persons to befriend him; that the officers would not take his word for a single copper; and that unless I stood up to John Doe and Richard Roe, through the medium of my two friends, he would be immediately committed to prison, whence, with detainers, &c. &c. it would be impossible for years, perhaps, for him to obtain a release. All the ceremonies which the law requires being gone through, Harry Lee marched out with all the honours usually attending such a war.

But, mark, gentle readers! as soon as the said Harry Lee obtained his liberty, he refused to comply with his solemn engagements; he, indeed, settled one of the actions; but would neither surrender himself nor settle the other. The consequence was obvious; having indemnified my brother and friend, we were obliged to pay, and, with the exception of fourteen pounds, the whole sum as smart money, for having been duped by Harry Lee.

Now, Mr. Editor, I am of opinion that if a man cannot satisfy his creditors, he ought, in honour, to release his bail by the surrender of his person, which Harry Lee positively refused. He was, however, not contented with this abominable usage of me, but went up and down the town circulating calumnies and lies against me, and threatened to beat me as soon as he found an opportunity; in short, he gave me such a challenge that I could not, consistent with honour or propriety, refuse.

The black ingratitude of Harry Lee is now very conspicuous; after cheating, deceiving, and I may say robbing his friend in need, he now wants to give him a kicking into the bargain; but I have no doubt but that I shall stop his career, and put in a blow of just indignation and honourable resentment, against a man whose conduct is a disgrace to any rank of life. I am, much against my inclination, forced to the fight, not from any fear of Harry Lee, but from a sense of violating those rules and peaceable conduct in which I had resolved to pass the remainder of my life. He who has been successful in upwards of 30 pitched battles; he who has disputed the palm of victory with the first and ablest men of his time, cannot surely be apprehensive of danger, either to his person or reputation, from Harry Lee!! I know that 'The race is not to the swift, nor the battle to the strong; but that time and chance happeneth to all men;' barring however all unforeseen accidents, I am fully persuaded that I shall make Harry sorely repent his unprovoked insolence; but I shall not gain by the contest the smallest sprig of laurel, because Harry Lee has none to lose. I am sorry thus to occupy the time of the public; and am, Mr. Editor, Daniel Mendoza.

Mendoza wrote from 5, Webber Row, off the Blackfriars Road, south of the river. Lee responded. There is a lightness in the orotundity that makes one almost suspect that Mendoza and Lee had hatched a cunning plan to convince the world of an enmity that did not exist ('haberdashery of complaints' is a fine phrase).

Mr. Editor, I have to thank you for your candid and manly manner in which you announced your intention to afford me an opportunity of confuting the charges brought against me by Daniel Mendoza.

Among the extraordinary events that fate or folly produce, I believe insanity itself never dreamt of an epistolary correspondence between

Daniel Mendoza and Harry Lee. What Devil could have provoked him to exhibit his wonderful stock of honour, virtue, and benevolence in so public a manner, I am at a loss to divine; but clear and certain I am, that all the advantage he promised himself he has already enjoyed; it is the curse of fools to be the heralds of their own disgrace; for mark, Mr. Editor, how a plain undisguised story, delivered by a plain unlettered matter-of-fact man, shall set him down.

Mr. Mendoza has thought proper to pester the public with a long narrative of his extravagant acts of kindness towards me; that he rescued me from the hands of a bailiff, the confines of a prison, and other disastrous perils. However, not to retail all the haberdashery of complaints he has thought proper to extend to an unreasonable length, I shall content myself with briefly answering the essence of his charge against me, and, I trust, shall have credit for doing it with truth and candour, without the aid of Mr. Mendoza's ingenuity. It is true, I was arrested on two writs of ten pounds each; a circumstance that has frequently happened to honester men than either Mendoza or Harry Lee. It is also true, that I called upon him to assist in procuring me my enlargement, which, by the bye, was but a slender tribute to the gratitude he owed me; he certainly procured me bail, upon my promise of settling both actions. As Mr. Mendoza admits, I did pay one; but I am very sorry, for his own sake, he did not keep a little nearer truth, with respect to the state of the other, as that might have relieved him from the reprobation that injustice, fallacy, and ingratitude merits. The second action, upon which I am accused of having run from my bail, and left Mr. Mendoza, under all the piteous, lamentable, and ruinous circumstances, to pay, stood exactly thus, at the time of his letter: the debt and costs came to sixteen pounds, the alternative was paying it or going to prison; fourteen pounds I raised and paid, so that all Mendoza could possibly be liable to, was the vast sum of two pounds, which I have also paid. And here, Mr. Editor, you must give me leave to declare, that I think no man living abhors the idea of deserting his bail, or deceiving his friend, more than I do. How far I have done either, in the present case, I leave to the determination of any man, Dan Mendoza excepted. Admit it, for a moment, Mr. Editor, that I had left Mr. Mendoza to pay a few pounds for me, for what he terms fixing my security, the offence, surely, could not be held in any very heinous light by him, if he will have the goodness to call to his recollection the situation in which he left all his friends who were security for his integrity when he commenced Sheriff's Officer. And now, Mr. Editor, I crave your attention to a few words more, which, I trust, will quench the thirst of Mr Mendoza for literary fame, and exhibit him as a paragon of ingratitude. I make great allowances for the passions of a man labouring to prove himself more conscientiously honest than myself; but I cannot help lamenting that he chose the subject of ingratitude for his purpose; and the daemon who whispered it in his ear was certainly unacquainted with the account current between him and myself upon the article of gratitude, which, in fairness, ought to have been stated. In fine, Sir, Mr. Mendoza has, upon some very urgent occasions, been driven to the solitary friendship of Harry Lee, who afforded it him in the most ample manner his capacity would permit. However, fortunately for Mendoza, it was sufficient for all his purposes. Upon two several occasions have I solicited the pecuniary assistance of my friends, in aid of what my own abilities could afford; and this, too, for the purpose of extricating him from the most irksome of all personal inconvenience, as well as to succour his almost famished family. Believe me, Mr. Editor, it is painful to me to upbraid a man with the services I have done him: nor should any consideration whatever have induced me to reveal them, had he not goaded and scourged me into the measure. Perhaps Mendoza has forgot the letters in my possession, expressive of the great obligation I had conferred on him, and which, I trust, will put both him and the Devil who instructed him to turn author, to the blush, upon a perusal, whenever he finds it convenient to give me an opportunity to publish them.

With respect to the language that may have passed between us, I admit it may not have been the most chaste; but, considering all things, not very illy adapted to our professions and habits of life. It is sufficient to say, that the public have learnt from Mendoza's statement, that it has brought about a challenge, which has been accepted, to determine the dispute by manual argument, and I will not envy the laurels he may gather on the occasion. I can only promise that I will do my utmost to prevent his tearing a single sprig from the brows of

Your most obedient humble Servant,
H. Lee.
Antigallican, Temple Bar.

Rather a good letter, and not unpersuasive. It has a kind of chuckle in it. If both men are sincere, then there was a misunderstanding. But £2 – which is what the argument comes down to – is very much more to a man whose family is starving than it is to a man without family, which one has to assume was the case with Harry Lee. Whatever the truth of the matter, 'Mendoza is about to re-enter the pugilistic lists' declared the newspapers, and with boxing once again fashionable, the stir was considerable. 'The cognoscenti hesitate not in betting very great odds on Mendoza,' this despite his not having fought for more than ten years. 'The only first rate bruiser of the Old School in existence' was the hot favourite, the odds at anything from three to five to one in his favour. Lee was in training somewhere near Epsom in Surrey under the tuition of the considerable fighter, John Gulley (later to make a fortune on the horses and become MP for Pontefract). He certainly needed all the help and training he could get. For all his pugilistic experience Lee had never actually fought a pitched battle, and was never to do so again. He was known principally as 'an excellent sparrer' (as Mendoza surely knew, having spent his life sparring with him).

They fought on 21 March, 1806, in the hamlet of Green Street Green, near Bromley in Kent, on the Hastings road. Lee was 5 feet and 9 inches tall and weighed about 12 stones, and was noted for his good looks and Gypsy-like appearance. It is said that he was an Irishman from Dublin, though at least one newspaper thought he was Jewish (or rather 'one of the tribe of Israel'.)[3] In terms of size, then, the fighters were evenly matched, though Lee had the greater reach.

Mendoza's fights with William Warr – far more important in boxing terms – had been comparatively ignored during the lull in the sport's popularity. Now the press was eager to report.

> Everything moveable in and about London from a coach and four down to a jack-ass was in requisition yesterday, to convey the fraternity of the fist, and the higher ranks of pugilistic amateurs, to Bromley to see the above battle.[4]

The new generation of boxers had never seen Mendoza fight, and there must have been appetite to see the great man at work one last time, however short the bout might turn out to be. It turned out that they may not have seen the best of Daniel Mendoza, but they certainly got a fight. Many of the write-ups were lengthy and detailed, which attests to the renewed popularity of the sport and the continued interest in Mendoza himself. 'It is almost incredible, the number of spectators that were present,' commented the

Morning Chronicle. The *Ipswich Journal* reported that nobles, amateurs and notable bruisers were compelled to sit on the wet grass 'under the authority of the lower orders who were in powerful array in the rear of the ring'.

MENDOZA *v* LEE
Green Street Green, Kent
21 March 1806

The ring is roped, 25 feet square, on turf. Mendoza enters around 12.30 p.m., looking composed, smiling. William Warr and Gibbons attend him. Lee arrives a little later, the Game Chicken (Henry Pearce) and John Gulley his seconds. As usual, it is raining.

They come to the mark, shake hands. They set-to. Lee attempts a sparring jab. Mendoza avoids and replies with a right-handed blow landing above Lee's left eye, which draws blood. He follows with a hit to the stomach, which puts Lee down. Odds go to ten to one. Round two: they exchange blows, Mendoza gets hit on the nose. They close and fall together. Lee is bleeding copiously. Third round: Mendoza hits Lee with left, then right. Lee falls. Fourth: Lee gets a good hit above Mendoza's left eye. They close. Mendoza throws Lee. Fifth: Mendoza hits Lee, who falls out of the ring. In the eighth round Lee gamely rushes Mendoza, gets hit and then thrown, cross buttock. In the tenth round Mendoza laughs at Lee. Lee, infuriated, runs onto another blow. The rounds begin to resemble each other, Lee rushing, Mendoza hitting, Lee falling. Lee lies himself down quietly from time to time in order to gain breath (both men are old for this kind of activity). Mendoza finds the whole affair amusing, laughing at his old friend's attempts to hurt him. Some in the crowd begin to hiss and boo, and call 'foul', so often does Lee go down. But while he goes down, he does not go out. By round twenty, Lee is visibly angry. Mendoza, with the dexterity of old, avoids Lee's punches. Dan seems as fresh in the twenty-sixth round as at the start of proceedings. Lee, however, is taking a tremendous pounding, the left side of his face seriously disfigured. But he does not give in, and, taking some encouragement from signs of tiredness in Mendoza in the thirty-second round, actually affects to be enjoying himself in the thirty-third. Mendoza does not take too kindly to this, and begins to put Lee under the ropes. By the forty-second round it is clear that Lee is finished, but he gamely continues until falling without a blow in the fifty-third, at which point the umpires call an end to the contest. Other than a cut above his right eye, and an already broken nose re-broken, Mendoza seems more or less unscathed, his fatigue momentary.

Dan had indeed won easily, 'showing himself a pleasing fighter, as he always has done'. What had ever been his weakness – his lack of a killer punch – was what had kept Lee in the fight (though one report suggested that Dan had damaged his right hand in the first round, making it difficult to make a fist. This may go a little further to explaining how long it took Mendoza to win). Within a fortnight Mendoza was teaching again at the Paul's Head Tavern, in what was Cateaton Street, and is now Gresham Street, and at the end of April he and William Warr were given a benefit at the Fives Court. Mendoza sparred with a new young Jewish fighter named Ikey Pig: 'This match afforded a little amusement in as much as it displayed the advantage of superior science in the art.' Dutch Sam sparred with Dan's 'son' (this seems unlikely. What was probably meant was nephew or cousin).

In July Mendoza attempted, in the Court of Requests at the Guildhall, to get his winnings from a bet on a recent fight – 2 guineas, probably staked on one of the fighters triumphant at Padnal Corner in Epping Forest early in the previous month – from a Leadenhall market butcher by the name of Leybourn, but the commissioners were of the opinion that 'all betters and backers on prize fights for money tended to excite a breach of the peace' and Mendoza's case was dismissed.

In September he was exhibiting in Margate and it is probably safe to assume that he continued his tours of the country, running from debtors, falling in with players, making himself liked and disliked in equal measure. In February 1807 he is tried for assault of a Thames waterman and acquitted. In Dublin an Irish woman defeated an English doorman, and is dubbed 'the fair Mendoza'. In July he and fellow Jewish boxer Isaac Bitton, originally from Amsterdam, are given a benefit at the Fives Court 'crowded in a manner never before witnessed'. Above all, he continues to second Dutch Sam – they are careful, it is said, 'to pick their customers'.[5]

The three-fight series between Tom Belcher and Dutch Sam, already mentioned, stirred memories of the great rivalry between Mendoza and Humphries, and indeed of the popularity the sport had previously enjoyed.

A 'numerous train of nobility', stretching, according to one paper, from Hyde Park turnpike to Twickenham (about 10 miles), turned up to watch Dutch Sam fight Tom Belcher on 8 February 1806, at Moulsey Hurst, by now the most favoured venue for London prize fighting. Almost half of the recorded prize fights between 1805 and 1824 were fought there. It was a multi-sport venue, also hosting horseracing, running, archery and cricket. Mendoza was Sam's second, Gulley was Belcher's. The fight swung back and forth, the bets favouring one and then the other. It came down, in the end, to sheer stamina and staying power. Dutch Sam had more. He was said to have fought 'very much in the Mendoza style ... and it was no inconsiderable advantage to have him [Mendoza] at his elbow'. Belcher's supporters felt their man had been the better boxer and on 28 July, once more at Moulsey Hurst, Dutch Sam and Tom Belcher met again. This time Bitton joined Mendoza in Sam's corner. Bill Warr and Bob Watson were second and bottle holder for Tom Belcher.

It was fairly brutal. By the fourth round Belcher's nose was already streaming blood, and Sam's eye was swelling. The fifth, according to *Boxiana*, was special: 'A better round was never witnessed in any fight whatever – science, activity and bottom were all upon the alert.' Slowly but surely Sam gained the upper hand. The fight ended in controversy in the thirty-fourth round. Belcher threw a punch that Sam evaded, and responded as Belcher fell to his knees with the momentum of his miss (and exhaustion). There were cries of 'foul' and long debates followed between the umpires. 'A man on his knees to be reckoned down', read Broughton's rule number seven. At the end, the fight was called a draw. A third event was required.

A month later, on 28 August 1807, the two great boxers met for the last time, at Lowfield Common, a little north of Crawley in Sussex on the London to Brighton road. The betting favoured Sam, and by the ninth round the odds had gone to four to one. In the seventeenth round Belcher again fell to his knees after being parried. This time Sam raised his arms, as if to stop himself landing a foul blow. In the nineteenth, Belcher was again on his knees: 'but Sam was on his guard, and only smiled.' Belcher was possibly the better pugilist – the reports are full of his 'science', and he seems to have been liked – but Sam was a real bruiser. He hit hard, and it was eventually obvious that he was going to win the fight. He stalked Belcher down, following him round the ring, 'dealing out death-like punishment'. Tom's brother Jem took him out of the ring after the thirty-sixth round, and placed him in 'a gentleman's chariot'. Sam 'dressed himself with perfect indifference before he left the ring'.

In October, at Newmarket, a fighter named Bob Gregson lost narrowly to John Gulley (the MP to be). Gregson had first appeared earlier in the year, in an exhibition with Isaac Bitton at the Fives Court, in which he had impressed the knowing ones. After the first Gulley fight, it was suggested that Gregson, for all his height and strength (he was known as 'the Lancashire Giant') might benefit from some technique, and who better to teach it than he whose 'knowledge of the art is well known to be the first in the kingdom', Daniel Mendoza.[6]

Dan had been at Newmarket, where he'd also been a spectator at the famous foot race between Captain Barclay (to whom *Boxiana* was dedicated) and Abraham Wood. The two men competed to see who could cover the greater distance in 24 hours. Barclay being an 'amateur' was given a 20-mile start. Barclay walked and Wood ran up and down a 1-mile course measured along the length of the Newmarket to London road. After 6 hours and 22 minutes Wood had covered 40 miles, before retiring complaining of stomach cramps. The reported 10,000-strong crowd was none too pleased, and Wood was turfed out of his Cambridge hotel and sent home to Lancashire. He complained that he had been poisoned.

Mendoza agreed to take Gregson on, and though Gregson was again to lose to Gulley, he did become champion before losing to Tom Cribb in October 1808 at Moulsey Hurst. A bust of Gregson can be found at the Royal Academy, where he was presented as the very model of male anatomical beauty. He later ran pubs, and, all too familiarly, died in impoverished circumstances in Liverpool at the age of forty-six. As the *Hampshire Chronicle* opined:

> The neglect which Gregson has experienced since his defeat, is another instance of the instability of popular favour, which depends alike on the momentary glory of its object, whether he be prime minister, an actor, a warrior or a professional bruiser.[7]

Or *sic transit gloria mundi* as it used to be more concisely put at papal coronations (1409–1958).

Dan Mendoza, it so happens, was down on papal coronations, or so it might appear. During the 1807 General Election he was heard leading a mob against a speaker for Catholic Emancipation, yelling 'No Popery! No Popery!' It seems likely that he was paid for this service, although it was known that the king, George III, and the government, was also against Catholic Emancipation, so it may be that Mendoza felt he was playing the true patriot. It is arguable that Catholics (and most especially poor Irish ones) were despised and abused to an even greater degree than Jews.

While running his pub, giving exhibitions, attending fights, being a second, it seems Mendoza kept up his contact with the amateurs. Oxberry, in *Pancratia*, describes him as being 'dressed in green and mounted in style' in the company of 'two or three well-known amateurs' for the Cribb–Horton fight at Woburn in May 1808.[8]

In that same year Daniel Mendoza dedicated his *Memoirs* to Berkley Craven, a high-gambling aristocrat, who committed suicide after losing a fortune on the 1836 Derby. (Reportedly, if he'd waited a couple of days before pulling the trigger he would have won the money back on the Oaks.) The book ends with an account of the fight with Henry Lee, so it seems likely that a first edition appeared soon afterwards – but no copy seems to have survived. The 'New Edition' of 1816 is that used by both Paul Magriel (1951) and Alex Joanides (2011) in their modern recreations. Whatever the date, the book seems to have garnered scant attention in the press, in spite or because of its being arguably the first sporting autobiography. Earlier memoirs had been written by amateurs, chiefly along huntin', shootin' and fishin' lines.

Published in 1756, there had been an autobiography by a fighter who called himself 'Buckhorse' (his real name was thought to be John Smith), but this had been a book that told more about his entry into the 'higher life' after his career as a boxer had finished and there was little in it about the sport itself. Daniel Mendoza's book, whether written or ghosted, is about the life of a boxer, and particularly a Jewish boxer. For not only were the *Memoirs* the first autobiography by a sportsman, they were the first autobiography, with the exception of the memoirs of the businesswoman Glückel of Hameln in the previous century, by a Jew who was not a Rabbi or a philosopher. It is occasionally prolix, but on the whole rumbles along at a good pace, and is spiced with good anecdotage (it was said in one late eulogy that Mendoza was 'possessed of a rare fund of anecdote of the doings of pugilists of the good old times').

His memory for dates is a little askew, and he confuses the order in which he did things, but he clearly saved much printed material. He was certainly literate. One can imagine a box of ephemera. Perhaps he kept a cuttings book. And perhaps he did have to delay until 1816 to publish, waiting for his activities of October 1809 to be erased somewhat from common recollection.

13

OPs

In the theatre, the Augustan age of Garrick had given way to the Romantic age of Kean and Macready and Mrs Siddons and Kemble, and the battle for supremacy between the two Theatres Royal, at Covent Garden and Drury Lane. The Licensing Act of 1717, which remained in force until 1843, created a monopoly for the performance of legitimate drama in favour of these two theatres (the King's Opera House in the Haymarket had a monopoly for opera). There were plenty of other theatres, which were licensed to put on variety and music. The Jewish population favoured the theatre in Wellclose Square, and Astley's. Astley took over the Wellclose Square theatre in 1800. It was an age of melodrama, a word that entered the printed English language in 1789, and by 1805 was in common usage: '*The Forty Thieves*, to be performed as a grand melodrama at the Theatre Royal Drury Lane, under the direction of R. B. Sheridan'. Both theatres succumbed to what was described as a 'mania' and a 'rage' for the genre. Stagecraft came to the fore, as every natural disaster imaginable was recreated for the delectation of an audience made up of every class. At times it came to resemble circus – indeed at times it *was* circus, as in Astley's theatrical presentations. Animals prowled across the stage. And pugilists.

Perhaps the greatest of these melodramas took place not on the stage, but in the auditorium, in the streets around the Covent Garden theatre and in the press: the Old Price (OP) Riots of 1809.

Not the least of those involved was a certain group of boxers. Pierce Egan had words for them:

> Boxing is not only a national, but a noble propensity; and, in its proper application, has raised the valour and manly intrepidity of the English nation, eminently conspicuous over all others, from its practice; but when unfortunately perverted by any of its professors, who turn it into an engine against that public by whom they have been supported and cherished, it degenerates into brutality, and renders its name despicable. Pugilism, we are sorry to observe, never lost its importance so much in the esteem of the nation, as in the O.P. disturbance of Covent-Garden Theatre, when some of its first-rate professors suffered themselves to be hired to intimidate and impede the people from obtaining their rights and liberties! Names might be mentioned, as we are in possession of them; but we trust that a friendly hint will prove more than sufficient to point out the impropriety of such proceedings, and that, in future, good sense will reign predominant, by preventing the repetition of such disgraceful conduct.[1]

While this paragraph did not specifically mention that the majority of these pugilists was Jewish, it was included at the end of Egan's chapter in *Boxiana*, which dealt with Mendoza's successor as fighting hero of the Jewish community, Dutch Sam. Mendoza was foremost among those who allowed themselves to be hired.

This was not the first time that Jews had disrupted proceedings at Covent Garden. In December 1802, on the first night and on several succeeding nights of Thomas Dibdin's opera *Family Quarrels*, Jewish members of the audience objected vociferously to a song, 'I Courted Miss Levi', on the grounds that it defamed Jewish women. Miss Levi, who double-crosses her admirer, is followed by an equally duplicitous Miss Abrams and then a Miss Moses.

> Then I courted Miss Moses
> Great big Miss Moses
> Lord, what a Miss Moses was she!
> I believe there are few ladies with such lips and such noses you'll see;
> Her brother was vastly rich, and had a great deal of money in the stocks;
> He was not so vulgar as to get it by trade, but he taught the great people how to spar and to box.

Oh, what a charming girl!
Miss Moses took lessons of her brother how to use the pretty little
    fists of her own,
Which caused me to leave off my visits at that end of town
For though married people may be allowed to spar a little bit,
    I should not like a wife who would knock me down.
Oh what a Miss Moses!
Great, big, thumping Miss Moses
Lord! What a Miss Moses was she![2]

The reference to Mendoza is unmistakable. The suggestion that he was 'vastly rich' is possibly simply an anti-Sephardi stereotype, but it may also be suggestive of the way in which Mendoza behaved – that when he had money, he spent it.

It is possible that part of the rancour was due to the participation of John Braham. Braham was one of Europe's leading tenors, and also a Jew, and possibly even more famous than Daniel Mendoza. Charles Lamb described his abilities in a letter to his sister:

> Do you like Braham's singing? The little Jew has bewitched me. I follow him like as the boys follow Tom the Piper. He cures me of melancholy as David cured Saul... Braham's singing when it is impassion'd is finer than Mrs. Siddons or Mr. Kemble's acting & when it is not impassion'd it [is] as good as hearing a person of fine sense talking. The brave little Jew![3]

Quite apart from performing, Braham was also responsible for some of the music. Whether the Jews who complained about the Miss Levi song were the same as those who were involved seven years later, in far more significant goings-on at Covent Garden, this time on the side of the management, is an intriguing, unanswerable question.

In the early hours of 20 September 1808 a fire broke out at the Theatre Royal, Covent Garden, and raged until the theatre was burned to the ground. Theatre fires were fairly common, due to the use of naked flame, and the amount of inflammable material such as drapes and wooden scenery. In the first decade of the century the Pantheon, the Royal Circus, Drury Lane and Covent Garden were all at some point reduced to cinders. Eventually, wet blankets, eight on each side of the stage, became mandatory (hence the term 'wet blanket' to describe someone of puritanical or sanctimonious opinion, or, more colloquially, a party pooper). The Covent Garden fire killed more than twenty people, but the inquest found no one to blame and rebuilding began the following January. By September the new theatre was ready to open, with the greatest actress of the period (and sister of theatre manager, part-owner and lead actor, John Philip Kemble), Sarah Siddons, in *Macbeth*. Obviously, the new building had cost a fortune, both in construction and in lost revenue. In order to recoup some of their losses the management raised the price of tickets. Boxes now went up 1*s,* to 7*s.* Tickets to the pit went up from 3*s/6d* to 4*s.* The number of cheap seats was reduced to make room for new and private boxes. There was uproar. Macbeth strutted and fretted to little avail, all was sound and fury.

It signified an absolute refusal on the part of those infuriated by the new prices and seating arrangements (the 'OPs' as they came to be known) to countenance these changes. The problem was exacerbated by the fact that the only other theatre in London licensed to show full-length plays, Drury Lane, had also burnt down in the previous February, and was still being rebuilt (its management learned how not to re-open).

The notably diverse and enthusiastic theatre-going public of London felt it was being played. And so throughout the first week the audience hissed and booed and heckled, and generally let its feelings be known. Kemble called the magistrates from nearby Bow Street, and the Riot Act was read, but it was drowned out by the audience – which, after all, had paid to assemble, and so to whom the Act could not be applied – singing 'Rule Britannia' and 'God Save the King'.

Having in the first instance relied on officers of the law to do the job of keeping order, by the beginning of October it was clear to Kemble they would not suffice. Other arrangements would have to be made, which involved inviting into the theatre a group capable both of intimidating, and not being intimidated by, the OP protesters. A group of professional pugilists was the answer. It would appear it was led by Daniel Mendoza, who brought his Jewish friends with him, among them Samuel Elias, Dutch Sam, then at the height of his fame and power, and regarded as 'the greatest fighter, pound for pound, the prize-ring had yet seen'.[4] More than likely, Mendoza was, as usual, in need of funds. A benefit at the Fives Court in May had been sparsely attended, and he was now responsible for Esther and seven children, four of whom were under the age of eight.

The Times thundered that on the night of 9 October the pit resembled 'a second Babel'. It was full, it reported, of 'Jews, Turks, Hibernians, Bow Street Officers, pugilists, pickpockets, all jumbled together'.⁵ A few days later the *Morning Chronicle* reported on some of the placards displayed in the pit by the OPs:

> The Covent Garden Synagogue – Mendoiza, the grand Rabbi
>
> BISH, the Detector of Fraud v Mendoza, the Leader of Hired Pugilists
>
> Shall Britons be subdued by the wandering tribe of Jersusalem?
>
> Oppose Shylock and the Jews!

The *British press* had more:

> Genius of Britain, espouse our cause,
> Free us from Kemble, and Jewish laws!
>
> By ruffian Jews assaulted;
> By Managers scorned;
> By Thief-takers ill-treated;
> But John Bull will not be subdued!
>
> Mendoza to fight
> Brandon to swear
> John Bull in the right
> Therefore don't care!

There were mocking calls: 'Turn out the fighting Jews!' 'Old clothes.' 'Lemons and oranges.' 'Any bad shillings?'

The law, as we have seen, took a fairly relaxed view of violence, being more stringent when it came to property or matters of a pecuniary nature. The *Morning Post* of 11 October reported that a man named James Andrews had been charged at the Bow Street magistrates' court with distributing the following 'inflammatory and forged hand-bill':

> MENDOZA AND KEMBLE
> It is a notorious fact, that the Managers of Covent-Garden Theatre have, both yesterday and to-day, furnished Daniel Mendoza, the fighting Jew, with a prodigious number of Pit Orders for Covent-Garden theatre, which he has distributed to Dutch Sam,

and such other of the pugilistic tribe as would attend, and engage to assault every person who had the courage to express their disapprobation of the Managers' attempt to ram down the New Prices.

James Brandon, who would nowadays be called something like Head of Security at the theatre (and referred to on one of the placards above), attended the hearing, and denied that the contents of the flyer were true. Andrews, a 'common lottery-bill deliverer', told Mr Read, the magistrate, that a gentleman had given him a shilling to deliver them.[6] But Thomas Bish – 'BISH the Detector of Fraud' – had actually seen Daniel Mendoza handing out tickets (the recognition is another indication of just how famous he was):

I saw him myself, and can bring twenty respectable persons who also saw him, to prove that Mendoza for several days past distributed a considerable number of orders of free admission to Covent Garden Theatre, to such persons as were more likely to break than keep the peace.[7]

Nor was he the only one:

Sir

In your paper of this day, it is asserted 'that Mr James Brandon declared on oath, that to his knowledge no orders for admission to the Covent Garden theatre had been issued by Mr Kemble to Daniel Mendoza, the prize fighting Jew and Dutch Sam, and that if such orders had been issued, he must of necessity have known it.' I therefore trouble you with the following facts: a tradesman with whom I am acquainted, came into a shop where I was, about two o'clock this day, and shewed two double orders for the pit. He said they had been given to him by Daniel Mendoza, the prize-fighting Jew, who cut them from a sheet of paper, of which he had two, covered with these orders for the boxes; that Dutch Sam was present, and was boasting of his exploits in breaking the peace, and of the mischief he had done to many of his Majesty's subjects at the theatre last night. Mendoza then offered to furnish any number of orders to persons who would make a damned row in support of the Managers. I requested one of these orders, which had been endorsed by Mendoza, in his presence, with the letter D on the back;

he then wrote me an order to Mendoza for a few more. I read the note, of which I enclose a copy, to a messenger, and then dispatched him to Mendoza. He has just returned with one double order, and Mr Mendoza's compliments to the gentleman, 'he was very sorry he had not taken more in the morning, for then he had offered him as many as he pleased.' His son was then gone into the theatre, and if the Messenger would wait till his return he should have as many as he wished.

I am, sir, your obedient servant, James Powell.

The contents of the flyer Andrews had been distributing were obviously true. 'Apparently predetermined contests took place in every part of the house... Neither the remonstrances of the peaceable, nor the distress of the female part of the audience, had the least influence on the conduct of the combatants,'[8] wrote *The Times* correspondent. But those arrested were the OPs rather than members of the 'pugilistic tribe'. With the exception of the *Morning Post*, which remained staunch for the proprietors, the newspapers didn't like this. One OP at least thought the paper (and indeed *The Times* as well) had been 'bought' by Kemble:

The Times and *Post* are bought and sold
By Kemble's pride and Kemble's gold

Jewish boxers had first entered the theatre on October 6, and remained active until October 14.[9] Quite how or why Kemble had approached Mendoza is unknown, but it is certainly the case that grandees of the Fancy were often patrons of both theatre and boxing. And in the case of Daniel Mendoza, in particular, the endeavours were not dissimilar. As has been remarked, he spent more time professionally on stages than in rings. We know too that he was a theatre-goer, have been spotted weeping at *The Deserter of Naples*. It is quite possible, then, that Kemble and Mendoza knew one another (perhaps even met at the Finish, or The Antigallican) or that an intermediary recommended one to the other. The *Memoirs* finish before the OP riots, and there is no attempt in the 'New Edition', published in 1816, to extend the history to cover them. I suppose it is possible that he was ashamed of his involvement,

Employing the Jewish boxers was a mistake, because the OPs fought back. Protest became riot. In Cruickshank's caricature,

Killing No Murder as Performing at the Grand National Theatre, Mendoza can be seen at the centre, uttering the words 'Down down to H--l with all OPs & say 'twas Dan that sent thee there'.

The perception that Kemble had hired the Jewish boxers coloured the rest of the conflict, even though Mendoza and his crew desisted from 14 October. Kemble himself was referred to as 'Jew Kemble', and his nose lent caricaturists a feature that fitted perfectly with the stereotypical Jewish phiz. Kemble also had the misfortune to be a Catholic, which, to many, was worse than being a Jew. On 5 November, Guy Fawkes Night, Kemble's home was surrounded by OP protesters threatening to burn it down.

Jewish elders were horrified. There were awful stories: Jewish boxers sparring in the lobby of the theatre while another gang pickpocketed the distracted theatre-goers; a John Tackle described how, having gone to the aid of a young OP spectator, he was set upon by a gang, 'all Jews', and dragged out of the theatre and beaten up. The Chief Rabbi, Solomon Hirschell, removed the names of 100 'itinerant' Jews from the charity list of the Great Synagogue for six months.[10]

It is arguable that his role in the OP Wars undid much of the good Daniel Mendoza had done for the Jewish community, but it should be remembered that this was, anyway, a deeply xenophobic period. The Jacobite rebellion was perhaps just an echo in the collective memory, but the American Revolution was relatively fresh in the mind. Most importantly, of course, the country was at war with post-revolutionary and now imperial France (on October 14, the day the boxers left Covent Garden, France and Austria signed the Treaty of Vienna, by the terms of which Austria ceded vast tracts of land to Napoleon). Anything remotely resembling the foreign was suspect. Mendoza may have felt that support for authority would emphasise his patriotism.

14

OWEN

The enthusiasm for prize fighting continued, even after Jem Belcher's loss to Hen Pearce, the 'Game Chicken', in 1805. Indeed it grew. Pearce was followed by John Gully (MP to be), Tom Cribb (who dominated the sport from 1808 to 1822) and Tom Spring (the last of the great names of the 'golden age' of the prize ring). The great black boxers Bill Richmond and Bill Molineaux arrived on the scene. Jack Randall, the 'non-pareil', reminded old timers of Mendoza's style (and impressed John Keats, who saw him defeat Ned Turner in Crawley in 1818).

Boxing became almost respectable. The Prince of Wales's interest never waned. In 1814, with Napoleon apparently safely exiled to Elba, the Prince invited his guests the King of Prussia, Tsar Alexander of Russia and General Blücher (the following year required at Waterloo) to watch a demonstration of pugilistic skill with him at the home of Lord Lowther, in Pall Mall, London. The boxers were picked by Jackson, so there was no Mendoza. Seven years later Jackson again excluded Mendoza from the select group of boxers invited to guard Westminster Hall at the coronation of the Prince as George IV. Boxing had come a long way from Hockley-in-the-Hole to the Palace of Westminster.

Despite, perhaps because of, its continued popularity, objections remained as common and vociferous as ever. One newspaper asked 'can true bravery, which is compound of every virtue, exist with barbarity, treachery, and fraud?' It went on:

> For of such precious materials are our Prizefighters composed. If we revert to ancient history we shall find, that a delight in spectacles of blood, and combats of gladiators, was esteemed an ominous symptom of the decline of a mighty empire; and, in modern times, the savage custom of boxing for money, and without even the pretence of revenging an affront, is despised and held in abhorrence by nations of peculiar military excellence. The French look upon it as opprobrious. A prizefight was never heard of in Prussia or Germany. The Scots, who are avowedly a military people, consider the practice as disgraceful, nor was there ever an instance of a Highlander disgracing himself by a pugilistic exhibition.[1]

Dan gets a mention – 'Mendoza made two speculative trips to Scotland and Ireland, and returned from both as he deserved – penniless and disregarded.' Not quite true. It is arguable that the great tradition of Irish boxing began with Dan's defeat of Squire Fitzgerald. This magisterial statement concludes thus: 'Magistrates can have no possible excuse for a laxity of exertion, and should recollect that "eluded Laws" are particularized by the moralist as the primary malady of a sinking State.' The evil was spreading. We find Virginians disapproving of Bostonians, Dan again taking the flak:

> In a Boston paper of the 10th we perceive a notice to the public that there would be a Boxing Match at the 'Sparring Academy' between Sampson the strong, and Mr Ryan the chicken – in which would be exhibited the 'double chopper' of Mendoza and 'the flanker by which he conquered Humphries'. – 'in the course of the evening sparring by several gentlemen – and the whole to conclude with an oration upon pugilism'. All this may be deemed very refined amusement by the Bostonians – but in Virginia we should consider ourselves disgraced were we to countenance such a brutal exhibition. It is certainly a grade lower than cock fighting.[2]

That was not the view of farmer's son Jean-Andoche Junot, Duke of Abrantès, one of Napoleon's most favoured generals, and said to be, along with several other French officers, a convert 'to the English pugilistic system'. He was of the opinion that 'an English blackguard learns more humanity and good morals, in seeing a regular boxing match, than it is probable he would, in hearing five dozen of sermons.' What was more, by taking up pugilism the French could learn to resolve arguments without spilling blood. It was thought that to further this aim, with the right encouragement 'Mendoza would be ready, on the return of peace, to open a school in the splendid metropolis of France.'[3]

As we have seen, Fewtrell had already tried his hand in the splendid metropolis, to little avail. There is no suggestion that Daniel Mendoza ever considered setting up a school in Paris once the Napoleonic wars were over.

Following the unhappy scenes at Covent Garden the previous year, Mendoza continued to tour, exhibit, teach and second. In April 1810 he was reported to be umpiring a bout in Leeds. In December he witnessed the famous and controversial first fight between Cribb and Molineaux at Copthall Common, of which he reportedly wrote:

> In the battle between Cribb and Molineaux, it is well known the latter had won three times. Some who had backed Cribb for hundreds, would have taken five pounds, before the battle was decided, for their money; but favouritism prevailed.[4]

In July an auction is mentioned in the *Morning Chronicle*. Abraham Goldsmid, a banker, known for his generosity and, like Nathan Rothschild, as a provider of financial support to the government in the war with France (and who committed suicide in 1810 after going bankrupt) had provided a cheap home for one D. Mendoza at The Royal Oak on Whitechapel Road (it is now an electrical goods shop). The 'well-known public house ... late in the occupation of Mr D. Mendoza, held for an unexpired term of about eighteen years, at the low rent of about fifty pounds per annum' was for sale. 'Early possession may be had.' It is not impossible that this was another D. Mendoza, though the fact that his name is mentioned suggests an advertiser's use of celebrity.

By the date of the advertisement, the Mendozas were certainly not living at The Royal Oak. A fortnight before its appearance, Daniel's wife Esther and daughter Sophia had been assaulted in their own home in Tower Street, St George's Fields. This was very close to the King's Bench prison, in the purlieus of which their husband and father was once again spending time.⁵ The *Morning Chronicle* carried a lengthy report of the trial proceedings.

Sophia, now around eighteen years old, with a friend, had been enjoying 'the beauties of a moonlight evening ... walking backwards and forwards on the pavement before her father's door'. A Mrs Houston, who lived opposite and was standing at her own front door, called out, 'I see there are Jew whores as well as Gentiles.' Sophia went inside and was told by her mother to ignore 'such vulgar, low-bred people', but also to stay indoors. A few moments later there was a loud knocking, and Esther opened the door to Henry Houston, who, 'in language not the most polished', accused Sophie of having abused his wife. Esther denied any such possibility and tried to close the door. Houston put his foot against it. Catherine Houston and a friend, John Davies, now turned up and told Henry to pull Esther out of the house. What happened then is unclear. Sophia attacked Mrs Houston, who knocked her down and bit her thumb. Esther went to her daughter's aid but was attacked by Henry Houston. 'A general scuffle ensued.'

All this was put to a jury, the judge bringing to its attention the fact that the defendants' stories were wildly contradictory. After a considerable time the jury acquitted Davies and found against Henry and Catherine Houston, and they were fined a shilling each. Had they stolen a handkerchief they might have been transported. In what was perhaps an imaginative extra piece of reporting in the *Globe*, Sophia apparently ventured out after the scuffle 'with her sleeves rolled up to her shoulders, calling on the party to "come out and fight"'.⁶

At the beginning of November Mendoza was free of the King's Bench, as he was seconding Gogharty against Hall at Portsmouth. 'The town and neighbourhood were nearly deserted by 10 o'clock ... the common was completely full,' remarked the *Morning Post*. Gogharty lost. Mendoza proceeded to Chichester, where Molineaux and his friends were giving 'public specimens of their science in the polite accomplishment of boxing'. Mendoza gave the same at The Fountain (a pub still standing, which, a few years after Mendoza's appearance there, was taken over by H. G. Wells's grandparents. It is now a local live music venue. It has a Roman wall. So the centuries pass). In the middle of the month a fight between one Docherty, seconded by Mendoza, and one Burns, seconded by Molineaux, almost resulted in what would have been a fight for the history books. Molineaux had taken exception to something Mendoza had been shouting at Burns. Mendoza took exception to Molineaux's taking exception and the two great fighters, the Jew and the black, 'shoved each other'. A buzz of excitement must have run around the ring, but nothing came of it.[7]

The following summer we find Mendoza, popular as ever in East Anglia, in both Norwich and Ipswich, where he sparred and exhibited with Dutch Sam and a fighter named Rogers. It was perhaps the Dutch–Jewish connection that made Mendoza so popular in this part of the world. However, there were still toughs wanting to take on the famous fighter. On the first night at Snow's Green, south of Norwich, a sailor – 'a pilot from Gorleston' – challenged him. They fought with gloves for six rounds before 'Jack, perceiving his inability to contend with his celebrated opponent, very wisely gave up the contest.'[8] The 'old school' man still had some tricks.

At these exhibitions, Mendoza, after sparring with Dutch Sam, would as before (and by most reports entertainingly), 'go through the various attitudes' of well-known boxers, not only those of the 'old school', such as Johnson, Perrins and Humphries, but also of Cribb, Pearce and Molineaux (and, 'maliciously', Warr).

In August 1814 a report in the *Morning Chronicle* mentioned that Mendoza had challenged a highly regarded boxer named Ned Painter, who was twenty years younger than himself. This, the report said, followed a well-attended benefit for Dan at the Fives Court, at which the master had sparred with Firby, and Tom Belcher knocked Ikey Pig 'through the railing of the stage', to be caught by spectators. The fight with Painter never happened, and it is highly unlikely that the challenge was ever made, other than by a newspaper.

In July 1815 Old Nosey beat Boney at Waterloo, and the Napoleonic Wars ended. The year before (when Napoleon's end was assumed), the Pugilistic Club had been founded, along the lines of the Jockey Club and the Marylebone Cricket Club. Members wore blue coats and 'yellow kersymere[9] waistcoats' with 'PC' embossed on the buttons. Pierce Egan, in *Boxiana*, declared that the club was formed 'for purposes of truest patriotism and national benefit'. He goes on, in characteristic vein:

> Men of rank associating together learn to prize the native and acquired powers of human nature. They then learn to value

other distinctions, besides those of fortune and rank; and by duly estimating them in persons in far inferior stations in life, they imbibe the principles of humanity and fellow feeling for our common nature.[10]

The inaugural dinner was held at The Thatched House Tavern in St James's. Many leading pugilists attended. We do not know if Dan Mendoza was among them, but he is not mentioned by Egan. Jackson was appointed Secretary. Increasingly, as argued by Adam Chill, with the end of the war boxing was being controlled not by the Fancy but by boxers themselves in association with highly influential journalists, such as William Oxberry, and Pierce Egan himself.[11] The mutually beneficial relationships between press and sport that continues to this day had already been illustrated by the early triumph of *The World*, which owed much of its success to the Mendoza–Humphries trilogy.

July 1816 was a busy month for Daniel Mendoza, and a disturbing one. His protégé Dutch Sam died on the 3rd, and on 18 July Mendoza's son Abraham was sentenced to death for highway robbery. Perhaps to relieve himself of this vicissitudinous coming together of events, Dan travelled to Colchester to train a 72-year-old man called Barnet who intended to cover a thousand miles by walking 1½ miles every hour until the task was completed. This was an example of 'pedestrianism', one of the weirder sports that the British developed in the eighteenth century. It was tremendously popular, and generally involved walking vast distances in quick time. For example, in 1788 Foster Powell walked 100 miles in 21 hours and 35 minutes. In 1809 Captain Barclay – later celebrated as the trainer of Tom Cribb, and to whom *Boxiana* is dedicated, and whom we met in a previous chapter racing at Newmarket – had walked a mile every hour for 1,000 hours. It was reported that Barnet was 'under the able care and direction of the celebrated pugilist Daniel Mendoza, who is determined to bring forward a game hero in pedestrianism, with the expectation of outdoing all the other pedestrian feats hitherto attempted'.[12] By 1 August, Barnet had completed 648 miles, and by the 6th he had finished. The *Colchester Gazette* reported the triumph in full:

Tuesday afternoon, at twenty minutes after one o'clock, Barnet, the Essex pedestrian, completed his most wonderful feat of 1,000 miles, at one mile and a half from his commencement, every successive hour; the like of which has not been as yet paralleled by any pedestrian. His last mile and a half he finished in presence of an immense crowd of spectators, who, on his coming in, cheered him it every direction for a considerable length of time. He then went an extra mile and a half, to the utter astonishment of every one present (his attendants keeping the ground clear), performing it in nineteen minutes. Barnet was decorated with blue ribands, and having finally finished the whole of his task, to the great satisfaction of the numerous assemblage was placed in a handsome chair, decorated with ribbands and wreaths of laurel, and carried into the town of Barking, preceded by a band of music and four men with colours flying. After parading in various directions, the company retired to the Duke's Head, where, on a lawn behind the inn, dancing immediately commenced, and booths being also erected, the company generally repaired to them, and kept up their merriment with great glee till a late hour. During the evening Barnet joined frequently in the dances with the fair visitors.[13]

I've no doubt Dan Mendoza enjoyed this triumph as much as the septuagenarian pedestrian. It had also become clear that his son Abraham would be transported rather than hanged.

The death of his protégé Dutch Sam must have been a blow, not only in personal terms but in terms both of Dan's professional status and his standing as a Jewish boxer. Sam had, in some sense, been Dan's and his community's representative in the ring. There was, however, another fine Jewish boxer now making a stir, and Mendoza took him under his wing. Abraham 'Aby' Belasco was the finest of four boxing brothers, and was declared the new 'champion of the Jews'. 'Belasco is the only one of the Mosaic tribe of this day that promises to maintain the name of a Mendoza or a Sam' was the opinion of *Trewman's Exeter Flying Post*. The two were distant cousins, Dan's grandfather Aaron was Aby's great grandfather. But 1817 proved a bad year for Belasco, with several defeats – one against Jack Randall – following two promising wins, so he left London to tour and exhibit with Mendoza throughout 1818 and 1819.

As before, boxing was promoted as morally superior to duelling, and there was nothing to upset the ladies. Everyone was welcome. Belasco made himself particularly popular by agreeing to fight local champions, such as the Winchcombe champion in Cheltenham and Joe Townsend in Coventry. While Mendoza had paved the way for acceptance of Jews – and Jews as fighters – in the regional towns and cities of the British Isles, there was bound to be a lingering sense among rural communities that they could be bettered by sound John Bull muscle. They never were.

On his return, Belasco, his reputation somewhat revived by a number of good victories, fell out furiously both with a rival, a fighter named Sampson, whom he had already beaten and who had called him a coward, and the *Weekly Dispatch*, to which he wrote a famous letter.

> Had Sampson challenged me in terms which one brave man usually addresses another, I should have contented myself with simply accepting his offer to meet me in the prize ring ... within one or two months. As, however, he has been pleased to give vent to his impertinence, in his letter ... by refusing to make the match with one of 'our people', I feel called upon myself to state, that I consider it no disgrace to belong to a community which boasts of a Mendoza and a Dutch Sam, and ranks among its members of the present day, gentlemen in the sporting world, not less remarkable for their honourable and gentleman-like conduct than for their liberality to men in the prize ring.[14]

Belasco probably suffered more anti-Semitic abuse than Mendoza. Unlike Dan's, Belasco's imitations of Christian boxers received short shrift, not least because he belonged to the 'tribe of Israel'. He even found it difficult to arrange, back or promote boxing matches, and his family was slandered as brothel keepers. Belasco was perhaps more active in his Jewishness than Mendoza, though probably no more proud. The community celebrated his final victory with a very well-attended benefit dinner at Howard's coffee house, which was attended both by members of the Fancy and senior figures of the Jewish community, including Nathan Rothschild. The proceeds Belasco squandered on opening a gambling house. He subsequently spent a year in prison for 'assaulting an officer', and thenceforth found himself often in trouble with the law.

There was a bizarre non-confession at the Old Bailey in 1844, during a trial after he had been the victim of a burglary. In answer to the question 'How long is it since you left off prize fighting?' Belasco declared:

> About eighteen years—my public-house is in Petticoat-lane—that is the right name—I decline saying whether I was in prison for

two years, or for a year before that—I do not wish to say whether I kept a house frequented by very young girls and men, or whether I had two years' imprisonment for that—I shall not say whether I was charged with uttering counterfeit money, or suffered a year's imprisonment for it—on my oath, I never buy property which is brought to my house—I have become honest and respectable—I do not buy anything—I have made that rule for ten years—I was always honest—it is ten years since I was in prison—the first time is so long since, I have almost forgotten it.[15]

The pub was The Gun and Star, which still exists, albeit in modern form and structure, as The Gun. Its previous incarnation closed in 2015, having been run by Karen Pollack and her son Marc, 'the last Jewish publicans in the East End'. There are few if any further records of Aby Belasco, but it looks as though among his last acts was making sure The Gun stayed in Jewish hands.

Dan Mendoza had continued to tour. It is unclear why he had given up teaching in London. Perhaps he was simply regarded as too 'old school'; Jackson, the 'gentleman', had become the go-to teacher (Byron among others took lessons), though in comparison with the man he had beaten in such controversial a manner, he knew very little. Or perhaps Dan Mendoza liked touring. He was, it seems, inveterately peripatetic, and was welcomed wherever he went. He was a natural show-off who preferred the stage to the ring; which makes his decision to fight Tom Owen so odd.

BOXING BETWEEN OWEN AND MENDOZA
or
Days of Old Revived
for fifty guineas aside, on Tuesday,
July 4, 1820.

Banstead Downs, fourteen miles and a half from London, was the spot selected to decide this rivalry of fame – this point of honour – this darling of reputation so allied to the hearts of all brave men!

By how much unexpected, by so much
We must awake endeavour for defence;
For courage mounteth with occasion.[16]

So ran the advertisement for Daniel Mendoza's last fight, almost certainly penned by Tom Owen himself, a man known for his ironic wit and white top hat, and who publicly declared that the ages of both boxers gave the contest 'rather a touch of the ridiculous'. Owen was fifty-one, and Mendoza would be fighting on the day before his fifty-fifth birthday (although most papers followed the 1764 birth date, and made it his fifty-sixth). 'These two old fools', the *Hereford Journal* scoffed.

It isn't entirely clear why they were fighting. *Boxiana* maintains that it was a kind of London grudge, encouraged perhaps by each man's supporters.

> This quarrel was not of that family extent like the Montagues and the Capulets, in Verona; neither did the Christians and Jews 'bite their thumbs' on passing each other in the street; but yet loud chaffing at the lushing cribs often occurred in Duke's-place and St. Kitt's, whenever the parties accidentally met together.

The two men had sparred with each other at the Fives Court and 'gave specimens of the old school, now superseded' at a benefit for Owen in June 1815 (in Belgium Napoleon was advancing swiftly towards Waterloo). One newspaper suggested that Mendoza challenged Owen to fight for 100 guineas in April 1818. It is not impossible to imagine Owen upsetting Daniel Mendoza with an offensive or ridiculing barb of one kind or another ('roars of laughter' tended to follow his remarks). Just the thing to set Dan off, he who was widely recognised as 'The Father of the Ring' at the time, but perhaps no less sensitive to insult than was the glass cutter's apprentice. Or perhaps this in itself was a title worth challenging. What seems most likely is that Dan needed the money, and perhaps, as before, wished to add some final glitter to his great and long career. Though he hadn't fought for fourteen years, he probably fancied his chances. He was certainly the favourite.

Tom Owen was a far from negligible boxer. He is often listed as a champion (some list him him succeeding John Jackson in 1797), and he is credited with the invention of the dumbbell. Known in his younger days as 'The Fighting Oilman', he had defeated all the local bruisers in his native Hampshire before going to London, being spotted by Jackson and matched, at his request, with the celebrated Hooper, 'the Tinman' (whom Mendoza had refused to fight) in November 1796. Owen beat the hitherto undefeated Hooper, though it was said that the Tinman had been 'but a shadow of his former self; luxury and debauchery had spoiled him'. Subsequent losses to Bartholomew and a likely Mendoza-trained Jewish boxer called Houssa rather dented Owen's reputation but he defeated one Davis at Deptford, and possibly bettered Jack Bartholomew in a 'turn up' at the Horseshoe and Hoop Inn on Tower Hill. He gave up prize fighting after being imprisoned for aiding and abetting Berks and the Game Chicken to fight a pitched battle. He took to sparring and seconding, and, it seems, writing, of which little appears to have come down to us, other than the advertisement above.

For all its folly, the fight garnered considerable interest, if only for 'the novelty of a fight between these old ones, so celebrated in the old school'. It was obviously a source of pub debate as to which 'school' was the better. The *Sporting Magazine* of January and February 1817 had set up imaginary bouts between various members of the opposing schools. Mendoza had been set against Tom Belcher: 'I tread on delicate ground, but I will give my opinion unbiased, and boldly maintain that Mendoza was superior to Tom Belcher.' Owen was not among the dozen or so 'old school' names selected.

Mendoza versus Owen, then, attracted 'immense numbers. The road was lined early in the morning, and from appearances, Petticoat-lane and the eastern haunts of the sons of Israel were deserted for the day, through eagerness to witness the last effort of the best Jew that ever stripped for combat. The patricians were also very numerous.'[17]

Banstead Downs are about 15 miles from London. The poet John Dyer eulogised them in 'The Fleece', a poem published some sixty years before the fight

> ... Spacious airy downs,
> With grass and thyme o'erspread, and clover wild,
> Where smiling Phoebus tempers every breeze,
> The fairest flocks rejoice –
> Such are the Downs of Bansted

Actually, even then they were known as a sporting site, for horseracing, hunting, footraces, and indeed prize fighting. As these goings-on attracted money, so they attracted highwaymen (a certain Miss Worsley saw one off with a whip).

MENDOZA *v* OWEN
4 JULY 1820
Banstead Downs

Very likely it is raining (apart from the fact that it seemed always to rain when Daniel Mendoza fought, the summer of 1820 was especially wet), and the water runs off the bare hills. The crowds are out from London. Indeed the East End of the town is 'completely drained'. The names of Mendoza and Owen have attracted a good muster of young swells from the West End, too. They have not seen either of the 'Ould Ones' fight. A great number of the oldest amateurs in the Fancy are also present, including Sir Thomas Apreece, Bart, who was Mendoza's umpire at Odiham thirty-two years before and is acting in that capacity again. The Pugilistic Club will have nothing to do with the occasion.

Tom Owen, attended by Cribb and Hudson, makes his entrance. Mendoza follows, with Randall and Lee (yes, that Lee). Mendoza walks around the ring with a coat around his shoulders, bowing to the crowd. Owen is taking his time. His famous white top hat has been handed to a minion, who receives it as a page might a crown. Instead of plain drawers Owen is wearing nankeen breeches. He is taking his time. Mendoza's second, Randall, approaches him.

> RANDALL: You're as long in getting yourself ready, as if you was going to be married.
> OWEN: Aye, we shall soon be married, and close together, I'll warrant ye, and hit each other a bit.
> HUDSON: Don't be in a hurry – we shall soon be about your house – too soon for Danny.

Owen's yellow ribbon is tied to the posts at the corners of the ring. Then Mendoza's 'blue silk bird's eye'.

They strip and come to the mark. Mendoza looks good for fifty-five. He seems confident. His eyes sparkle. However, nothing much happens as the two old ones circle around one another. It is a long time since either of them hit or was hit in earnest. Finally they tangle and fall, Mendoza underneath. Tom gets some encouragement from the crowd. The second round is equally cautious, but Mendoza gets a left-handed hit in before the two go to ground, Mendoza again underneath. Mendoza hits with right and left before Owen lands a hard punch below Mendoza's left eye. The 'claret' is flowing. Mendoza is down, but up again in sprightly fashion. Randall is none too pleased.

Mendoza now gets in a good punch to Owen's body and then throws his opponent, but both go down. The odds are changing. Owen is beginning to look like the favourite. In the seventh he lands a heavy right hander on Mendoza's ear. This follows his use of the celebrated 'Owen's Stop' (only ever used by Owen).

Now it is the ninth round, and both men are struggling for breath. The blood is running in streams from the lacerations around Mendoza's eyes. Owen gets Mendoza's balding head under his arm, and begins to pummel. A right goes into Mendoza's kidneys, and then another at the back of his head. Owen has always been a hard hitter. In the eleventh round Owen hits Mendoza twice with his left. Mendoza is visibly weakened now. The next round sees the end.

Was Mendoza shocked by the defeat? Very likely. In his heyday he had turned down fights he knew he could not win. It is possible he underestimated Owen's strength of punch or overestimated his own abilities. Had he properly prepared for the fight, or gone back to his teenage approach, 'never being very attentive in training' and relying on 'the excellence of [his] constitution'? *Boxiana* reported that 'Mendoza, in appearance, is quite an altered man, as a pugilist; he could scarcely make a decisive hit – and his once fine science was looked for in vain.' It was a sad end, and the tone of some of the newspaper reports reflected that.

Thus was this gallant professor of his day beat in 10 minutes and 27 seconds.: – he who had fought thirty-three battles, and shown himself at all times the pride of the prize-ring: he who had subdued the vauntings of Bill Warr, and curtailed the boxing notions of Humphries... In this battle it was Mendoza in shadow and in attitude, but not in measurement nor in action. He had no chance of getting at his adversary, and perhaps he is more beat than ever he was in his life. Owen is a heavy right-handed hitter, and had length and strength over him. He won his fight well with Hooper, and is not to be scoffed at now.[18]

The melancholy that attaches both to the event itself – men of this age should not be fighting – and to the result was perfectly expressed in *Blackwood's Magazine*, which published a sonnet with a lengthy preface. Both are well worth reprinting.

SONNET

On the Battle between Mendoza and Tom Owen,
at Banstead Downs, July 4th, 1820.
BY W. W.

Is this Mendoza?–This the Jew
Of whom my fancy cherished
So beautiful a waking dream,
A vision which has perished.

(Extempore on seeing the battle. W. W.)

* Query—The Fancy ?. But no. I crush the ungenerous sentiment. Mendoza's reputation has not perished in the souls of the Fancy. His imaginative faculties may have been clouded by age: they were mortal, and faded away; but his former deeds—his brilliant qualities—his undoubted valour—his unrivalled science, are written with a pencil of light, and, incapable of injury, will flourish as long as water flows, or tall trees bloom. When I said that the vision my fancy had formed had perished, I only meant, that the ideal creation I had figured to myself of Mendoza, had vanished in the cold consciousness of knowing his existence through the gross medium of the external senses. For, as the picture of the actual Yarrow flowing before the eyes, beautiful as it is, is less delightful than the imagined stream; so is the actual Mendoza than the fancied. W. W.

'Superfluous lags the veteran on the stage,'
Said Samuel Johnson many a year ago,
In stately verse; and now its truth we know
When we behold Mendoza, bent with age,
Throw up his hat at Banstead, and engage
Tom Owen –That the diamond of the ring
In eighty-nine, the eastern star, the king

Of scientific pugilists, in the page
Of Boxiana, hymned by Fancy's pen
As one long swathed in glory, should forego
His old renown, appears to thoughtful men
Most ominous! O Daniel, Daniel O!:
Why, when you cried, I go to fight Owen,
Did no kind genius echo back N–O.[19]

Even had a kind genius been about, it is unlikely that Mendoza would have declined to fight. It was, in a sense, easy money, and he almost certainly thought he was going to win.

However, once defeated, Mendoza knew he had fought his final prize fight, and shortly afterwards, on Thursday 31 August 1820, he made a Farewell Address to the Fancy at the Fives Court. Pierce Egan described the scene, and transcribed the speech:

After the stage had been kept waiting, as the actors say at the playhouse, the veteran of the ring appeared, made his bow, seemed rather depressed, and addressed the audience in the following words:

'Gentlemen,—I return you my most sincere thanks for the patronage you have afforded me to-day, and likewise for all past favours. To those persons who have set-to for me to-day, I also acknowledge my gratitude; and their services will never be forgotten by me. Gentlemen; after what I have done for the pugilists belonging to the Prize Ring, I do say, they have not used me well upon this occasion; in fact, the principal men have deserted me *in toto*. Gentlemen; I think I have a right to call myself the father of the science; for it is well known that prize fighting lay dormant for several years after the time of Broughton and Slack. It was myself and Humphries that revived it, in our three contests for superiority, and the science of pugilism has been highly patronised ever since.—(Hear, hear! from some old amateurs.)—Gentlemen; I have once more to thank you for the present, and all other past favours; nay, more, I now take my leave of you; and I trust that I shall never trouble you for another benefit. (Applause.) I have now only to say—farewell.'

Abraham Belasco offered to put on the gloves with Mendoza, but the latter did not exhibit. It was not a lucrative benefit. Few, if any, boxers have had such opportunities of making a fortune as

Mendoza. In the milling circles he was quite the fashion for several years; and his numerous benefits in London, Scotland, and, indeed, in most of the provincial towns in England, were overflowing.[20]

Frustratingly, Egan offers no explanation as to how Mendoza managed to squander so much money, though even today it is reckoned that athletes are not great bookkeepers. Boxers Mike Tyson and Evander Holyfield have both lost fortunes of hundreds of millions of dollars.[21]

This 'farewell' was to be very far from Mendoza's final benefit.

LIFE

END OF PRIZE FIGHTERS
Mendoza – Most celebrated of the old school. Now in a state of destitution – his daughters on the streets and his sons transported.

This notice, from the *United Services Journal*, was reproduced in numerous newspapers, from the *Devon and Wiltshire Gazette* to the *Caledonian Mercury*. The puritanical glee that sees a sinner punished simmers beneath the bald facts. There was no Welfare State, no pugilistic charity, to support the man who had more or less invented the modern sport of boxing.

There was no support to be had from his family. His father, Abraham, had died at seventy-four on 30 December 1805. His mother, Esther, in 1813. Of his ten siblings, five died very young. His sister Benvenida had died as early as 1784. Newspaper reports often mention that Daniel sparred with his brother. This may have been either his elder brother Isaac (born 1758) or, later on, Raphael (born 1772). More likely it was his brother-in-law Aaron.

Daniel Mendoza's decline was slow but how else could it be, his high coming almost fifty years before his end? He continued to second fighters, and to exhibit where he could. But he was emphatically now of the 'old school'. He remained popular outside London. In Bristol in July, 1821 'The Nestor of the Ring ... the *great little man*, Mendoza ... in a set-to with Sam Portch, astonished and delighted the connoisseurs by a display of those *happy stops* and quick hitting, which rendered him worthy of the title – "The Father of the Ring".'[1] It is hard to imagine he did not enjoy fight days, when the crowds turned up in their hundreds or thousands, such as in the West Country in 1821, when he and Aby Belasco seconded a fighter named Winterflood of Bath against Hazell of Bristol, on Durdham Down, just to the north of Clifton. Hazell won. 'The ring was crowded with amateurs; and every species of conveyance was in requisition, from the humble donkey to the barouche, and the veriest daisy from Kingswood to the thorough "bit of blood", forming a grotesque and motley group.'[2]

These years are punctuated by unsatisfactory benefits at the Tennis Court in Windmill Street (Jackson only reluctantly allowed Mendoza to take them at the Fives Court). He did not lose his impetuous wit, though – was once told off for using it with a boxer called Oliver (not 'Death'). ''Tis not because a man is old that he has a licence to be saucy.'

There was trouble, too, with his offspring. How many children Daniel and Esther had is not entirely clear, but the best guess is ten. Their first child, Sarah, died as a baby. Five at least survived. We know because at least four of them ended up in Australia, not all by choice.

Already, in 1816, Abraham had been transported. Born in February 1790, perhaps apprenticed as a shoemaker, married to Rachel Anidjar in 1813, he was found guilty of assaulting Joseph Wood in the King's highway (Petticoat Lane), on 7 April 1816, 'for putting him in fear, and taking from his person, and against his will, a watch, value £15, a chain, value £4, two seals, value 30 shillings, and a key, value 5 shillings'. In other words, highway robbery. Abraham had a bit of 'previous', six years earlier having been indicted for stealing a silk handkerchief. On that occasion he was found not guilty. Now he was sentenced to death. This was 'respited' to transportation for life on 18 September. The *Morley* sailed for New South Wales in November 1816.[3] Abraham found work as a shoemaker and died on 18 December 1839. It is possible that he returned at some point because he is cited in an 1830 case of dispute with his brother Daniel, both identified by the *Morning Post* as 'sons of Daniel Mendoza, the ex-pugilist'.

More offspring were to go involuntarily. Sophia, 'the fighting man's daughter', born in 1792, whom we have already met involved in a fracas in Tower Street, was described by a London policeman, Robert Marston, as 'a bad character'. She was involved in a theft of feathers (among other things) worth some £7 from the bed in the room that she had been renting with a Mr Jones, living as his wife. Jones it was who was arrested by the Thames Police, in Tower Street. Sophia escaped any kind of prosecution for that, though the evidence in Jones's trial does seem to point very directly towards her as the chief wrongdoer. The feather heist took place in February 1828. Three months later Sophia herself was arrested and found guilty and 'indicted for stealing, on 19 of April, 1 tea-pot, value 5 shillings.; 1 tea-caddy, value 3s.; 7 chimney ornaments, value 7s.; 1 basin, value 3s.; 2 spoons, value 1s.; 1 rummer-glass, value 2s., and 1 pair of boots, value 3s., the goods of John Williams'.[4] She and a friend had helped a distressed young woman to her home before proceeding to purloin everything they could pocket. The punishment was seven years' transportation. She sailed on board *Harmony* on 9 September 1828, arriving at Van Diemen's Land (Tasmania) on 14 January the following year. Thirty-four years old at the time of her conviction, Sophia was described as 'a servant of all work', which almost certainly included prostitution. She was 5ft 1 inch tall, her complexion and hair were 'dark'. She had an 'oval face, high cheekbones, aquiline nose, Jewish countenance'. She had arrived with three fatherless children. Repeatedly in colonial courts for various offences, she did not receive her 'Certificate of Freedom' until 1855, in which year she died. In 1844 she had married a man named Daniel Denyer.[5]

Daniel Mendoza, born in March 1799, was identified by a man called Joseph Hook who claimed that Mendoza had attacked him with a knife in the graveyard of Stepney church. A sailor named Evan Davies was a witness.

> On the 15th of September I saw the prisoner and Hook together in Stepney Church-yard. The prisoner said to him, 'You are afraid to strike me.' Huke said, 'Do you want to fight me in earnest? I know you, and you may be as good a man as your father for what I know.'

The case was thrown out when it was discovered that Hook and Mendoza were well known to each other; nonetheless it had been a bloody incident. One wonders what Daniel senior thought of his son's knife play.

A year later, in May 1820, this same Daniel was found guilty of pickpocketing and sentenced to transportation for life. There is, however, no evidence that he was sent to Australia. It is probable that he served his time on a hulk (a prison ship), because he is known to have died in London in 1838.

Isaac Mendoza, born in July 1808, married a Sarah Bell at Bevis Marks Synagogue in January 1832. He stole a handkerchief and was sentenced to seven years' transportation (compare this with the shillings his father was forced to pay, having been found guilty of assault). He sailed, like his sister Sophia, to Van Diemen's Land. The ship, *John*, left on 3 August and arrived on 1 December 1833. And like his brother Abraham, he became a shoemaker. He died in Melbourne in 1881.

Daniel and Esther's (possibly) last-born, Matilda, also ended up in Australia. She had married a man named Samuel Michael Simmons, probably shortly after her father's death in 1836. It is conceivable that he was related to the Simmons, or Symonds, with whom Mendoza sparred (and who was Dan's bottle holder in the fight with Jackson). Matilda was attacked 'in a most wanton manner' by two cabdrivers a couple of years after her father's death. Whether this was because she was her father's daughter, or Jewish, or whether it was a sexual assault, we simply do not know. It was not enough to make her emigrate before having had seven children. She and Simmonds emigrated to Australia in November 1853. Simmons seems to have died in an asylum in 1881. Matilda lived until 1897 and died in her home on Elizabeth Street, Strawberry Hills, Sydney.

There are various Mendozas mentioned in the newspapers as being children of Dan and Esther who do not figure in any official records. There's a 'Lewis', a 'Michael' (who was commended for going to the aid of a policeman who was being attacked), and a 'Julia Simons', apparently a daughter, who was charged with robbery, and described in the *Morning Post* as 'a long-nosed and ancient Jewess, [who] stood at the bar with features arranged with the greatest possible propriety'. 'Simons' is close to 'Simmonds'. Perhaps Julia was Matilda.

The old man found himself in trouble with the police in May 1827, when he was charged with 'a dirty action'. He was accused of throwing some 'filthy stuff' into the face of a Mr Lyons. This Lyons had attended a benefit for Mendoza at the Fives Court, and had accused Mendoza of being 'an informer', of having 'laid information against him, Lyons'. Mendoza declared that he 'never did a "dirt action" in his life', and that he had never informed on anyone. In the office of the magistrate, Lyons shouted 'You lie!' and clearly got very worked up. The magistrate was unimpressed, and said that Lyons' conduct was 'enough to provoke any man', and suggested that if Mr Lyons wanted to take the case further then so he should, but he was dismissing the charge. The two men kept yelling at one another, and the magistrate warned them not to commit a breach of the peace.

By 1824 a 'Young Mendoza' had appeared. This was Sam, born in 1800, and probably a nephew of Daniel's. He sparred with Belasco, and seems to have turned up loyally to his uncle's benefits. At the Fives Court in 1824 the benefit was well attended and though Mendoza himself apologised for not exhibiting, due to physical infirmity, Belasco and Sam 'showed what thoroughbred *sheenies* can do'. ('Sheeny' was a vulgar name for a Jew, a term of obscure origin).

On 13 November 1825 Mendoza took yet another benefit at the Tennis Court. It was a catastrophe, receipts on the door amounting to not much more than 3 guineas. The evening finished with Mendoza and Aby Belasco setting-to, but before this happened, Daniel Mendoza made another farewell speech (though he was to have more and more benefits the further he fell into destitution and despair). It is worth reproducing in full, as it was reproduced in newspapers throughout the country. He began by thanking those who had come, and then continued.

But, Gentlemen, like fighting itself, I am going out of fashion. I have fought as many battles as most men, and in this, at least, the evening of my days, I have the satisfaction to say I never deceived my friends. Proud should I be if I could say my friends never deceived me; but unfortunately promises, in modern days, are like pie-crusts, they are made to be broken. Several of my friends, as they call themselves, promised to be here to set-to for me, but they are not here – I am sorry for it for your sakes – I am sorry for their own sakes – for I am sure that those who will not endeavour to assist old age cannot expect to be assisted. Jem. Ward, the champion, as he calls himself, faithfully pledged himself to be here, and set-to with me, but he has not come; if he does not keep his faith better with his backers,

I am afraid he will not gain much respect. In this state of things, my friend, Aby Belasco, has kindly volunteered to do what he can, and I entreat that you will accept our efforts to please, as a proof, at least, that we wish to do our best.[6]

It is impossible not to hear the bitterness, the sense of disappointment. What is more, he was right about fighting going out of fashion. The previous year had seen John Jackson shutting up his rooms in Bond Street (the fencing academy of the Angelos remained until 1830, when it moved to St James's Street); Moulsey Hurst shut down by local magistrates; Tom Spring retiring; and the last volume of *Boxiana* published. The Golden Era was over.

Daniel Mendoza had eleven more years to live – 'the lamp of life was fast expiring,' as Henry Holt put it when at the beginning of 1827 he – 'the Orator of the Ring' – appealed to the Fancy after yet another Mendoza benefit. Reference to Dan's 'misfortune' is never specific, and yet it turns up again and again. Sophia had yet to be transported.

Sir Thomas Apreece himself attended the 1827 benefit, by which Mendoza was touched. It had been a long association. Whether Sir Thomas was in a position to help his old friend out seems unlikely, because by November of the year *Bell's Life* was reporting as follows

Poor old Mendoza is in the greatest distress, with a large family; his goods are about to be seized for rent. It is to be hoped the remembrance of his past services may prompt the humane to lend a hand to him whose hands were always ready to sustain his character as a man.[7]

It seems to have been a matter of feast or famine, with little to be absolutely relied upon. In the following year, he had benefits at Howard's Coffee House and in September at the Tennis Court. The latter was 'very respectably attended', and Dan 'received the approbation due to his former good conduct'. It was reckoned he may have made up to £30, once expenses were paid. A tidy sum, but nothing to retire on, something around £2,500 in today's money.

Jews, like Catholics, like Dissenters, did not benefit from the Poor Law, which was organised along parish lines, and the accelerated influx of Jews into the country at the end of the previous century had put a great strain on the synagogues' ability to provide relief for the destitute. It is possible, too, that Mendoza's behaviour in 1809, during the OP riots, told against him. More likely his very reputation as a pugilist did not sit well with the Jewish elite, which strongly disapproved of boxing, more strongly still than the Anglican establishment. The Jews' Hospital, founded in 1807, was essentially an Ashkenazi institution. Most Jewish boxers were, oddly, Sephardi – of Iberian or Mediterranean origin. Oddly because as between the two tribes, the Sephardi were the more anglicised and on the whole much better off. Whatever the reason for Mendoza's increasing destitution, what he had done for his co-religionists in terms of status, not just in making Jews less vulnerable to physical abuse on the streets, but also in promoting their reputation in wider society, appears to have gone unrewarded.

He now spent his time dwelling on his glory days, at the Castle Tavern, Tom Belcher's pub in Holborn, 'the undisputed unofficial headquarters of the ring'.[8] He would have rolled home to Horseshoe Alley, from which most of the furniture would have been hocked: 'Mendoza is without a bed to lie on,' reported *Bell's Life in London* in August 1830. The following month another benefit at the Tennis Court 'was a complete failure – the money at the door did not suffice to pay the expenses of the court. The unfortunate man is in the most miserable state, and was almost in despair at his failure.'[9] The only pinpoint of light in that sentence is the 'almost'. In October 1835 *Bell's* reported that Mendoza had contracted palsy, and was 'quite blind'.

Daniel Mendoza died at his home in Horseshoe Alley, Petticoat Lane, on 3 September 1836 at 1.30 a.m., 'after a long and lingering illness, embittered by poverty and a succession of vicissitudes'. He was buried the following day at the Nuevo Cemetery for Spanish and Portuguese Jews at Mile End. In 1855, 7,000 graves were moved to Brentwood, in Essex. Mendoza's is unmarked. What became of Esther has gone unrecorded.

* * *

I am very far from being an expert, but it seems to me that great boxers have almost always been quick of mind and body. Obviously strength, and resilience and courage – 'wind' and 'bottom', to be Georgian – are essential qualities, without which you can be no kind of boxer, but the truly great are both intelligent and fast. This is what Daniel Mendoza was. All his contemporaries recognised his 'lightning' speed of thought, parry and blow. The frequent references to his pre-eminence as a 'professor' suggest acknowledgement of a fine, acute intelligence. His weakness as a fighter at a time when there were no weight divisions was his relatively small size and the lack of a killer punch. But even in the obvious mismatch with Jackson he had been more than holding his own before his antagonist chose a less than gentlemanly method of forcing victory. Dan had grown up as a boy fighting men; he had taught himself how to beat those who were bigger, heavier and stronger than himself. For the aficionado, watching Daniel Mendoza box must have been a pleasure.

The scale of his contribution to the development of boxing is unarguable. He can be credited with turning what was a kind of superior cock fight into a sport, emphasising defence and in-fighting, and demonstrating new techniques and tactics in lessons, in exhibition, on the printed page, and in prize fights themselves. His never-ending tours took boxing to almost every corner of the British Isles, from Duke's Place to Dundee and Dublin.

His legacy as a boxer extended to inividuals in the form of a surge in the number of Jewish pugilists who became active in the opening decades of the nineteenth century. Dutch Sam, Aby Belasco (and brothers) and Isaac Bitton have been mentioned. There were also Youssup, Solly Solicky, Bernard Levy, Young Dutch Sam, Elisha Crabbe, Yokel, Barney Aaron, Black Abey, Lazarus, Little Puss, Cat's Meat, and Ikey Pig, not forgetting Ugly Baruk (who fought to a draw with Symonds at Hornchurch).

His *Memoirs* stand as the remarkable first shout of a genre that has led us in recent years to outstanding sports autobiographies such as Andre Agassi's *Open* and *Beware of the Dog* by rugby player Brian Moore. Mendoza's memoirs ramble, are unreliable as to dates, and end too soon. They remain immensely readable and unexpectedly candid (with the possible exception of eliding the odd excursion to the coast of Africa). While Mendoza knew his worth and was proud of his achievements, he could have had no idea how important his life has come to be seen.

In the introduction I wrote that Mendoza is too far away from us to be properly knowable as an individual. Nowadays he is regarded as a symbolic figure, as seminal in the development of the integration of Jews into British life, as important in the development of boxing – and as a conferrer of dignity in both realms. He is used by academics to illustrate issues of late-eighteenth-century masculinity, or to demonstrate the nature of English nationalism. These descriptions and claims for him all have truth about them, but they also help to diminish Daniel Mendoza as a distinct individual. Whether the preceding pages have managed to present what was a living being is not for their author to judge, but I hope to have gone a little way to doing so. For all his brutalities, Daniel Mendoza makes me smile. The *Memoirs*, along with the words of others, and gleanings from the ephemera of the time, I think reveal that his view of the world was essentially comic. He recognised, I believe, absurdity.

His story is also sad. Real lives don't have arcs. They might be seen as graphs, though even these can only tell an outsider's view. Success doesn't always align with happiness. The story goes: a young man, born into a relatively pious East End family, learns enough Hebrew to be proud of himself, finds that people whom he likes appear to be badly treated, finds too that he has the physical wherewithal to protect them, ends up using that skill to make money, more money than he can otherwise earn, though he'd rather bake biscuits than hand out 'facers'. He comes to the attention of the highest in the land. And they appear to like him not only as a boxer, but as company. And he likes theirs. He earns a good deal more money but in the company of people wealthier than Croesus, and he attempts to keep up. Eventually he loses a boxing match to a young man who actually, unlike him, *looks* like a member of the nobility, who perhaps aspires to a higher social class, something Mendoza, for all his rousting with the Quality has never done. His is still a name to reckon with. He has made a fortune touring; he has been to almost every town and city in the country at least once. And he continues to teach. But the money, the keeping of the money, is hard. Like so many in the country, he spends time in debtors' prisons, in London, in Carlisle. Eventually he 'settles down', becomes landlord of a popular East End pub. The graph line, however is heading downwards from 1795, when he turns thirty years of age. He continues to teach, to exhibit, but more and more often he is seeking benefits for himself. The papers begin to refer to him familiarly as 'Dan'. No longer the fighting Jew, he is 'old school', revered but no longer an item. He gets himself tangled up with the OP Riots, probably for money; he becomes an anti-papist, probably for money. There is no welfare, no Retirement Home for Distressed Pugilists. Despite the lingering power of his name, the memory of his glory is fading, and soon he is to be found at a corner table in the famous Castle Tavern in Holborn, where old fighters go to retell the stories of their youth, and maybe fall asleep over a pint of porter... Eventually the graph axes run out, and Daniel Mendoza is sans eyes and soon, sans everything. A young man's glory is so often a terrible curse. How bright the star of the east burned, and how dark his final days.

* * *

I have seen many Jews hooted, hunted, cuffed, pulled by the beard, spit upon, and so barbarously assaulted in the streets, without any protection from the passers by or police, as seems when compared with present times, almost impossible to have existed at any time. Dogs could not be used in the streets in the manner many Jews were treated. One circumstance among others put an end to the ill-usage of the Jews...

About the year 1787 Daniel Mendoza, a Jew, became a celebrated boxer and set up a school to teach the art of boxing as a science, the art soon spread among the young Jews and they became generally expert at it. The consequence was in a very few years seen and felt too. It was no longer safe to insult a Jew unless he was an old man and alone.[10]

The idea, originating with these words of Francis Place, and promulgated ever since, that Daniel Mendoza freed his 'tribe' from contempt, that he liberated Jews from fear of attack by making them, in some people's eyes 'the bullies of London', is attractive and largely true, but Daniel Mendoza did not extinguish anti-Semitism in London. Jews remained different – 'other'. The poet Robert Southey, under the satirical *nom de plume* Don Manuel Alvarez Espriella, wrote, as if home from abroad (i.e. England):

At one of the public schools here, the boys on Easter Sunday rush out after prayers, singing

He is risen, he is risen
All the Jews must go to prison[11]

The year was 1813. It took another half-century before a practising Jew was allowed to take his seat in the House of Commons.

What Mendoza did do was to destroy a particular stereotype of the Jew as craven and submissive and un-English. He did this not only by hurting gentlemen like Richard Humphries and blackguards like William Warr, but by spending time with the upper echelons of the Fancy, by chatting with the king. He was brutal, he was stylish, he was mischievous, and he did not appear to have any sense of social inferiority. As with most people, his character was full of contradictions. He hated cruelty and beat his servants, he wanted to be a baker and he was a boxer, he practiced mercy on his antagonists and laughed in their faces, he was very rich and very poor, a proud Jew who fought on the Sabbath, the plaything of the nobility, and a despiser of the haughty. He was a Professor of Pugilism, a convicted thief, and a violent stabber.

Pierce Egan described him as 'intelligent and communicative', and his friendships with Decastro, Apreece, Wolcot, as well as the *Memoirs*, with their references to Anacreon and Fielding and Shakespeare attest to that. But he was not a good father, and as a husband failed, in the end, catastrophically. Many people have claimed direct descent from him, including the great comic actor Peter Sellers, but his children could not be said to have flourished. There were clever genes about certainly: Daniel's great nephew, Rufus Daniel Isaacs, son of an importer of fruit, became Lord Chief Justice, Viceroy of India, and 1st Marquess of Reading. He was said to have had 'a prodigiously retentive memory'. One suspects it was more accurate and forensic a tool than his great uncle's.

Daniel Mendoza was almost certainly a little more thuggish than the image that currently obtains – that of the curly-tressed, handsome, charismatic figure, a kind of romantic hero, as much at home on the stage as in the ring, a Byronic liberator of the English Jews. Actually, he was a bruiser. But he was revolutionary. He did change boxing and he did change popular perceptions of the Jews. He was the first true sporting superstar in British history. In Michael Shapiro's book *The Jewish 100: A Ranking of the 100 Most Influential Jews of All Time*, he is ranked number 82. He is sandwiched between Arthur Miller above and Stephen Sondheim below. Stagey. He would have liked that. Five years after his death, Dowling in *Fistiana* wrote:

> In poetry, in painting, and in music, we have our natural geniuses, who soar above all competitors in the brilliancy of their works; and so it would seem it is in the rougher paths of manly exercises. Mendoza was a natural genius in the elegant and effective use of his fists.[12]

In these present times, with a resurgence of antisemitism and infectious varieties of political extremism, with native-born people being told to 'go back home', it is worth reflecting, with a due understanding of the times in which he lived, on the identity and life of Daniel Mendoza, Londoner, Englishman, Briton, memoirist, champion boxer, fighting Jew.

NOTES

INTRODUCTION

1. Joyce Carol Oates, *On Boxing*, p.63
2. Mark Kram, 'There Ain't No Others Like Me', *Sports Illustrated: 50 Years 1954–2004*. New York, Little, Brown and Company, 2004)
3. David Halberstam, 'Chasing 'Ghosts of Manila' http://www.espn.com/page2/s/halberstam/010815.html

PROLOGUE

1. http://www.oldbaileyonline.org/browse.jsp?ref=t17711204-39
2. ibid
3. *Newgate Calendar* http://www.exclassics.com/newgate/ng323.htm
4. ibid
5. *The Annual Register for the Year 1771*
6. William Jackson, *The New and Complete Newgate Calendar*, Vol.5, p.21

CHAPTER ONE: TYNE

1. Bevis Marks Records: The circumcision register of Isaac and Abraham de Paiba (1715–1775), quoted in Gee, Tony, *Up to Scratch* p.35
2. Lewis Edwards, 'Daniel Mendoza', *Transactions (Jewish Historical Society of England)* Vol. 15 (1939–1945), pp.73–92
3. T. M. Endelman, *The Jews of Georgian England, 1714–1830*, p.119
4. ibid
5. *Memoirs*, pp.5–6 (Joanides, p.23)
6. Markman Ellis, 'The Philosopher at the Tea Table', Lecture, Queen Mary, University of London, 2010

7. Owen Swift, *A Handbook to Boxing*, p.30
8. Endelman, p.139
9. David S. Katz, 'Gibbon's Jews – Dead but Alive in Eighteenth Century England', in *Jewish Culture in Early Modern Europe*, ed. Cohen, Dohrman, Shear, Reiner, Hebrew Union College Press / University of Pittsburgh Press, 2014, p.275
10. *Memoirs*, pp.12–14 (ed Joanides, p.26)
11. M. Dorothy George, *London Life in the Eighteenth Century* (1925, 1966) p.263
12. George, p.265, quoting Place's *Autobiography*
13. George *op. cit.* p.272
14. Old Bailey Proceedings Online (www.oldbaileyonline.org, version 8.0, 29 March 2019), September 1782, trial of DANIEL MONDOCA (t17820911–101).
15. Emma Christopher, *A Merciless Place*, p. 215
16. Pierce Egan, *Boxiana*, Vol. 1, p.92
17. *Memoirs*, pp.33–34 (Joanides, p.32)
18. Jerry White, *London in the 18th Century: A Great and Monstrous Thing*. p.145
19. Endelman, pp. xx–xxi
20. The Jewish Naturalization Act, May 1753
21. Letter from Walpole to P. Yorke, September 1753, quoted in Dana Rabin, 'The Jew Bill of 1753', *Eighteenth-Century Studies*, Vol. 39, No. 2 (Winter, 2006), pp. 157–171
22. *The Scots Magazine*, May 1754
23. William Romaine, *A Modest Apology*, quoted in Endelman, p.124
24. Daniel Defoe, *A tour thro' the whole island of Great Britain, divided into circuits or journies*
25. *Memoirs* pp.47–48 (Joanides p.38)
26. *Memoirs*, p.55 (Joanides, p.41)

CHAPTER TWO: MARTIN
1. William Oxberry, *Pancratia*, p.72
2. *Whitehall Evening Post*, October 21, 1786
3. Karia Boddy, *Boxing: A Cultural History*, p.37
4. Misson, Henri, *M. Misson's memoirs and observations in his travels,* trans. John Odell (London 1719) vol 1. p.304, quoted in Boddy, p.37
5. Dennis Brailsford, *Bareknuckles*, p.28
6. Letter from Rome, *Morning Post and Daily Advertiser*, July 25, 1783
7. *Morning Herald and Daily Advertiser*, January 27, 1783
8. *Whitehall Evening Post*, September 1, 1785

9. Walter Thornbury, 'Hockley-in-the-Hole'. *Old and New London: Volume 2*. pp.306–309. *British History Online*. http://www.british-history.ac.uk/old-new-london/vol2/pp306–309.
10. And if you quiz a local they will tell you it is the birthplace of Boadicea.
11. Steven Marcus, 'Annals of the Prize Ring', *Commentary* magazine, December 1956
12. *Morning Chronicle and London Advertiser* May 19, 1786
13. *Public Advertiser*, April 14, 1787
14. *Morning Chronicle and London Advertiser*, April 18, 1787
15. *Public Advertiser*, April 19, 1787
16. Lewis Edwards, 'Daniel Mendoza', Jewish Historical Society, 1938, quoting from Bohun Lynch's *The Complete Boxer*, 1925
17. *Boxiana*, p 113
18. *Chelmsford Chronicle*, 20 April 1787
19. *Oxford Journal*, 21 April 1787
20. *Public Advertiser*, April 19, 1787
21. *The World and Fashionable Advertiser*, April 18, 1787
22. *Memoirs* p.61 (Joanides p.43)
23. *Memoirs* p.59 (Joanides p.43)

CHAPTER THREE: HUMPHRIES 1

1. *The World and Fashionable Advertiser*, November 7, 1787
2. ibid.
3. *London Chronicle*, January 10–12, 1788
4. *The World and Fashionable Advertiser*, September 21, 1787
5. *Memoirs* pp.60–62 (Joanides pp.43–44)
6. ibid, p.63 (Joanides p.44)
7. ibid, p.105 (Joanides p.59)
8. ibid, pp.67–68 (Joanides p.46)
9. ibid, pp.69–71 (Joanides p.47)
10. ibid, p.66 (Joanides 46)
11. *Boxiana*, Vol 1, p.249
12. *Memoirs* pp.76–79 (Joanides pp.49–50)
13. *Morning Chronicle and London Advertiser*, June 26, 1787
14. *The World and Fashionable Advertiser*, June 26, 1787
15. *Chester Chronicle*, May 31, 1811
16. 'The chopping blow, or as it is generally called, "the Mendoza", from the address with which it is struck by the celebrated pugilist of that name, is given by raising up the fist with the back of the hand, towards your adversary, and bringing it down with violence upon his face, thus cutting him with your backhand knuckles.' *The Modern Art of Boxing*, (1789) p. 16
17. *Memoirs*, p.80 (Joanides p.50)

18. *The World and Fashionable Advertiser*, July 16, 1787
19. *The Public Advertiser*, July 23, 1787
20. *Boxiana*, Vol 1, p.76
21. *Morning Chronicle*, August 14, 1787
22. *The World and Fashionable Advertiser*, September 14, 1787
23. *The World and Fashionable Advertiser*, September 17, 1787
24. *Memoirs*, pp.73–74 (Joanides 48)
25. *The World and Fashionable Advertiser*, October 13, 1787
26. The Spread Eagle, on Kingsland Road, in East London, is still there, though neither Humphries nor Mendoza would recognise it.
27. *The World and Fashionable Advertiser*, October 15, 1787
28. *The World and Fashionable Advertiser*, October 22, 1787
29. *Whitehall Evening Post*, October 30, 1787
30. *St James's Chronicle*, October 16, 1787
31. Stuart Reid, ODNB, https://doi.org/10.1093/ref:odnb/12195
32. ibid.
33. *Daily Universal Register*, December 12, 1787
34. *Oxford Journal*, December 22, 1787
35. *Daily Universal Register*, December 26, 1787
36. *Daily Universal Register*, December 7, 1787
37. *Boxiana*, 94
38. Adam Chill, *Bare Knuckle Britons*, p.37
39. Reid, ODNB
40. *Boxiana*, Vol 1, p103
41. *The Odiad*
42. *Gazetteer and New Daily Advertiser*, January 4, 1788
43. 1788 was one of the driest years ever recorded in England
44. Admiral Harry Powlett, 6th Duke of Bolton (6 November 1720–25 December 1794) was a British nobleman and naval officer, and Lord Lieutenant of Hampshire.
45. *Whitehall Evening Post*, January 10–12, 1788
46. *Boxiana*, Vol 1.
47. *London Chronicle*, January 10–12, 1788
48. *Morning Herald*, January 10, 1788
49. *The Scots Magazine*, January 1, 1788 [sic]
50. *Morning Post and Daily Advertiser*, January 10, 1788
51. *Memoirs*, pp.83–84 (Joanides, pp.51–52)
52. 'The cross-buttock throw is one of the most dangerous throws that can be given. It can only occur when your own and your adversary's right sides, in closing, happen to be in contact; in which case, you are to take a low hold of the waistband of his breeches with your right hand, and of his right shoulder with your left, and by this means cant him over your right hip, head foremost on the ground.' *The Modern Art of Boxing*, 1789, p. 23

53. *Morning Post and Daily Advertiser*, January 10, 1788
54. *Whitehall Evening Post* January 12–15, 1788
55. *The World*, January 12, 1788
56. *General Evening Post*, January 15, 1788
57. last two from the *Morning Chronicle*, March 28, 1788

CHAPTER FOUR: WAR OF WORDS

1. White, *op.cit.*, pp.253–254
2. Pierce Egan, *Sporting Anecdotes*, pp.10–13
3. Gerald Reitlinger, The Changed Face of English Jewry at the End of the Eighteenth Century', p.40
4. *Morning Chronicle and London Advertiser* February 5, 1788
5. *Boxiana*, Vol 1, p.110
6. Dighton became successful enough to open his own shop in Charing Cross, selling both his own and work by others. In 1806 he was discovered to have stolen prints from the British Museum, and had to lie low for a few years.
7. *The World*, January 10, 1788
8. *Morning Herald*, January 10, 1788
9. *Morning Chronicle and London Advertiser*, February 2, 1788
10. Delpini had a superstitious fear of the number eight, and thought he would die in 1788. Actually he died at the age of eighty-eight, in 1828.
11. *Boxiana*, Vol 1, p 249
12. *Critical Review*, Vol 65, p. 403
13. Aston, one of the 'steady and firm patrons of pugilism' according to Egan, was famed as a cricketer (playing for both Hambledon and the MCC). He was to die in a duel in India, one of the consequences of which was the promotion of a certain Arthur Wellesley.
14. *Memoirs* pp.110–111 (Joanides p.61)
15. *Memoirs* pp.112–121 (Joanides pp.62–65)

CHAPTER FIVE: HUMPHRIES II

1. 'Half a crown in every half-guinea went to the man who built the amphitheatre' *Whitehall Evening Post*, May 7–9
2. *Morning Post and Daily Advertiser*, April 29, 1789
3. http://www.historyofparliamentonline.org/volume/1790–1820/member/combe-harvey-christian-1752–1818
4. *General Evening Post*, May 7–9, 1789
5. *Felix Farley's Bristol Journal*, May 9, 1789
6. *The World*, May 8, 1789
7. *Diary or Woodfall's Register* (London), Thursday May 7, 1789
8. *General Evening Post* (London) May 7–9, 1789

9. *Diary or Woodfall's Register* (London), Thursday May 7, 1789
10. *Memoirs of the Life of Daniel Mendoza*, ed. Joanides, Alex (London: Romeville, 2011) p. 79

CHAPTER SIX: HUMPHRIES III

1. *Argus*, January 2, 1790
2. *Memoirs*, p.159 (Joanides p.79)
3. *The Boarding House, or Five Hours at Brighton*, a play reprinted in *The Sporting Magazine*, and quoted by Sharron Harrow in *Sporting Literature and Culture in the Long Eighteenth Century*
4. *Public Advertiser*, March 2, 1790
5. *The Sporting magazine*, II, May 1793, 85 (quoted in Brailsford *op. cit.* below)
6. Brailsford, p.30
7. *English Chronicle or Universal Evening Post*, November 24–26, 1789
8. *London Chronicle*, January 16–19, 1790
9. *Whitehall Evening Post*, January 14–16, 1790
10. It is worth reading Egan's description of Hooper's decline, to be found in an extended footnote on pages 5–6 of Volume 1 of *Boxiana*.
11. *Boxiana*, Vol 1, p.115
12. 'The learned Doctor, in himself, was another *striking* proof of pugilism being a national trait, by having a regular set-to with an athletic brewer's servant, who had insulted him in Fleet-street, and gave the fellow a complete milling in a few minutes.' *Boxiana*, Volume 1, pp 18–19
13. *St James's Chronicle*, March 1790
14. *Whitehall Evening Post*, August 12, 1790
15. *Diary or Woodfall's Register*, October 2, 1790
16. *London Chronicle*, September 30–October 2, 1790

CHAPTER SEVEN: SQUIRE FITZGERALD

1. *Fistiana*, p.85
2. *Evening Mail*, June 6, 1791
3. *Whitehall Evening Post*, May 15, 1790
4. *Memoirs*, p.203 (Joanides pp.96–97)
5. *Boxiana*, Vol 1, p.245
6. Swift, *op.cit..* p.29
7. The umbrella was an eighteenth-century invention. Hackney cab drivers would use their whips on them as they passed, furious at potential custom being so lost.
8. *Whitehall Evening Post*, January 15–18, 1791
9. *Diary or Woodfall's Register*, January 18, 1791

10. ibid.
11. *Memoirs*, pp. 203–205 (Joanides p.97)
12. *Memoirs*, pp.178–179 (Joanides p.86)
13. Memoirs, pp.187–188 (Joanides pp. 89–90)
14. Dublin wasn't exactly a haven of the pacific: rival gangs known as the 'Liberty Boys' – mostly weavers from the Liberties – and the 'Ormonde Boys' – butchers from Ormonde quay on the northside – fought bloody street battles with each other, sometimes heavily armed and with numerous fatalities.
15. *Morning Post and Daily Advertiser*, October 12, 1791
16. *Memoirs*, pp.207–208 (Joanides pp.98–99)
17. *Whitehall Evening Post*, November 22, 1791
18. Joseph Moser, *The Adventures of Timothy Twig, Esq*, London, R& T Williams, 1794, Letter VII, p.45

CHAPTER EIGHT: WARR

1. Alan Booth, 'Popular Loyalism and Public Violence in the North-West of England, 1790–1800', *Social History*, Vol 8, No. 3 (Oct 1983) pp. 295–313
2. *General Evening Post*, May 12, 1792
3. https://www.youtube.com/watch?time_continue=15&v=BY9a_Q75CRk
4. *Morning Herald*, May 21
5. *Memoirs* p.221 (Joanides, pp.104–5)
6. *Boxiana*, Vol 1, p.6
7. *Diary or Woodfall's Register*, June 28, 1793
8. *Morning Post*, November 4, 1793
9. *Oracle and Public Advertiser*, March 1, 1794
10. *The World*, January 9, 1794
11. White, *op.cit.*, p.447
12. ibid, p.446
13. *Memoirs*, pp.250–251 (Joanides, pp.117–118)
14. *Morning Post*, March 26, 1795
15. *Oracle and Public Advertiser*, Nov 13, 1794

CHAPTER NINE: JACKSON

1. Brailsford, *op. cit.*, p.68
2. Oxford Dictionary of National Biography
3. *Boxiana*, Vol 1, p.287
4. *Morning Chronicle*, April 17, 1795
5. Joanides, pp. 111–115
6. *Morning Chronicle*, April 17, 1795
7. *Pancratia*, p.120
8. *Oracle and Daily Advertiser*, November 26, 1801

9. *Boxiana*, Vol 1, pp.294–295
10. *Lloyd's Evening Post*, October 26–28, 1795

CHAPTER TEN: MRS JORDAN

1. Henry Downes Miles, *Pugilistica: The History of British Boxing*, Vol 1, p.79
2. J. Bowditch, *Imprisonment for debt: A letter on the present state of the law of arrest:* The duty of the sheriff and his officer, their fees, &c. as fully laid down, with a few hints in practice on the law of bail and render, intended as a guide to the merchant and tradesman: to which is added the recent decision of the Court of Queen's Bench in the case of a sheriff's officer
3. *Memoirs* pp. 244–261 (Joanides p.118)
4. Imprisonment for debt *op. cit*
5. *Memoirs* pp. 251–254 (Joanides p.120)

CHAPTER ELEVEN: NOT BELCHER

1. https://www.parliament.uk/about/living-heritage/
2. *Memoirs* p.260 (Joanides pp.121–122)
3. *Telegraph*, Feb 23, 1797
4. *The Sporting Magazine*, Volume 9, pp.280–282
5. ODNB Harriet Pye Esten https://doi.org/10.1093/ref:odnb/39766
6. *London Packet or New Lloyds Evening Post*, March 16, 1798
7. *Oracle and Daily Advertiser*, May 30, 1798
8. *Morning Herald*, Sept 27, 1798
9. *Oracle and Daily Advertiser*, May 15, 1799
10. *Memoirs* pp.279–280 (Joanides, pp. 128–129)
11. *Memoirs* pp.284–285 (Joanides, p. 130)
12. *Pancratia*, p. 236
13. *Memoirs*, p.294 (Joanides, p.133)
14. *Oracle and Daily Advertiser*, December 23, 1800
15. *Memoirs*, pp.299–302 (Joanides, pp.136–137)
16. *Morning Post and Gazetteer*, Nov 27, 1801
17. *Memoirs*, pp.304–305 (Joanides, p.138)

CHAPTER TWELVE: LEE

1. Walter Thornbury, *Old and New London,* Vol 1
2. Fewtrell, *Boxing Reviewed*, p.81
3. *Morning Post*, Feb 27, 1806
4. *Jackson's Oxford Journal,* March 29
5. *Jackson's Oxford Journal*, April 9, 1808
6. *Hereford Journal*, November 25, 1807
7. *Hampshire Chronicle*, May 16, 1808
8. *Pancratia*, p 310

CHAPTER THIRTEEN: THE OPs

1. *Boxiana*, Vol 1, p.333.
2. Edwards & Knibb, *Encyclopedia of comic songs, English, Scotch, and Irish, both of old times and new, etc...* pp.385–386
3. Charles and Mary Lamb, ed. E. W. Marrs, *The Letters of Charles and Mary Lamb*, Vol II, p.273
4. John Ford, *Prizefighting*, p.103
5. *The Times*, October 10, 1809
6. *Morning Post*, October 11, 1809
7. *The Times*, October 12, 1809
8. *The Times*, October 14, 1809
9. James William Baker, 'The Covent Garden Old Price Riots: Protest and Justice in Late-Georgian London', Open Library of Humanities, 2(1), p.e4. DOI: http://doi.org/10.16995/olh.13
10. Endelman, *op. cit.*, p.222

CHAPTER FOURTEEN: OWEN

1. *Public Ledger and Commercial and General Advertiser*, November 4, 1808
2. *Savannah Republican And Savannah Evening Ledger*, April 5, 1810
3. *The Sporting Magazine*, Volume 38, 1811
4. Luke G. Williams, *Richmond Unchained*, p.156
5. https://www.thegazette.co.uk/London/issue/16508/page/1480
6. *Globe*, October 17, 1811
7. *Saunders' News Letter*, December 17, 1811
8. *Norfolk Chronicle and Norwich Gazette*, July 11, 1812
9. A twilled fine woollen cloth of a peculiar texture, one-third of the warp being always above, and two-thirds below each shoot of the weft (OED).
10. *Boxiana*, Vol. 2, p.26
11. Chill, *op. cit.* pp.99–123
12. *Morning Post*, July 16, 1816
13. *Colchester Gazette*, August 10, 1816
14. *Weekly Dispatch*, January 19, 1823, quoted in Chill, op. cit.
15. *Old Bailey Proceedings Online* (www.oldbaileyonline.org, version 8.0, 26 March 2019), September 1844, trial of SOLOMON PARKER JOSHUA JACOBS (t18440916-2232).
16. *Boxiana*, Vol 3., p.60
17. *Morning Chronicle*, July 5, 1820
18. *Morning Post*, July 5, 1820
19. *Blackwood's Edinburgh magazine*, v.8 1820–1821 Oct–Mar
20. *Boxiana*, Vol III, pp.489–90
21. Russ Alan Prince, 'Why Star Athletes Lose Their Fortunes', *Forbes Magazine*, September 23, 2014

CHAPTER FIFTEEN: LIFE

1. *The Fancy*, Issue viii, p.183.
2. *Bristol Mercury*, July 28, 1821
3. *Old Bailey Proceedings Online* (www.oldbaileyonline.org, version 8.0, 22 January 2019), July 1816, trial of ABRAHAM MENDOZA (t18160710-7).
4. *Old Bailey Proceedings Online* (www.oldbaileyonline.org, version 8.0, 21 January 2019), May 1828, trial of SOPHIA MENDOZA (t18280529-170)
5. J. S. Levi, *Australian Genesis*, p.188
6. *Berkshire Chronicle*, Nov 19, 1825
7. *Bell's Life in London*, November 18, 1827
8. Brailsford, *op. cit.*, p.68
9. *Bell's Life in London*, Sept 26, 1830
10. Francis Place, *Autobiography*, quoted by M. Dorothy George in *London Life in the Eighteenth Century*, pp137–138
11. Robert Southey, 'Jews in England' (Letter LXIII), *Letters from England by Don Manuel Alvarez Espriella, Vol 3* p.144
12. *Fistiana*, pp.32–33

Appendix A

THE ART OF BOXING

THE ART OF BOXING
by Daniel Mendoza, P.P.

Printed and sold for Daniel Mendoza, No 4 Capel Court,
And No. 2 Paradise Row, Bethnal Green
(PRICE FIVE SHILLINGS)

PREFACE

After the many marks of encouragement bestowed on me by
a generous public, I thought that I could not better evince my
gratitude for such favours, than by disseminating to as wide an
extent; and at as cheap a rate as possible, the knowledge of an art,
which though not perhaps the most elegant, is certainly the most
useful species of defence. To render it not totally devoid of elegance
has, however, been my present aim, and the ideas of coarseness and
vulgarity which are naturally attached to the science of pugilism,
will, I trust, in a great measure, be done away, by a candid perusal
of the following pages. *Boxing* is a national mode of combat, and
is as peculiar to the inhabitants of this country as *Fencing* to the
French but the acquisition of the latter as an art, and the practice
of it as an exercise, have generally been preferred, in consequence
of the objection which I have just stated as being applicable to the
former. That objection, I hope, the present treatise will obviate,

and I flatter myself that I have deprived boxing of any appearance of brutality to the learner, and reduced it into so regular a system, as to render it equal to fencing, in point of neatness, activity, and grace.

The Science of Pugilism may, therefore; with great propriety, be acquired, even tho' the scholar should feel actuated by no desire of engaging in a contest, or defending himself from an insult.

Those who are unwilling risk any derangement of features in a real boxing match may, at least, venture to practise the art from sportivenss; and sparring is productive of health and spirits, as it is both an exercise and an amusement.

The great object of my present publication has been to explain with perspicuity, the science of pugilism, and it has been my endeavour to offer no precepts which will not be brought to bear in practice, and it will give me peculiar satisfaction and pleasure to understand, that I have attained my *first* object, by having taught any man an easy regular system of so useful an art as that of boxing; and that I have proved successfully in my *second*, by having removed any prejudices which, from the misstatement of others, might have been unfavourable to my character.

D. MENDOZA
No. 4, Paradise Row,
Bethnal Green
April 20, 1789

BOXING

The first principle to be established in Boxing is to be perfectly a master of the equilibrium of the body, so as to be able to change from a right to a left handed position; to advance or retreat striking or parrying; and throw the body either forward or backward without difficulty or embarrassment.

The second principle to be established is, the position of the body, which should be an inclining posture, or diagonal line, so as to place the pit of the stomach out of your adversary's reach. The upper part of your arm must stop or parry the round blow at the head; the fore-arm, the blows at the face of stomach; and the elbows, those at the ribs: both knees must be bent, the left leg advanced, and the arms directly before your throat or chin.

It must be an invariable rule to stop or parry your adversary's right with your left, and his left with your right; and both in striking and parrying, always to keep your stomach guarded, by barring it with your right of left fore-arm.

It is always better to avoid a blow by throwing the head and body back, at the same time covering the pit of the stomach, than to attempt to parry it.

Both hands must never be up or down at the same time. If your adversary strikes either at your face, stomach or side, with his left hand, parry or stop with your right, covering the stomach with your left; if he strikes with his right, let your left oppose it, covering your stomach with your right.

It is proper to exercise the scholar in changing both arms and legs from alternate positions of right handed to left handed, and to make him master of the equilibrium of the body, advancing and retreating.

LESSON I
Master strikes with his left arm at your face.

Parry with your right fore-arm, barring at the same time your stomach with your left fore-arm, throwing your head and body back.

Master strikes with his right at your face.

Parry with you left fore-arm, barring at the same time your stomach with your right fore-arm, throwing your head and body back.

Master strikes round at your right ear with his left.

Parry with your right arm, turning up the elbow so as to cover the side of the head, barring the stomach with the left fore-arm, and throwing head and body back.

Master strikes round at your left ear with his left.

Parry with your left arm, turning up the elbow so as to cover the side of the head, barring the stomach with the right fore-arm, and throwing head and body back.

Master strikes at your stomach with his left.

Bar your stomach with your right fore-arm, keeping your left opposite his nose, throwing your head and body back.

He strikes at your stomach with his right.

Bar your stomach with your left fore-arm, keeping the right opposite his nose, throwing head and body back.

His left strikes at your right side.

Stop with your right elbow, keeping your left fist opposite his nose, throwing head and body back.

His right strikes at your left side.

Stop with your left elbow, keeping your right fist opposite his nose, throwing head and body back.

LESSON II

1, 2.

Master makes the feint 1, 2, at your face, striking first with his left at your face (which is the feint) in order to hit you in your face with his right.

Parry first with your right fore-arm, and secondly with your left fore-arm, covering the stomach with the right fore-arm, and throwing head and body back.

Master feints in the same manner, beginning with his right.

Parry first with your left arm, and secondly with your right fore-arm, covering the stomach with the left fore-arm, and throwing head and body back.

His left feints at your stomach, to hit your face with his right.

Bar your stomach with your right fore-arm, and parry the blow at your face with your left fore-arm, throwing head and body back.

His right does the same.

Bar your stomach with your left fore-arm, and parry the blow at your face with your right fore-arm, throwing head and body back.

His left feints at your right side, to hit your face with his right.

Stop with your right elbow, and parry his blow at your face with the left fore-arm, throwing head and body back.

His right does the same.

Stop with your left elbow, and parry his blow at your face with the right fore-arm, throwing head and body back.

N.B. Observe, that the three foregoing feints are at the face, i.e. 1, 2 at the face – secondly, 1 at the stomach, 2 at the face; and next 1 at the side, 2 at the face.

The feints at the stomach and side are not 3 as those at the face, but only two – for example:

Master strikes 1 at the face, 2 at the stomach, with alternate arms.

Parry the first with the proper fore-arm, and the second with the proper bar; that is, if he strikes with his left at your face, and the right at your stomach, parry his left with your right fore-arm, and his right with your left across your stomach; if he strikes first with his right at your face, and his left at your stomach, parry his right with your left fore-arm, and his left with your right across your stomach.

Master strikes 1 at the side and 2 at the stomach.

Parry with the proper arms, first by catching the blow on the proper elbow, and secondly, parrying the blow at the stomach with the proper fore-arm; that is, if he strikes with his left first, catch it with your right elbow, and bar his right with your left across his stomach, and vice versa of his right.

He strikes at the face 1, and 2 at the side.

Parry each with the proper forearm and elbow.

He strikes at the stomach 1, and 2 at the side.

Bar the first with the proper fore-arm, and catch the other with the proper elbow.

This 2d Lesson consists of 1, 2, at the face, stomach and sides.

1 at the face 2 at the face		
1 at the stomach 2 at the face	}	1,2, at the face
1 at the side 2 at the face		
1 at the face 2 at the stomach	}	
1 at the side 2 at the stomach		1, 2 at the stomach
1 at the face 2 at the side	}	
1 at the stomach, 2 at the side		1, 2 at the side

LESSON III

1, 2, 3

Master strikes with his left at your face 1; with his right ditto 2; with his left at your stomach 3, the blow intended.

Parry the 1st with your right fore-arm – 2d with your left fore-arm – the 3d with the right fore-arm barring your stomach, throwing head and body backward.

Master strikes with his right at your face 1; with his left, do 2; with his right at your stomach 3.

Parry the 1st with your left fore-arm – the 2d with your right fore-arm – the 3d with your left arm, barring your stomach, throwing head and body backward.

N.B. – The above is 1, 2, 3 at the stomach.

1, 2, 3,
AT THE FACE

Master strikes at your head 1 with his left; do. 2 with his right, at your face; and 3 with his left, the intended blow.

Parry the 1st with your right – the second with your left – 3d with your right, your fore-arm covering ultimately your stomach, throwing head and body back.

Master strikes at your head 1 with his right; do 2 his left at your face; and 3 with his right, the intended blow.

Parry the 1st with your left; 2d with your right; 3d with your left, your fore-arm covering ultimately your stomach, and throwing head and body back.

N.B. – The above is 1, 2, 3, at the face.

1, 2, 3,
AT THE SIDE

Master strikes with his left hand at your head 1; his right do 2; and his left at your side 3, the intended blow.

Parry the first with your right fore-arm – second left fore-arm – third right elbow.

Master strikes with his right at your head 1; left ditto 2; right at your side, the intended blow.

Parry the first with your left fore-arm; second right fore-arm; third left elbow.

LESSON IV
RIPOSTS
Master's left strikes at your face.

Parry with your right fore-arm; and return at his face with your left, which he catches in his open hand.

His right strikes at your face.

Parry with your left fore-arm, and return at his face with your right ditto.

Master's left strikes at your stomach.

Stop by barring with your right fore-arm, and return at his face with your left, which he catches.

His right strikes at your stomach.

Stop by barring with your left fore-arm, and return at his face with your right.

Master's left strikes at your right side.

Stop by catching the blow on your right elbow, and return at his face with your left.

His right strikes at your left side.

Stop by catching the blow on your left elbow, and return at his face with your right.

Master's left chops at your face.

Parry with your right fore-arm, and return at his face with your left.

His right does the same.

Parry with your left fore-arm, and return at his face with your right.

Master's left strikes at your stomach.

Parry it down with your right, and return a back handed blow with the same hand, covering your stomach with your left arm.

Master's right strikes at your stomach.

Parry it down with your left, and return a back handed blow with the same hand, covering the stomach with the right arm

Master's left strikes again at your stomach.

Parry it down with your right, and return a straight blow at his face with the same hand.

His right does the same.

Parry it down with your left, and return a straight blow at his face with the same hand.

LESSON V

1, 2,
AT THE FACE
RIPOSTS

The Scholar strikes 1, 2, beginning with the left.
Master parries with his left, and riposts with his left at your face.

Parry this riposst by catching the wrist with your left fist, and striking a back-handed blow across his face with your left hand

Do the same with your right hand, i.e. beginning 1, 2, with your right.

This he will parry with his right, and ripost with the same, when you catch it with your right fist, and return with a back-handed blow across his face.

RIPOSTS

1, 2, 3 at the face, beginning with the left.
Master will parry with his right, and ripost at your stomach with his left.

Stop this with your right fore-arm, and return with your left at his face.

1 at the face, and 2 at the stomach, beginning with your left.

This he will stop with his left, and ripost 1, 2, at your face, beginning with his left. Parry with your left, and return 1, 2 at his face.

1 at the face, 2 at the face, and 3 in the stomach, beginning with your left, keeping your right fist opposite his face.

This he will stop with his right, and ripost the same again, 1, 2, 3, at your stomach, which you must bar.

Do the same with the other hand, i.e. beginning with your right.

This he will stop with his left, and ripost the same again, 1, 2, 3, at your stomach, which you must bar.

The Scholar strikes with his left at the face, the Master parries with his right, and riposts with his left at the stomach.

Knock the blow down, and return strait at the face.

Do the same with the other hand.

LESSON VI

Scholar strikes 1, 2, at the face, beginning with the left.

Master parries, and riposts the same.

Scholar strikes 1, 2, 3, at the face, beginning with the left.

Master parries and ripostes the same.

Scholar strikes 1, 2, at the face and 3 at the stomach, beginning with the left.

Master parries and ripostes the same.

Scholar strikes 1, 2, at the face and 3 at the side, ditto ditto.

Master parries and ripostes the same.

The Scholar should always use himself to cover either the stomach by barring or the head by projecting the fist.

At this period the scholar should parry and stop, but not return all feints for some time, and when perfect herein, he may
SET-TO OR SPAR LOOSE.

RULES OF BOXING

After having thus explained the order of the lessons, and the proper method of practising them, I would impress upon the reader's mind the following precepts, which will be brought to bear in fighting, and found equally easy and necessary.

Parry the blows of your adversary's right hand with your left, and those of his left hand with your right.

This rule ought never to be disregarded, except when you see a safe opportunity of catching a blow of his right hand if aimed at the face on your right, and striking him in the loins with your left; or of stopping his left-arm stroke on your left, and directing your right fist to his kidneys.

If your adversary aims all round blows,

which is generally the case with a man ignorant of Boxing, you should strike straight forward, as a direct line reached its target sooner than one which is circular.

If he gives way, or is staggered by a severe blow,

You should not be anxious to recover your guard and stand on the defensive, as this will only be giving him time to recollect himself, but take advantage of his momentary confusion and follow up the blow.

Advancing,

Is practised by placing the right foot forward at the same distance from your left, as your left is from your right in the first attitude; you then throw your left foot forward so as to resume your original position, and thus keep gaining on your antagonist as he recedes.

Retreating,

Which is used when your adversary approaches too violently upon you, or when you feel yourself embarrassed and wish to recover your guard, is practised by placing your left leg about as far behind the right, as the right in the original position is removed behind the left, then throwing the right hindmost so as to regain your former attitude, and thus continue receding from your antagonist just as the circumstances of the battle shall render necessary.

If you are long-armed,

You will have an advantage over your antagonist, as your guard will keep him at a distance, and your blows, by reaching further, will be struck with more force.

If short-armed,

Your superiority over your antagonist will consist in close fighting. You must endeavour to get within the compass of his arms, and aim straight blows, which will reach him before he can strike at you, and if he does strike at you, his fists will go over your shoulder.

If your adversary is ignorant of Boxing,

He will generally strike round blows, or plunge head-forward. If he strikes round blows in an awkward, slovenly manner, content yourself with aiming at his face and stomach, in a straight forward direction. If he strikes them quickly, stand chiefly on the defensive, stopping his blows, and throwing in the return whenever you find it convenient. And when you perceive him winded, hit as fast as possible, and follow up your blows. If he butts, or plunges at you head-long, you may either strike straight forwards and catch his face on your fist; or turn round on your left heel, and let him fly over your thigh; or jump on one side, and strike him with one hand as he advances, and the other as he passes by.

In the preceding lessons and precepts, I have endeavoured to explain the *Art of Boxing* perspicuously, and to reduce it within as narrow a compass as possible. In order still further to illustrate my instructions, I have inserted two plates in the book, – one – viz. the frontispiece – representing the guard or first position, and the other, the method of guarding then face and body. I shall now proceed to lay before my readers such information relating to the approaching battle with Mr Humphreys, as a statement of whatever has passed between us on the subject, since our last boxing match at Odiham can possibly afford.

If any instructions in the preceding pages appear difficult or obscure, I shall be happy to give every necessary explanation to those who will have the goodness to apply to me, for that purpose, at No 2 Paradise Row, Bethnal Green; or No 4 Capel Court, behind the Royal Exchange.

Appendix B

THE CORRESPONDENCE OF HUMPHRIES AND MENDOZA IN THE PAGES OF *THE WORLD AND FASHIONABLE ADVERTISER*, JANUARY 1788 AND MAY 1789

MENDOZA to The World, 12 January 1788

Mr MENDOZA'S Letter in Vindication of his Behaviour at the late Contest between him and Mr HUMPHREYS

Understanding, with no little degree of anxiety, that some gentlemen have disputed the propriety of my conduct, on Wednesday last, in the battle between Mr. Humphreys and myself, I am induced to exhibit the following facts; on the proof of which, I will hazard every credit from a generous Public, whom I never have, and never will deceive.

At ten minutes after one o'clock, I set to with Mr. Humphreys, and, for nearly 20 minutes, I had most evidently the superiority. Finding with ease I could stop most of his blows, and though I was frequently closed by Mr. Humphreys, (a mode of fighting I could wish to avoid) I found an ability to throw him.

My strength and spirits were superior to my adversary, till the last fall but two, when I fell directly on my head, and by the force, pitched quite over. I then found myself much hurt in my loins, indeed so much, that it was with extreme difficulty I could stand up right;

but by the last fall I received, I was scarcely able to breathe; and it was with great pain that I could sit on the knee of my Second. When Johnson asked me, if I had done, I could only answer him by a sign.

By this untoward accident alone, I lost a battle, on which my warmest hopes were fixed.

To my friends and patrons on that occasion I owe much; to the public, I owe still more; the confidence of which I never have betrayed. With this assurance I shall only add, that if the world is desirous of renewing the conflict, and should Mr. Humphreys be willing, I shall be more than happy to engage him.

D. MENDOZA.
No. 9 White-street, Houndsditch.

P.S. Mr. Henry Saffory, surgeon, Devonshire-street, Bishopsgate-street, is the gentleman who now attends me. The following attestation Mr. Saffory has permitted me to publish:

At the immediate request of some gentlemen of my acquaintance, I visited Mr. Daniel Mendoza this morning on his return from Odiham. Having very minutely inspected his various bruises, and fully investigated his complaints; I do declare, from every appearance, that it was impossible for him any longer to maintain a conflict, in which he was so severely hurt. The seat of his complaint is in his loins; and I have no doubt but the excruciating pains he must then have experienced, was sufficient to deprive him of the ability to stand.

HENRY SAFFORY
Thursday, Jan. 10, 1788.
Devonshire Street.

HUMPHRIES to The World, 14 January 1788

Notwithstanding my declaration, previous to the Battle between me and Mr Mendoza – that whether I was beaten, or I beat him, I would never fight again; yet, as in his Address to the Public, he has insinuated – that in his late contest with me, at Odiham, his being 'beaten was the mere effect of accident' – I do now declare, that I am ready to meet him at any time, not exceeding three months from the present date – on condition, that as it is merely to oblige him that I once more enter the lists with him, the sum we fight for, shall not be less than two hundred and fifty guineas a side.

The terms of fighting to be exactly the same as the last, excepting, that the whole door money shall go to the winner of the battle. The stakes to be held by the same gentleman as before.

RICHARD HUMPHREYS

A copy of the above is sent to Mr. Mendoza, with a request, that he will give a positive answer before the expiration of the week; as his longer silence will be construed as a disinclination to renew the contest.

MENDOZA, *16 January 1788*

It is with some concern, that I feel the least inducement to give a negative to the challenge of Mr. Humphreys; but I flatter myself I shall stand fully justified in the opinion of a candid public, when the conditions of that challenge are properly considered.

The first proposition of Mr. Humphreys, is to fight for 250 guineas a-side. This the public will readily perceive, is conveying (in an oblique direction) a negative in the challenge itself. The right of odds may very fairly be expected, both from the recent victory of Mr. Humphreys, and the opinion which the friends of that gentleman so warmly support, of his superior skill in the art of boxing. Yet I am bold to say, that neither these circumstances, nor any inconvenience the deposit of so large a sum may subject me to, shall prevent the contest.

The second proposition, is not altogether the most liberal; to fight within three months. Mr. Humphreys surely must be informed, that a complaint in the loins, is sometimes an unwelcome companion through life: the proposition on the one hand exhibits an hidden wish to prevent a contest, or on the other a want of feeling that can do little credit to his most sanguine friends.

The last proposition, – the winner to have the door, however it may breathe an affected sense of superiority on the side of Mr. Humphreys, I most cordially agree to. The time which was limited for my reply, being one week, is a circumstance, that will not impress the public with any additional opinion, either of the courage or candour of Mr. Humphreys.

As I have unavoidably denied my acceptance to the challenge of Mr. Humphreys, it may be expected, I should make some propositions myself: which if they appear liberal in the public eye, I shall be indifferent to any answer he may convey; whether to meet me on the stage, or rather wear: hose laurels, with which chance has crowned him.

The first proposition is, that I will meet Mr. Humphreys on the same sized stage as at Odiham, i.e. 24 by 24, and fight him for 250 guineas a side.

The second proposition – the victor shall have the door. And as the world is decidedly of opinion that Mr. Humphreys is superior in the art of boxing, the third proposition that I make is, the man who first closes shall be the loser. The time of fighting, it is impossible to mention, since the injury I have received on my loins, may continue its effects to a distant period; by the moment I am relieved from that complaint, and declared capable by the gentleman who now attends me, I shall chearfully step forward, and appoint the day.

The acceptance or denial of Mr. Humphreys to the third proposition, wilt impress the public with an additional opinion of his superior skill, or they must conclude that he is somewhat conscious of his inferiority in scientific knowledge. In imitation of the challenge of Mr. Humphreys, I shall not distress him for an immediate reply: but leave him to consult his friends, and his own feelings, and send an answer at his leisure.

I remain, Sir,
Your obedient servant, DANIEL MENDOZA.
9 White Street, Houndsditch,

HUMPHRIES, 20 January 1788

Without replying to the invidious reflections so bountifully bestowed on me by Mr. Mendoza, (which, unless we were to abide by common sense, must only expose us to the derision of a discerning public), I first observe, – that it affords me infinite pleasure, when I consider, after a week's reflection on my Answer to his Challenge, it does not contain a sentiment I could wish amended: And I mean unequivocally to abide by my first engagements, even to the article of odds; for how can he reconcile the justice of his remark on this head, with his assertion, 'that I am indebted to Chance for the Victory.'

Yet I cannot help remarking, that neither Mr. Mendoza nor his friends, seemed decided where they should fix this unlucky disaster. At first it was his ankle; and there were people who would have sworn they saw three of the bones come out – Then the disorder moved gradually to his hips; from whence, (lest it should be mistaken for a rheumatic complaint), it settled with most excruciating pains, in his loins; where I am aware it may abide as long as he finds it convenient. His relying on his Surgeon for the moment when he shall be pronounced recovered, is ridiculous; his complaint being of such nature, that himself must be the best, and only judge, when he is free from it.

It may be true, what he observes of the strain in his loins, 'that it is sometimes an unwelcome companion through life'; but does it follow, that I am to stand engaged to meet him, whenever he shall think proper to call upon me? Is there no time when a man may be supposed past his prime for boxing? Or if not, shall he never have the choice of retiring from scenes, which at once involve the hazard of his life, and reputation?

The proposition which sentences, 'the first man who closes, to be the loser,' I must confess does not more surprise me for its absurdity, than that it should come from the man, who in the last contest, was himself the first to close – not to mention the folly in depriving himself of the opportunity of gougeing, and practicing other unmanly arts, the effects of a defeated spirit. Whoever considers the above proposal, must be surprised it did not occur to him, to declare against hard blows; 'a mode of fighting' he may also 'wish to avoid' – But it is endless to trace his absurdities, – indeed, both his mode of reasoning, and the nature of his proposals, are such, that it is wonderful no one should have reminded him, that the offering them to the consideration of the Public, must be deemed an insult, where it cannot but be his interest, at least, to make a show of respect.

In fine, the sentiments of justice and liberality are readily conceived, and as easily conveyed: Presuming on this, I thought that I gave sufficient time for a direct answer; – but to give colour to artifice, that it may bear the semblance of candour, requires at least a week's meditation – or, it would be too easily detected.

Once more, I repeat it, that I shall meet him only on the conditions stated in my first letter; with this additional one, that should I be beaten through accident, he shall give me an opportunity of re-establishing my credit in another contest. It is clear, that should I accede to his ridiculous propositions, it would only be driving him to new straits – for the whole tenor of his letter only proves, that Parrying, not Fighting, is the end of his wishes.

RICHARD HUMPHREYS.

MENDOZA, 23 *January 1788*

To analyze the production of Mr. Humphreys, which appeared in your Paper of Tuesday last, would be a task, the result of which would furnish the public with but little information either useful or entertaining; yet, as there are a few points which deserve some comment, I shall stand excused in the opinion of the World for this intrusion.

The prefatory part of the address of Mr. Humphreys, is explicable only by the author; but his assertion – 'that he is determined to abide unequivocally by his first engagements, for after a few week's reflection upon his challenge, it does not contain a sentiment he could wish to amend' – is a contradiction that his pretensions to common sense, surely should have taught him to avoid: if the addition of a new proposition to his former challenge, leaves it unequivocally the same, a catalogue of conditions, from the prolific invention of Mr. Humphreys, may soon follow (like the preceding) as the intended obstacles to any future battle.

The second paragraph in the letter of Mr. Humphreys, is a distant reflection on the surgeon who attends me; but his professional abilities are too eminent, to be affected by so pitiful an attempt. The only inducement I had to abide by the declaration of my surgeon, was to exempt me from the charge of being even able to make any artificial excuse. The same paragraph fully explains the propriety of that remark; for as a specimen of candid implication, Mr. Humphreys has inserted, that the complaint in my loins may remain as long as I find it convenient.

The subsequent paragraph must meet the general current of observation: that however he may praise his good fortune for being led from the scene of battle with his life, he has, alas! too much reason to lament the loss of reputation.

However, to prevent Mr. Humphreys the apology of wasting his prime of life in the expectation of my recovery, I will engage, at all hazards, to fight him by the Meeting in October.

The assertion of Mr. Humphreys, that I closed first, is a positive falsehood; indeed, it is rather unfortunate, that this doctrine has remained so long silent: Its appearance in the Boxing-Calendar is so very ill-timed, that a candid world cannot pay it the least tribute of respect.

The opportunity of gougeing, and the practice of other unmanly arts, being totally done away in a scientific display of Boxing, should operate as assistant inducements to Mr. Humphreys to accept my challenge; particularly, since hard blows must tell. But the simple facts are there: Mr. Humphreys is afraid; he dare not meet me as a Boxer: – he retires with the fullest conviction of his want of scientific knowledge; and though he has the advantage of strength and age; – though a teacher of the art, he meanly shrinks from a public trial of that skill, on which his bread depends. To intrude any further on the indulgence of a candid Public, would be altogether improper; as such, I shall conclude this address with the addition only of one observation; that though conquered by Mr. Humphreys in the battle at Odiham, I entertain a meaner opinion of his abilities as a Professional Boxer, than when I first met him on the stage.

I remain, Sir, yours,
DANIEL MENDOZA.
No. 9, White-Street, Houndsditch.

HUMPHRIES. 24 January 1788

I entirely agree with Mr. Mendoza, 'That it is highly improper to intrude farther on the indulgence of a candid public' – and, therefore, it is my determination, not to enter into the particulars of his last letter, though replete with evasion, absurdity, and falsehood. Thus much I do venture to pronounce – tho' no Critic – a character which Mr. Mendoza has, in the opinion of every one, very unsuccessfully aimed at some fame as a Boxer, I flatter myself, I am entitled to – as such, and on the terms already proposed on my part, I am ready to meet him; and with his immediate and unreserved acceptance or refusal of these terms, shall end our literary intercourse.

Mr Mendoza says, 'I am afraid of him' – The only favour I have to beg, is, that he, or any of his friends, will be kind enough to tell me so personally, and spare me the trouble of seeking them.

RICHARD HUMPHREYS

MENDOZA, 27 January 1788

To prevent the tedious necessity of a reference to the several letters which I have written, and which have appeared in your paper; I am induced to take my leave of the public, with the insertion once more of the conditions of my challenge to Mr. Humphreys; and I beg that the world will consider them, as open to the acceptance of that gentleman, whenever he may think better of his boxing abilities.

The first condition is, that I will fight him for 250 guineas a side; the second, the victor to have the door; third, the man who first closes to be the loser; fourth and last, the time of fighting to be in the October Newmarket Meeting.

Mr. Humphreys would do well to insert this challenge in his memorandum book; and as a teacher in the art of boxing, it would not be amiss to have it well penned, neatly framed, and hung up in his truly *Scientific Academy*.

I remain, Sir, your humble servant,
DANIEL MENDOZA
No. 9, White-street, Houndsditch

HUMPHRIES, *11 May 1789*

As many reports have been circulated in consequence of the issue of the late engagement between myself and Mendoza, highly injurious to my character, and without the smallest foundation, I think it a duty to myself to offer some public vindication of my conduct, being conscious of having acted with the most honest endeavours to gratify the expectations of my friends, and the curiosity of the public. Prejudices of the kind which I allude to, are easily received into the minds of people who are rendered more susceptible of them by disappointment, but are always removed with great difficulty. Having, therefore, so arduous a task to perform, I fear I shall be under the necessity of trespassing longer than I could wish on the public attention, in giving a full detail of the most material circumstances which attended the battle: I shall, however, state them with so strict an observance of truth, as to compel an admission of them, from the most interested and partial friends of my opponent.

It will be unnecessary to give a minute account of the battle previous to that dispute to which I attribute the issue of the contest: it will be sufficient to declare, that uniformly from the beginning till that time, the odds were two to one in my favour.

After the battle had continued near half an hour, I attacked Mendoza with such exertion and success, as to produce a change sufficiently apparent to heighten the betts as far as three to one. It has since transpired, and the assertion I am now about to make will be supported by the testimony of many respectable persons who were witnesses to the declaration of Ryan, that Mendoza at that time whispered to his bottle-holder, that he was unable any longer to continue the engagement. However, at the instance of

Ryan, he was persuaded once more to meet me, at which time, as a last effort, he aimed a blow with all the strength he was then possessed of, which I receiving on my left arm at the very moment when I was in the act of stepping backwards, I unavoidably fell to the ground. Upon this Mendoza instantly undertook to decide the battle in his own favour, by withdrawing himself from the ring, and declaring the fall thus unavoidably occasioned, to be unfair. Sir Thomas Apprice, who was then present as Mendoza's umpire, threw up his hat as a signal of his concurrence. Upon this Mr. Coombe, who stood in the same relation to me as Sir Thomas did to Mendoza, went up to enquire what reason he assigned for thus endeavouring to assume the victory, at the same time declaring upon his honour, that he had seen the blow which had thus unavoidably occasioned my fall. Sir Thomas only declared that he had not seen it, but would not take upon himself to declare that such blow had not been received. Thus far I thought the determination of the umpires was sufficiently decisive to have prevented any further protraction of the battle; yet notwithstanding I went up repeatedly to Mendoza, and challenged him to renew the contest, although the time for setting to again had been repeatedly called by my umpire; after I had advanced into the middle of the ring and thrown up my hat in token of defiance, as well as to mark my claim to the victory in consequence of his not obeying the summons of the umpire to appear, Mendoza still persisted in an obstinate refusal to meet me for the space of an hour and a quarter. At this time Mendoza was told, that unless he would come forward to the engagement, he should not be allowed any part of the money collected at the door, and was thus at length persuaded to meet me once more. At the time when this dispute arose I was in a profuse sweat, but being thus obliged to remain for so long a time inactive, the perspiration was checked, and I then felt the effects of a rheumatic complaint, with which, it is universally known, I had been last winter very severely afflicted, although I had so far recovered from it as entirely to remove all apprehension of feeling such consequences during the time of my continuing to perspire.

Under these disadvantages I was to meet a man again, who had enjoyed a long and uninterrupted series of good health, who could by no means feel the same inconvenience from such interruption, but who on the contrary had a manifest advantage in thus obtaining time sufficient to recover himself, in a great measure, from the effects of the blows which he had received.

After the renewal of the battle, and the further continuance of it for a considerable time, I made a blow at Mendoza, and in endeavouring to retreat from his return blow, I sunk down, without the power of recovering myself, which not being deemed by the umpires to be an accidental fall, the battle was decided against me. As I am very confident after a battle obtained against me under such circumstances as are here related, and after one decisive victory on my side, that the superiority is not on the part of my antagonist, I have this evening sent Mendoza the following challenge.

R. HUMPHREYS.
Bernard's Inn, May 11

To Mr. MENDOZA

I have stated to the Public the reasons which induced me to send you this challenge, which I offer on the following terms.

1st. That you meet me at any time in October next that you will fix.

2dly. That there shall be no money collected at the door, in order to obviate any suspicion which may arise, that that was the object of our meeting. 3dly. You shall name the sum which you wish to fight for.

4thly. I leave the terms of our engagement to your own appointment.

R. HUMPHREYS.

MENDOZA *May 16 1789*

Mr HUMPHREYS,

It has not arisen from inattention, that I have delayed a reply to your challenge, but solely to arrange my engagements in the manner that will best enable me to comply with your wishes.

I have made at Manchester, Liverpool, and other places, appointments to exhibit publicly, and to teach the art of Boxing, which take place the middle of June, and will necessarily detain me in the country for some months: I am under the necessity, therefore, of declining your offer to meet in October; but submit the following terms to your consideration.

1st, I will either meet you on any day within the first week of the month of June next, or on the 5th day of May, 1790.

2dly, I do not insist on a collection at the door: but to obviate any idea that that is the object of our meeting, I propose that the money so collected, after defraying unavoidable expenses, shall be given to the poor of the parish where we fight.

3dly, I will fight you for love – or the same sum for which we fought at Stilton.

4thly, I will fight you on turf, inclosed in a circle of equal dimensions as at our last contest – a stand-up fight – the person falling without a blow, to lose the battle.

5thly, That both Seconds, at the setting-to of the parties, shall retire to the sides of the place enclosed. The place of fight, umpires, and other preliminary conditions, to be settled at a previous meeting of our respective friends.

I am,
Your very humble Servant.
DANIEL MENDOZA
No. 3, Paradise Row, Bethnal Green

Appendix C

DANIEL MENDOZA'S PRINCIPAL FIGHTS

Tom Tyne	7 November	1785	Wanstead	L
Tom Tyne	July	1786	Croydon	W
Sam Martin	17 April	1787	Barnet	W
Richard Humphries	9 January	1788	Odiham, Hampshire	L
Richard Humphries	6 May	1789	Stilton	W
Richard Humphries	29 September	1790	Doncaster	W
Squire Fitzgerald	2 August	1791	Dublin	W
William Warr	14 May	1792	Smitham Bottom, Croydon	W
William Warr	12 November	1794	Bexley heath	W
John Jackson	15 April	1795	Hornchurch	L
Harry Lee	21 March	1806		W
Tom Owen	4 July	1820	Banstead Downs	L

Appendix D

CAPTION TO JAMES GILLRAY'S PRINT OF THE FIGHT AT ODIHAM

Foul Play, Or Humphreys And Johnson A Match For Mendoza

Dedicated to Wilson Braddyl esqr., Gymnastico Generalissimo. This extraordinary Match was Fought at Odiham in Hampshire Jany. 9th 1788, after 25 Minutes Contest, Mendoza by his superior Skill carrying off the Honors of the day from his Antagonist, when Johnson after having recovered Humphries (who was nearly deprived of Life from a Knock-down Blow) by pouring cold water on his Stomach, finding him still weak & staggering from another blow, & Mendoza aiming another which must have decided the Battle very Judicously steped in between, & by his address entirely changed the Scene; in consequence of which, several Gentlemen (who did not wish to gain by collusion) withdrew their Betts. Humphrey [sic] relying on such another Step, has thought proper to accept Mendoza's Challenge for another Combat, but like a bold Briton! has proposed such terms, as he knows his antagonist cannot possibly comply with from the state of his finances!!!— "I have done the Jew!" . . . Humphries Letter to Braddyl.'"

GLOSSARY

An amalgam of Georgian definitions. Those of a more sardonic tone come chiefly from John Bee's *Slang*.

Advancing – This is necessary when your opponent gives way. It is done by stepping a pace forward with the leg that is foremost, and then with your hindmost foot, so as never to lose your original position. If he continues to retreat methodically, follow him in that manner; but if he runs from you, it would be folly to advance according to method.

Arguefy the topic – a phrase used of boxing matches by Captain Topham

Bodiers – blows upon belly or ribs, including breast

Bar – To bar a blow is to stop its effect, by placing your arm on the part which it is aimed at.

Blue ruin – gin

Boring-in – when one man hammers away at another, pressing forward *a la* Scroggins

Bottle holder – An assistant to the second, so termed from his carrying a bottle of water on the stage, for the use of the person fighting.

Bottom – to have this is to have physical resources, stamina, staying power; substance, strength of character, dependability. (OED)

Box, boxer, boxing – 'To box', to fight; he who fights is a boxer, and the pair are then boxing. Very inelegant when used in the second person; for he boxes' he fights is substituted. 'Tis 'A boxing bout' when two commoners meet; but 'a battle' or 'a fight' is adopted for a manly contest between men of scientific attainment.

Breadbasket – the stomach area

Brisket or breast cut – showy but harmless

Champion – no emolument ever arose from this honour, but casual presents often, and the acclaim of all the Fancy.

Chancery – A man whose head is under his antagonist's left arm while the right is punishing out his day-lights, is 'in a Chancery suit,' from which Lord Eldon could not relieve him, though old Thurlow might.

Chopper – A blow that descends straight down the features, the knuckles making fine work thereon. Not a desirable strategie; originating with Dan Menduzca; now little used.

Claret – Not fit to drink. A softened term for the stream of life.

Commissary-general – Bill Gibbon, in whom centres the news as to where fights are to take place, he having the care of the P.C. ropes, stakes and whips, for making a ring. His pay, three quid.

Conk – the nose

Counter-hit – When both hit from the same side, as a left-hander for a right.

Crib – a house

Crimps – persons employed in procuring seamen for the merchants during war: mostly Jews, and invariably cheats. None employed for the army since 1792.

Cross-buttock – When one man can get his hip-bone hard against his antagonist, equally low down, twisting him with head and limbs off his balance, any how, the latter receives a heavy fall or throw on his head – 'tis a settler for him.

Daffy – gin

Dropping – Falling on your breech, your knee, or your back, to escape the coming blow of your adversary.

Drops – A blow by which a man is sent down on the spot where he stands, like being shot.

Facer – a straight blow imparted on the face

Feint – A blow aimed at the head (say) but not sent home, while the other hand alights on the mark.

Fighting in-fighting – where the men come close together; perhaps lay hold, struggle, chancery suit, and ultimately fall. It is frequently the termination of off-fighting; which consists in placing a blow, parrying it, and returning with the like hand; or counter hitting, then recovering the guard, or position, and defending the vital parts as at first. **Out-fighting** a man is mostly applicable to Millers, but may extend to all classes of boxers: when a man repeats his blows more fast and heavy than his opponent, the latter is 'out-fought.' Bacon, that gumptious fellow, says, 'An Irishman fights before he reasons; a Scotchman reasons before he fights; an Englishman is not particular as to the order of precedence, but will do either, to accommodate his customers!'

Fist – In the ring, they are to be made up with the thumb outside, covering the first knuckle of the fore-finger, and a little more of the middle one: he who covers his thumb must not hit – even a woolpack; he is then coney-thumbed. Neither does a pugilist quite close his fist until, the blow is let go; millers and haminermen slobber-away as they like. Fist is wholly masculine: when a female makes up a fist, she is no longer a woman, and must be floored like a man.

Flabbergasted – In ring-affairs, a man may be flabbergasted by a flush hit between the eyes, whether with the gloves or without them.

Flash – knowing

Floorer – a knock-down blow. But a man may be floored by losing all his blunt, or having the house burnt about his ears. 'Floored him clean,' a knock down at full length.

Game – to be so meant to 'maintain one's spirit and endurance to the last'. (OED) Hardiness to endure, and resolution to stand against, the severity of an adversary's blows.

Gouging – Screwing your knuckles into the eye of your adversary. A practice not very frequent, nor much commended amongst boxers. Mendoza once played Humphreys this trick during their battle at Odiham.

Grappling – Closing in upon your opponent.

'Grassed neatly' – is a prettier expression than floored, when the act is performed on Nature's natural garb!

Guard – The posture best calculated to prevent your adversary from striking you, more commonly applied to the first position.

Hammer – when a man hits very hard, chiefly with a favourite hand, his blows are said to fall like those of a sledge-hammer. Such boxers are hammering fighters, that do not defend their own vitals, cannot make sure of a blow, and are termed hammerers and hammermen. They are not Pugilists.

Hammering boxers—are great country loobies, who possess no one quality for the exercise but strength, the consciousness whereof gives them pluck. These hammer away for an hour or two, hearken not to the call of time, 'and turn a deaf ear to enough,' always act most unfairly in other respects, and sometimes commit murder – for which they deserve the halter.

Heavy wet – beer

Hebrews – Jews are so called from the language spoken, and they are treated as a distinct nation, though 'tis evident a Jew may be an Irishman or an Englishman. 'You may as well talk Hebrew,' said of jargon; because the Hebrew (so called) spoken by the Jews is of the German dialectic; the character of which also differs from that of the sacred, as both do from the Rabbinical.

Hit – A blow or stroke that actually takes place.

Ivories – teeth

Jackey – gin

Manoeuvre – Any piece of skill in fighting, by which you accomplish your own intentions, and frustrate those of your adversary.

Mark – The pit of the stomach. So called, from its being the object at which a stroke most likely to put an end to a battle can be aimed.

Mauleys – boxing gloves

Max – gin

Millers – second-rate boxers, whose arms run round in rapid succession, not always falling very hard, or with determinate object; and they seldom win against equal strength in a scientific opponent – but by accident. Gas was a miller; the Hudsons were nothing else – but Josh. improves. Shelton is a reformed miller: Scroggins, an incorrigible one.

Moulder – a lumbering boxer.

Mufflers – gloves with wool stuffed upon the knuckles, for boxers to spar withal, and not hurt each other TOO MUCH; claret comes sometimes.

Muzzler – a blow slanting upwards placed on the upper lip or tip of the nose.

Nob – the head

Ogles – the eyes

One-two – when both hands are applied to the antagonist quickly, a saying created in Bristol.

Out and Outer – someone who sticks, no matter what.

Parry – to prevent blows landing on the body, whereupon the receiver should return with the same hand.

Philistines – sheriffs' officers and their followers; revenue officers; the press-gang, and police officers.

Phiz – the face

Practice – in Boxing, as in every other science, is the great requisite to acquire a perfect knowledge of it. It should not be neglected while you have a friend to spar with, or a glass to stand before. A glass will, indeed, set you right with regard to the securest attitude, and you may strike and practice the lessons before it. The same use may be made of a candle, if you stand between its light and the wainscot, on which your shadow may be observed with much advantage. A companion to spar with, is, however, of still greater service than either, as he obliges you more closely to unite practice with theory. If you happen to be where there is neither candle nor glass, you may amuse yourself by striking forward with each arm successively. By repeating this you will find yourself able to strike much oftener and quicker in any certain, limited space of time, than you could at first. The same may be done with a pair of dumb bells in your hands, of a weight just adapted to your age and strength.

Purr – the rushing in, Lancashire fashion, with the head against the opponent's guts. Return blow – one having planted a hit, the other within a colon-pause, returns with like hand.

Ring – the roped space within which pugilists display their science or their hardihood usually about 24 feet each way, and by an easy transition, applied to those who look on, or take delight in the manly, peaceful contests there exhibited. 'I leave it to the ring.' 'Not a voice was heard all round the ring.' They are divided into amateurs (persons of property) and the men, or boxers, part of whom only are pugilists. The word is derived from a certain circular space enclosed with rails in Hyde Park, by command of George II. Having a large oak in the middle; the area is now planted with young limes and the railing is decayed; going strait up from Grosvenor-gate, the ring lies about 550 steps into the park.

Round – when boxers set-to, they fight till down, and that is a round; the next round begins not until half a minute, at least, has expired. Any deviation, attended with fatal consequences, is an act constituting manslaughter, on the part of the assistants.

Rush – when a milling cove runs in at his opponent hitting away hard and sharp, his head is more or less low. Such must be received by sharp right and left nobbers, continuing to retreat; and tis fair and safe to tumble over the ropes, or drop, as if from the blows.

Scratch – can be real or supposed

Second – (seldom performed completely) one who aids with advice the actual pugilist, or, indeed, boxer; who, when his principal is down, raiseth him up, bodily, supports him on his knee, gives advice as to the opponent's weak points, admonisheth him if neglectful – cheers him up – moisteneth his lips with water or orange, and, as the contest is protracted, with brandy diluted, – who, if an accident happens, takes prompt means of alleviation. He must be furnished with a lancet, to let out the extravasated blood below the puff'; and never desert his man on account of reverse of luck.

Shiver – 'Shiver his fist' when a boxer means mischief and nothing else, he shakes his hand, and generally lets fly with it. This happens early in the battle, usually; but 'tis a symptom of gayness that leaves a man, as the contest approaches towards 'finis'.

Shifting – Running from your adversary whenever he attempts to hit you, or to come near you, or when you have struck him: this is practised with a view of tiring him out.

Spurr (Spar) – fighting demonstrated: lessons in the art. Game chickens are said to sparr, when they fight for the mastery, which it is desirable one or the other should obtain soon, to prevent everlasting rows in the walk. Pugilists learn the art of personal defence, with gloves on, that are stuffed upon the knuckles; this is sparring; if they would learn the mode of attack, let them begin early the actual set-to. Dr. Johnson spelt the word with one (r) only; but, saving his prescience, he knew nothing at all about sparring, he being but a single-fight man, having once floored Tom Osborn, the bibliopolian. His spar is a long – it pole, used on board ships; and a fine piece of fun it would have been to see the old gent riding like a bear astride one of these up Streatham-hill where was his den. He gives no etymology, but simply says, 'Spar, v. N. To fight with prelusive strokes.' Whereas, every cocker and pugilist knows right well, that 'tis any thing but fighting: it comes from the verb to spare, which in the gerund takes an additional [r], and keeps it when we return to the infinitive again; for the earliest use of the word, which is in *Froissard's Chronicles*, the distinction was drawn to a great nicety: he says, The Englishmen on one parte, and the Scottes on the other, be goode men of warre; for when they doe mete, there is a hard fighte, without sparynge.

Stop – a blow – to prevent its alighting on the part intended by means of the guard or position of defence – i.e. The forearm or elbow. 'But this was effected differently by the several schools: the Broughtonian caught the coming blow on the perpendicular arm, which enabled them to take a quick return, cutting downwards. Mendoza's consisted of throwing up the arm from the elbow, catching the adversary at the wrist or higher, which disabled the muscle and spoiled that arm awhile – when he chopped.

Tom Owen's Stop – the left hand open, scrawling over the antagonist's face, service with the right.

Toss – one of the preliminaries of a regular fight; he who wins the toss plaving his back towards the sun at each setting-to. At Blenheim the Bavarian had his face to the sun and got diddled by Marlborough.

Wind – Breath. By too violent exertion in fighting a person becomes winded, or out of breath. The wind may be much improved by frequent practice, and greatly recovered when lost in fighting, if the person fatigued acts judiciously. He should play with his hands to and fro, fight only on the defensive, and if struck, fall, and lay flat on the ground until his second picks him up; by thus easing himself, his powers of respiration will gradually return.

BIBLIOGRAPHY

Online Sources
British Library Newspapers 1600–1950
The British Newspaper Archive
Convict Records of Australia
Jewish Roots
Newspaperarchive.com
Oxford Dictionary of National Biography
The Proceedings of the Old Bailey, 1674–1913

Primary Sources
The Annual Register
Anon, *The Sporting Magazine*, Volume 9, Rogerson & Tuxford, 1797
'A Friend to Rational Debate' – 'Arguments upon Boxing or Pugilism' – *The British Forum*—1806
A Highland Officer, *Anti-Pugilism; or, the Science of defence, exemplified in ... lessons for the practice of the broad sword and single stick*. London, J. Aitkin, 1790
An Amateur of Eminence, *The Complete Art of Boxing*, according to the modern method; wherein the whole of that manly accomplishment is rendered so easy and intelligent, that any person may be an entire master of then science in a few days, without any other instruction than this book. London, Printed for M. Follingsby, 1788

Astley's Cuttings – British Library

Bee, John (John Badcock) *Fancy-Ana; or, A History of Pugilism, From Figg and Broughton's Time to Spring and Langan's, including every transaction in the prize-ring, and every incident worthy notice (whether of spree, turn-up, boxing-match, or prize-fight) from 1719 to 1824, inclusive – Third edition, corrected and enlarged,* London, printed by W. Lewis *c.*1825

Bee, John (John Badcock), *Slang. A dictionary of the turf, the ring, the chase, the pit, of bon-ton, and the varieties of life, forming the completest and most authentic lexicon balatronicum ... of the sporting world, etc.* London, T. Hughes, 1823

Bevis Marks Records: The circumcision register of Isaac and Abraham de Paiba (1715–1775)

Bowditch, J., *Imprisonment for debt: A letter on the present state of the law of arrest: The duty of the sheriff and his officer, their fees, &c. as fully laid down, with a few hints in practice on the law of bail and render, intended as a guide to the merchant and tradesman: to which is added the recent decision of the Court of Queen's Bench in the case of a sheriff's officer* Hume Tracts, 1837

Defoe, Daniel, *A tour thro' the whole island of Great Britain, divided into circuits or journies,* London, JM Dent & Co, 1927 (originally published 1727)

Dowling, Frank Lewis, *Fistiana; or, The Oracle of the Ring. Comprising a defence of British boxing; a brief history of pugilism from the earliest ages to the present period; practical instructions for training; together with chronological tables of prize battles, from 1700 to 1840, inclusive, alphabetically arranged with the issue of each event. Scientific hints on sparring, etc, etc, etc New rules of the ring. Form of articles, duties of seconds, bottle-holders, and umpires and referees; hints on sparring and boxing; attributes of a pugilist, training, its use and practice; with copious instructions.* London, William Clement, Jun, 1841

Doyle, Sir Arthur Conan, *Rodney Stone,* 1896

Edwards & Knibb, *Encyclopedia of comic songs, English, Scotch, and Irish, both of old times and new, etc.* London, 1819

Egan, Pierce, *Boxiana; or Sketches of Ancient and Modern Pugilism, from the days of then renowned Broughton and Slack, to the Championship of Crib,* Vols I & II, London, Sherwood Neely and Jones, 1818

Egan, Pierce, *Boxiana; or Sketches of Ancient and Modern Pugilism, from the days of the renowned Broughton and Slack, to the Championship of Crib to Spring's Challenge to all England*, Vol III, London, Sherwood Neely and Jones, 1821

Egan, Pierce and Jon Bee, *Boxiana, or sketches of modern pugilism, containing all the transactions of note, connected with the prize ring, during the years 1821, 1822, 1823*, Vol IV, London, Sherwood, Jones and Co, 1824

Egan, Pierce, *Boxiana*, London, G. Vertue, 1830 (facsimile, Adamant Media Corporation, 2006)

Egan, Pierce, *Sporting Anecdotes*, London, Sherwood, Jones & Co., 1825

Fewtrell, Thomas, *Boxing Reviewed, or, The Science of Manual Defence*, London, 1790

Hazlitt, William, *Selected Essays*, London, The Nonesuch Press, 1946

Henning, Fred. *Fights for the Championship – The Men and Their Times*, London, Reprinted from the 'Licensed Victuallers' Gazette', 1900

Jackson, William. *The New and Complete Newgate Calendar*, 8 vols, London, 1800–1812

Lamb, Charles and Mary, *The Letters of Charles and Mary Lamb*, Vol II, Cornell University Press, 1975–8

Mendoza, Daniel, *The Art of Boxing*, London, 1789

Mendoza, Daniel, *The memoirs of the life of Daniel Mendoza: containing a faithful narrative of the various vicissitudes of his life, and an account of the numerous contests in which he has been engaged, with observations on each: comprising also genuine anecdotes of many distinguished characters, to which are added, observations on the art of pugilism; rules to be observed with regard to training, etc. – A New Edition*, London, Hayden, 1816

Mendoza, Daniel (ed. Alex Joanides), *Memoirs of the Life of Daniel Mendoza*, London, Romeville Enterprises, 2011

Mendoza, Daniel, (ed. Paul Magriel), *The Memoirs of the Life of Daniel Mendoza*, London, Batsford, 1951

Miles, Henry Downes, *Pugilistica: Being One Hundred and Forty-Four Years of the History of British Boxing.*, London, Weldon & Co, 1880

Oxberry, W., *Pancratia, or, A History of Pugilism*, London, Oxberry / Sherwood, Neely & Jones, 1812

Swift, Owen, *The Hand Book to Boxing,* London, Nicholson, 1840

Thornbury, Walter, *Old and New London, Volume I,* London, Paris & New York Cassel, Petter, Galpin & Co., 1875

Thornbury, Walter, 'Hockley-in-the-Hole.' *Old and New London: Volume 2.* London: Cassell, Petter & Galpin, 1878. 306–309. *British History Online.* Web. 21 March 2018. http://www. british-history.ac.uk/old-new-london/vol2/pp306-309.

Secondary Sources

Allen, Julia, *Swimming with Dr Johnson and Mrs Thrale – Sport, Health and Exercise in Eighteenth-century England,* Cambridge, Lutterworth, 2012

Amelang, James S., *The Flight of Icarus: Artisan Autobiography in Early Modern Europe,* Stanford, Stanford University Press, 1998

Baer, Marc, *Theatre and Disorder in Late Georgian London,* Oxford, OUP, 1992

Baker, James William, 'The Covent Garden Old Price Riots: Protest and Justice in Late-Georgian London' https://olh.openlibhums. org/articles/10.16995/olh.13/ *Open Library of Humanities*

Berkowitz, Michael and Ruti Ungar, *Fighting Back: Jewish and Black Boxers in Britain,* London, Department of Hebrew and Jewish Studies, University College London, 2007

Blady, Ken, *Jewish Boxers' Hall of Fame,* New York, Shapolsky, 1988

Boddy, Kasia, *Boxing, A Cultural History,* London, Reaktion, 2008

Booth, Alan, 'Popular Loyalism and Public Violence in the North-West of England, 1790–1800', *Social History*, Vol 8, No. 3 (Oct 1983) pp. 295–313

Brailsford, Dennis, *Bareknuckles: A Social History of Prize-Fighting,* Cambridge, Lutterworth Press. 1988

Braverman, R. Spectator 495: Addison and 'The Race of People Called Jews' *Studies in English Literature, 1500–1900,* 34(3), 537–552. (1994). Retrieved from http://www.jstor.org/stable/450881

Brodie, Daniel 'The Jewish Strong Man: Daniel Mendoza and the Assault on Stereotype in Late Georgian England', Unpublished Master's thesis, McGill University, 2011

Chancellor, V. E., 'Anti-Racialism or Censorship? The 1802 Jewish Riots at Covent Garden Opera and the Career of Thomas John Dibdin', *The Opera Quarterly,* 18.1 (2002), pp.18–25

Chill, Adam, *Bare-Knuckle Britons and Fighting Irish: Boxing, Race, Religion and Nationality in the 18th and 19th Centuries*, Jefferson, North Carolina, McFarland & Company, 2017

Christopher, Emma, *A Merciless Place*, Crows Nest NSW, Allen & Unwin, 2010

Cruickshank, Dan, *The Secret History of Georgian London*, London, Random House, 2009

Davison, Neil, 'Pugilism in *Ulysses*: Round Two', *James Joyce Quarterly*, vol 32, No. 3 / 4. 1995

Edwards, Lewis, 'Daniel Mendoza', *Transactions (Jewish Historical Society of England)* Vol. 15 (1939–1945), pp.73–92

Endelman, Todd M.. *The Jews of Georgian England, 1714–1830: Tradition and Change in a Liberal Society*, Ann Arbor. University of Michigan Press, 1999

Foer, Franklin, and Marc Tracy, *Jewish Jocks, An Unorthodox Hall of Fame*, New York, Twelve, 2013

Ford, John, *Prizefighting – The Age of Regency Boxing*. Newton Abbot, David and Charles, 1971

Gartner, L. 'Emancipation, Social Change and Communal Reconstruction in Anglo-Jewry 1789–1881', *Proceedings of the American Academy for Jewish Research*, 54, (1987) pp.73–116. Retrieved from http://www.jstor.org/stable/3622581

Gee, Tony, *Up to Scratch: Bareknuckle Fighting and Heroes of the Prize-ring*, Harpenden, Queen Anne Press, 1998

Gee, Tony, 'Daniel Mendoza', *Oxford Dictionary of National Biography* http://www.oxforddnb.com/view/10.1093/ref:odnb/9780198614128.001.0001/odnb-9780198614128-e-18556

George, M. Dorothy, *London Life in the Eighteenth Century*, Harmondsworth, Penguin, 1976 (Reprint, original 1925)

Harrow, Sharron (ed), *Sporting Literature and Culture in the Long Eighteenth Century*, London, Routledge, 2015

Hartley, R. A. *History and Bibliography of Boxing Books*, Alton, Hants, Nimrod Press Ltd, 1989 (?)

Hartnoll, Phyllis, *A Concise History of the Theatre*, London, Thames & Hudson, 1968

Harvey, Adrian, *The Beginnings of a Commercial Sporting Culture In Britain, 1793–1850, Aldershot*, Ashgate, 2004

Henriques, 'The Jewish Emancipation Controversy in Nineteenth-Century Britain,' *Past & Present*, (40), (1968). pp, 126–146. Retrieved from http://www.jstor.org/stable/650071

Inglis, Lucy, *Georgian London, Into the Streets,* London, Penguin, 2013

Jacobs, Joseph, 'England', *The Jewish Encyclopedia,* New York, Funk & Wagnall, 1906

Joy, Peter, 'Champion of England', *Jewish Quarterly* Vol. 52, No. 4 (2005) pp.54–62

Levi, J. S., *Australian Genesis: Jewish convicts and settlers 1788–1850,* Adelaide, Rigby, 1974

Liberles, R. 'The Jews and Their Bill: Jewish Motivations in the Controversy of 1753', *Jewish History,* 2(2), (1987). 29–36. Retrieved from http://www.jstor.org/stable/20101042

Liebling, A. J., *The Sweet Science, Boxing and Boxiana: A Ringside View.* Penguin Classics, 2018

Mailer, Norman, *The Fight,* London, Hart-Davis MacGibbon, 1975

Matar, N., 'The English Romantic Poets and the Jews', *Jewish Social Studies,* 50(3/4), (1988). 223–238. Retrieved from http://www.jstor.org/stable/4467425

McIlvanney, Hugh, *McIlvanney on Boxing,* London, Mainstream Publishing, 1996

Oates, Joyce Carol, *On Boxing,* London, Bloomsbury, 1997

Oxford Dictionary of National Biography

Popkin, R. David Levi, Anglo-Jewish Theologian. *The Jewish Quarterly Review,* 87 (1/2), 79–101. (1996). Retrieved from http://www.jstor.org/stable/1455218

Rabin, D. The Jew Bill of 1753: Masculinity, Virility, and the Nation. *Eighteenth-Century Studies,* 39(2), (2006). 157–171. Retrieved from http://www.jstor.org/stable/30053433

Ragussis, M. 'Jews and Other "Outlandish Englishmen": Ethnic Performance and the Invention of British Identity under the Georges', *Critical Inquiry,* 26(4), 2000, 773–797. Retrieved from http://www.jstor.org/stable/1344330

Reid, J. C. *Bucks and Brusiers: Pierce Egan and Regency England,* London, Routledge & Kegan Paul, 1971

Reitlinger, Gerald R. 'The Changed Face of English Jewry at the End of the Eighteenth Century', *Transactions & Miscellanies (Jewish Historical Society of England),* vol. 23, 1969, pp. 34–43. *JSTOR,* www.jstor.org/stable/29778784.

Ribalow, Harold U., *Fighter from Whitechapel – The Story of Daniel Mendoza,* New York, Farrar, Strauss and Cudahy and the Jewish Publication Society, 1962

Rubens, Alfred, 'Jews and the English Stage, 1667—1850' *Transactions & Miscellanies (Jewish Historical Society of England)* Vol. 24 (1970–1973), pp. 151–170

Rude, George, *The History of London: Hanoverian London 1714–1808,* London, Secker & Warburg. 1971

Schama, Simon, *Belonging: The Story of the Jews, 1492–1900,* London, The Bodley Head, 2017

Schechter, Ronald and Liz Clarke, *Mendoza the Jew: Boxing, Manliness and Nationalism,* New York, Oxford, OUP, 2014

Smith, R. 'The London Jews' Society and Patterns of Jewish Conversion in England, 1801–1859', *Jewish Social Studies,* 43(3/4), (1981). 275–290. Retrieved from http://www.jstor.org/stable/4467142

Snowdon, David. *Writing the Prizefight: Pierce Egan's Boxiana World,* Bern, Peter Lang, 2013

Warner, J. 'Violence against and among Jews in An Early Modern Town: Tolerance and Its Limits in Portsmouth, 1718–1781', *Albion: A Quarterly Journal Concerned with British Studies,* 35(3), (2003) pp.428–448. Retrieved from http://www.jstor.org/stable/4054062

White, Jerry, *London in the Eighteenth Century: A Great and Monstrous Thing,,* London, Vintage, 2012

Williams, Luke G., *Richmond Unchained,* Stroud, Amberley, 2015

TIMELINE

YEAR	MENDOZA	JEWS	BOXING	POLITICS	OTHER
1290		Jews expelled from England			
1653	Birth of Abigail Penha Castro (great-great grandmother)				
1655	Birth of David Mendoza (great-great grandfather)	Menassah ben Israel meets with Cromwell			
1656		Resettlement of the Jews in England			
1657		First synagogue			
1684	David Mendoza marries Abigail Penha Castro				
1692		Great Synagogue			
1700		Sir Solomon di Mendina knighted			
1701		Bevis Marks Synagogue founded			
1707		Hambro Synagogue founded			

YEAR	MENDOZA	JEWS	BOXING	POLITICS	OTHER
1709	Grandfather Aaron Mendoza born Grandmother Benvenida Tobi born				
1730	Aaron Mendoza marries Benvenida Tobi				
1740					
1743			Broughton's rules		
1746				Jacobite rebellion – Culloden	
1750			April – Slack defeats Broughton		
1751					
1752	Abraham Mendoza (father) marries Esther Lopez				
1753		Jew Bill passed and then repealed			
1754					
1755					
1756				Seven Years War	
1757					
1758	Isaac (brother) born				

1760		Board of Deputies founded	George III succeeds to the throne	
1765	DM Born 5 July			
1766				
1767				
1768				RA founded. *Encyclopaedia Britannica* begins publication
1769				Australia and NZ declared British colonies
1770			Lord North PM	
1771		Chelsea murder		First cotton mill
1772		Partitions of Poland. Emigration to Palestine	Slavery outlawed in England	
1773			Inclosure Act. Boston Tea Party	Stock Exchange formed at Jonathan's coffee house. *She Stoops to Conquer* – Covent Garden
1774				

YEAR	MENDOZA	JEWS	BOXING	POLITICS	OTHER
1775		Mob violence against Jews in Hebron		US War of Independence	
1776		17 December Official fast to wish success against the rebels in America		US Declaration of Independence	
1777					*School for Scandal*
1778				First iron bridge built	
1779					
1780	DM fights a tea porter			Gordon Riots: protest against Catholic Relief Act of 1778	
1781				Yorktown – defeat of British in America Freedom of religion in United States	
1782	DM found guilty of robbery, transported to west coast of Africa [?]				Sarah Siddons at Covent Garden
1783					
1784	DM's sister Benvenida dies DM defeats Harry the Coal heaver at Mile End [?]			Pitt reduces tax on tea from 119 per cent to 11 per cent	First mail coach London to Bristol

1785	7 November beaten by Tom Tyne in Wanstead				
1786	Defeats John Matthews at Kilburn Wells Defeats Tom Tyne at Leytonstone		Fight between Tom Johnson and Bill Love, in Barnet 5 May Martin v Humphries, Newmarket		
1787	17 April Defeats Sam Martin, the Bath butcher, at Barnet 22 May marries Esther Opens Boxing Academy at Capel Court Sept – set-to with Humphries	Conversion of Lord George Gordon	18 Jan Tom Johnson v Bill Warr at Oakingham 19 Dec Tom Johnson v Michael Ryan at Wradisbury (DM second for Ryan)		Newspaper, *The World*, founded by Captain Topham
1788	9 Jan loses to Richard Humphries at Odiham Sarah, daughter, born and died.		9 June John Jackson beats Tom Fewtrell near Croydon Aug – Tyne kills Earls	Transportation to Australia starts Regency Crisis	*The Times* first published The Thames freezes over, 25 November 1788 to 14 January 1789.

YEAR	MENDOZA	JEWS	BOXING	POLITICS	OTHER
1789	20 April – publishes *The Art of Boxing* 6 May – defeats **Humphries** at Mr Thornton's Park, Stilton		11 Feb Johnson beats Ryan 22 Oct Johnson beats Perrins	July – French Revolution – storming of the Bastille	Very wet summer Bentham William Blake – *Songs of Innocence*
1790	Abraham Mendoza born, 12 February Beats up Joe Ward at the Finish coffee house 29 Sept defeats **Humphries** at Doncaster Nov 5 – Cherokee chiefs at Lyceum				28 Oct – Cherokee chiefs arrive
1791	Feb–March in Birmingham June – Sheridan described as 'the Mendoza of wit' June – attempted mugging 2 August – defeats **Squire Fitzgerald** August – with Fewtrell in Edinburgh Oct – in Bury St Edmunds		Tom Johnson (DM is bottle holder) loses to Ben Brain		Paine / Burke D of Clarence & Mrs J Trial of Warren Hastings begins

1792	Feb–March exhibits in Dublin 14 May – defeats **Bill Warr** at Croydon 26 May – sparring resumes at Lyceum and Capel Court November – 'keeps a snuff shop in Dog's Row'			First Coalition London Corresponding Society – radical society influenced by French revolution	Raeburn skater Vindication of the Rights of Women *Sporting Magazine* first published
1793	Oct – exhibiting with Johnson in Bath Nov – tried for fraud – found Not Guilty DM in 'rules' of King's Bench debtors' prison London road shop Takes job as Recruiting Officer			War with France	
1794	12 Nov defeats **Bill Warr** at Bexley		Death of Ben Brain		Blake – The Tyger 16 August – Astley's Royal Amphitheatre of Arts burns down

YEAR	MENDOZA	JEWS	BOXING	POLITICS	OTHER
1795	15 April – defeated by John Jackson at Hornchurch August – sparring Oct – appointed Sheriff's Officer Oct – tried for assault, fined 50 shillings	Norwood Orphanage founded			
1796	Sheriff's Officer				Edward Jenner cures James Phipps of smallpox, by vaccination
1797	Exhibiting in Preston		Moulsey Hurst used for first time as venue for prize fight.	Spithead mutiny	Coleridge – Kubla Khan
1798	Exhibiting in York	Nathan von Rothschild, age 21, establishes a business in textiles and banking, in Manchester		Battle of the Nile	
1799	Exhibits in Liverpool – arrested			Trade unions outlawed (Combination Act)	

1800	August – exhibiting in Carlisle Arrested in Carlisle for debt Sept – exhibiting in Dumfries?	March – exhibiting in Newcastle Oct 13 – Benefit at Astley's Royal Amphitheatre	23 Dec – Jem Belcher defeats Gamble. (DM, Gamble's second, is late for fight)	Income tax at 10 per cent	
1801	July 17 – Second to Bitton v Jones August – becomes landlord of The Children in the Wood in the Whitechapel Rd. Changes name to The Lord Nelson			Act of Union – United Kingdom formed	First census (9 million people)
1802	Jan 18 – Margaret Lowe found guilty of defrauding DM by use of a bad shilling at The Lord Nelson Dec 17 – Court of King's Bench: charged with owing £10.00 – let off as not enough evidence.	First use for sparring of the Fives Court in St Martin's Street		Treaty of Amiens – peace with France	Political Register founded by anti-Semite William Cobbett. Pro boxing. Radical.

YEAR	MENDOZA	JEWS	BOXING	POLITICS	OTHER
	18 Dec – Court of King's Bench: charged with owing £18 – let off as not enough evidence				
1803	8 Feb – enters King's Bench debtors' prison			War with France again	
1804	Sept – Application for discharge from Kings Bench by means of Insolvency Act refused Oct – discharged from King's Bench		7 Aug – Dutch Sam defeats Caleb Baldwin	July – Insolvency Act	
1805	May – present in Chertsey for Tom Belcher v Ryan 30 Dec – Father dies	N M Rothschild, bankers, established in London	8 Oct Hen Pearce (the Game Chicken) defeats Jem Belcher, becomes Champion.	Battle of Trafalgar	
1806	March – defeats Harry Lee April – teaching again July – goes to Court to try and extract winnings from a bet; thrown out. Sept – exhibiting in Margate		6 Feb – Dutch Sam, seconded by DM defeats Tom Belcher	January – PM, William Pitt, dies	

1807	8 April Cribb beats Jem Belcher 28 July Dutch Sam draws with Tom Belcher (DM is Sam's second) Aug 21 Dutch Sam defeats Tom Belcher for. (DM is Sam's second) Oct 14 Gulley beats Gregson	Abolition of slave trade
1808	10 May Gulley defeats Gregson (DM is Gregson's Second), Dutch Sam defeats Cropley (DM is Sam's second) 25 Oct – Cribb defeats Gregson (DM is Gregson's second)	First edition of *Memoirs?*
1809		October: Old Price Riots
1810	31 May – Dutch Sam defats Ben Medley (DM is Sam's second) 10 Dec – Tom Cribb defeats Tom Molyneaux	

YEAR	MENDOZA	JEWS	BOXING	POLITICS	OTHER
1811			*Pancratia* (Oxberry) published	Regency	Luddites A 12-year-old Dorset child, Mary Anning, discovers at Lyme Regis a 21ft (6.4m) fossil of an ichthyosaur Jane Austen – *Sense and Sensibility*
1812	Mother dies			Assassination of Perceval	
1813			First publication of *Boxiana* in book form		Elizabeth Fry
1814	Tsar, King of Prussia and Blücher invited to witness the art of self-defence. Champions include Jackson and Cribb but not DM		22 May – Pugilistic Club inaugurated Tom Belcher becomes licensee of the Castle Tavern in Holborn.	Police force	
1815				Battle of Waterloo Corn laws	

	1816	1817	1818	1819	1820	1821	1822	1823
	Canova gives statue of Napoleon to Wellington		Shelley – Ozymandias			Constable, Gericualt Hazlitt		William Webb Ellis picks up the ball
				Peterloo	Death of George III			
	Dutch Sam dies aged 42					19 July – Coronation of George IV – pugilists as pages *Boxiana* Vol 3 (Egan)	Hazlitt's *The Fight* published	
	16 July – Trains Blackheath pedestrian 19 July – Abraham Mendoza (son) sentenced to death for highway robbery, subsequently transported to Australia *Memoirs of the Life of Daniel Mendoza – A New Edition* published				4 July fights Tom Owen on Banstead Downs			

YEAR	MENDOZA	JEWS	BOXING	POLITICS	OTHER
1824		Alliance Assurance founded by Rothschild and Montefiore	*Boxiana* Vol 4 (John Bee)	Combination Acts repealed	Dickens working in blacking factory
1825					The Stockton and Darlington Railway, the world's first public passenger railway, opened
1826		UCL Founded			
1827			Death of Richard Humphries		
1828	Daughter Sophia transported to Australia				
1829				Catholic Emancipation	Metropolitan Police formed
1830				Death of George IV	
1831				Riots over 1832 Reform Bill	
1832				Great Reform Act	
1833	Son Isaac transported				
1834				Poor law	
1835	October – reported as having the palsy and being 'quite blind'				

1836	3 Sept Dies
1837	Moses Montefiore knighted
1890	Complete equality of citizenship granted to (male) Jews and Catholics
1954	Elected to The Ring Hall of Fame
1981	Inducted into the International Jewish Sports Hall of Fame
1990	Inducted at its inauguration into the International Boxing Hall of Fame

INDEX